James Brown and His Money Man

Fred Daviss

with Jones DeVere

James Brown and His Money Man

Front cover photo credit: Fred Daviss Collection
Back cover photo credit: Fred Daviss Collection and ChrisSavas.com

Song Lyrics Acknowledgements
The Tennessee Waltz
Redd Stewart
Be Thankful for What You Got
William DeVaughn

ISBN 978-0-9972203-1-5

Dedication

To the three ladies in my life – my wife, Cynthia, and my daughters Kelley and Pepper. Probably none of them will read this book because they've already heard me telling these stories hundreds (if not thousands) of times, plus I can always quote the book to them any time they want.

Contents

Introduction

I was James Brown's best friend for over 40 years. In all that time, I had never seen him do any physical work. There was always an entourage of people around him to take care of every chore, but this time, the two of us were wrestling all these large duffel bags, trying to dispose of the contents.

It was a secret that only Mr. Brown and I shared. Nobody knew where we were or what we were doing. We covered our tracks so thoroughly that our actions could never be traced, and we never really spoke about it for the rest of his life.

As we were leaving one of the banks, Mr. Brown leaned over and grinned. "Missa Daviss, just think—if our plane goes down over the Atlantic, nobody will ever know." (For the sake of complete honesty, James Brown called me "Missa", not "Mister.")

I said, "Don't you care if your children ever get any of it?"

He explained that he had made generous allowances for his children—besides he was mad at his kids—he thought they were greedy and spoiled, and he believed he should first squirrel away some cash for himself. Considering all the chaos in his life with his taxes and his personal life, Mr. Brown really had a sound business plan. He explained it to me—"I split my bucks into three groups … one third goes to pay the business expenses, one third goes to building up the business, you know, making things better, improvements, that sorta thing … and then the last third is my F-You Money. That's the money I'll always have even if they take everything away from me … I'll still have plenty of money to say, *F-You*."

And that's what he did. In the U.S. he buried cash in rural church yards and in hollow trees out in the countryside. I was with him one night in South Carolina when he ran into the dark woods and came back with $15,000 in cash. In Europe, it was a little different, and in the course of 10 to 15 years, little by little, we placed currency into large safety deposit drawers in foreign banks. All tax free.

Now you may want to put a gun to my head and force me to hand over this money, but I can't. Only James Brown can retrieve the cash—it's like I can take you to Fort Knox, but there's no way in hell I can pull out a gold bar. Plus the people who safeguard the money aren't aware, or able, to acknowledge its existence … and I ain't talkin' either.

All those duffel bags we dragged around held $100,000,000. That may seem to be a lotta money, but back then, it was worth even more. At that time, you could buy a four bedroom house for $40,000. A new car cost $4000. A nice meal was $10. Now, everyone seems to be a millionaire—or a billionaire … so due to inflation, that hundred million in cash would be close to a billion dollars now. That's not a small amount, but Mr. Brown wanted that money to stay there. It would be his message from the grave. Even dead, he could still have control over his family, his business and the world.

That's the way he was. I know him better than anyone else in the world, and the real James Brown does not mesh at all with the public perception, and that's kinda the theme of this memoir. This book is about my relationship with James Brown—IT'S NOT HIS BIOGRAPHY—but through my story you will learn the real truth about his life. Forget what you think you know. At heart, James Brown was a straight-laced guy … he rarely smoked or drank (never saw him drunk), he almost never used profanity, he was a Baptist, a Republican, a health nut, and didn't do any hard drugs until his 50s. He worked every day of the year. No vacations, and I don't think he ever walked barefoot on the beach. He didn't have any friends, except me and a few others, and he didn't have any interests or any hobbies. Just work.

There's much more to him than you could ever imagine, and I'm doing my best to explain it to you.

During his lifetime, two autobiographies and several biographies were written about his career, and because of his overbearing control, he was able to censor the content of these books which only ended up showing himself as a two dimensional person. It was only part of the story.

For over 50 years, his public image had been well defined. Everybody had seen his stage performances, read his interviews, and even witnessed *his version* of the public meltdown with the police and his time in jail. But nobody really knew what happened once the curtain closed after the show … nobody knew what he thought, or what he feared, because he kept it all so carefully hidden. He could always close the curtain to his fans … and even with those closest to him, he was able to insulate his inner feelings and soul in a protective veil of bravado.

I was privileged to work behind that curtain, and I know I am the best-qualified person to tell his story even though I'm just a good ol' white boy from south Georgia who became his *Money Man*. You see, for over 40 years I've been a member of the James Brown family. And even though we were not bound by blood, we were still one family … his kids/my kids … his wives/my wives … his parents/my parents.

For you to understand James Brown, you have to know me and have to get into our relationship, because the deep commitment to each other defines us as individuals. You can't study James Brown by looking at him like he was some sort of lab specimen … you have to understand how he reacted to things, and learn about his opinions, his inspiration, his genius and his weaknesses. In reality, James Brown was larger than the legend, and more outrageous and more talented than you can ever imagine. But what he worked so hard to hide was his vulnerability and his kind, and often broken, heart.

Although most of the personal things I talk about have never been publicized, everything is the truth. Some of it is funny … some is sad … and some simply falls into the category of being *unbelievable* … unbelievable that I was so close to this unique musical legend.

CHAPTER 1

How I Became The "Money Man"

I saw James Brown resting comfortably with his head on a pillow. I had seen him asleep many times at his home and in hotel suites around the world, waiting for him to get up so that we could start another business day. At times, I'd sit by his bed and occasionally notice the little details … the scars on his hands and even how small his feet were.

This time, I quietly crept up to him—I didn't want to disturb him—and I hunched up over him and said, "You rat! You rat!" I know he heard me, and I kinda expected him to open up one of his eyes and smile. The "rat" comment was part of a funny little episode we had once shared at Graceland the night after Elvis died.

But he didn't smile not even when I patted him on his chest or touched his hands … the strange thing was, somebody had put some white gloves on him … something he never wore.

Soon after I stepped back from him, they closed the lid, and I walked back to my seat. And I could see people whispered to each other … wondering what I had said to Mr. Brown and asking each other, "Who in the hell is the white boy?" I suppose it was a reasonable thought. I mean, I was like a fish outta water, and people might not have understood why some white guy would have been honored to be one of the last mourners to see Mr. Brown.

Millions of people around the world knew James Brown ... but his fans didn't know about me. And even though all those accounts about tax evasion, record company lawsuits and his disagreements with the Federal Communications Commission were a recurring headline in the news, few knew that I, Fred Daviss, was the person behind the story. Now let me say real quick, I didn't create the problems ... as James Brown's employee, I just took the heat for him and made things work out, and that was my responsibility for almost the last 45 years of his life. Ironically, it was a job I didn't really apply for, but in the years that we were together, I did my part to help James Brown develop into one of the world's greatest musical legends.

I just wanted to do the best job I could, whatever it was. And I was probably the most unlikely guy imaginable to be associated with James Brown ... *who would have ever thunk it?* ... a southern white boy with a thick south Georgia accent becoming part of the Godfather of Soul's family. Now I know what's going on in your mind ... we all share the same stereotypes and misconceptions ... you're probably thinking that I'm your average southern, racist redneck and that Mr. Brown was some sort of wild, egotistical superstar. Well, there may be a bit of truth in every stereotype, but every stereotype also lacks a critical depth of understanding. And I know that I understood James Brown better than anyone else in the world.

Actually, James and I were family ... and I was probably closer to him than any one of his blood relatives. Closer than his parents, his wives and his children. They may have shared his blood, but when a man goes on the road for 300 concerts a year like I did, I had the unique opportunity to share his time, his life and his dreams.

Not that we didn't have our disagreements. We had good times ... we had bad times ... and we would argue. But it was like having a spat with your wife ... then we'd hug and make up.

As I mentioned, I really didn't plan to work for James Brown. I knew who he was, I had even been to one of his concerts in Macon, Georgia, but I was a college-educated banker living in Atlanta with a wife and two small daughters. My initial thought of working for Brown was not very attractive … do you think I was fixin' to leave home and drag around to one-night stands all across the world? The truth was, I had just been hired by Eastern Airlines as a pilot and was days away from resigning from the bank and accepting a significant increase in pay. My career was taking off!

However, the rest of my life pivoted on one brief moment while I was working at the bank … it was a powerful moment when our eyes locked and I said, "Mr. Brown, I know who you are." After that, my life was never the same. It was far better than I could have ever imagined!

Brown called me his *Money Man*, but officially, I was his Executive Vice-President and Comptroller. I also helped to manage his three radio stations, several corporate offices, publishing houses and production companies. I negotiated his recording contracts, paid his bills and handled hundreds of millions of dollars … mostly in cash. I kept him out of jail … fought his battles (in court with lawyers and in parking lots with my knuckles) and at times I held him when he cried. So to say I was *James Brown's Money Man* would be true, but there was a lot more to it.

I want people to know about the personal side of James Brown, the kinda stuff that his fans have never been privy to. I've seen how they wanted to touch him … how they wanted to talk with him or grab on to a little piece of him. I could tell you a lot of little things about him … hell, he wore a 7 ½ shoe … he was left handed, but he was also a complex person and a contradiction in so many ways. He was a different kind of man who had unbelievable charisma, talent and a huge intellect. There's no telling what his IQ was. With only a seventh grade education, he would casually insert little addendums in the margin of a recording contract that would later yield millions of dollars. That way, he beat the corporate lawyers with his own little pencil simply because of their inability to recognize his intellect!

And James Brown put out a strong aura … almost a supernatural thing that just reeked outta his skin from somewhere deep in his gut. This powerful force came from being a "Chosen Child." These are the things I want to tell. Not all the sensational stuff that the press exploited … just the true stuff.

A lot of our relationship had to do with race. It's a subject that's hard to understand, and harder to explain, because anytime you talk about race, someone is going to think it sounds racist. When Brown and I were in the presence of other people, I often had to walk a narrow path concerning what I said or did … otherwise, something was bound to be misinterpreted by outsiders. But when James and I were alone together, we could speak one-on-one about any racial matter, honestly and without fear of being misunderstood. First, he had to educate me. I'll never forget the first time he gave me his views on race. He told me there were four different groups in the black community. There was The Colored Folk who continued to shuffle and "yessuh" the whites. There was The Negro who never quit trying to act white … and then there was The Nigger, and as Mr. Brown said in an offhand way, "Everybody knows who he is … " Finally, there was The Black Man who could stand up and be proud of his heritage. By the way, I was in Los Angeles the night he wrote and recorded *Say It Loud, I'm Black and I'm Proud.* James Brown was not just The Black Man. Foremost, he was a celebrity, and once a person becomes a celebrity, their past is inconsequential. Fame trumps everything. And many times I've seen white women rush up to Brown and kiss him. If he wasn't famous, they would have never dreamed of even touching a black man. And I've also seen white men push their wives into Brown's arms for a photograph. Brown was a little uncomfortable with it, like, *What are these crazy people doin'? Are they getting turned on by seeing me huggin' up their wives?* No, but James Brown understood that they liked the idea of their wives embracing a celebrity.

Here's an example of the complexities of race … I was always trying to save money for Mr. Brown, so I suggested that he get a 727 to carry the band members plus all their equipment in the front of the plane while creating a private living quarters in the rear for himself. By getting rid of the tractor-trailers and tour buses we would be able to move the band quickly from one venue to the next. But Mr. Brown snapped back, "I know you're always looking to save money, but Missa Daviss, do you really think I'm gonna let all those niggers ride on my airplane? They don't even stay in the same hotel with me—they're employees!"

And he meant it in a good way … it wasn't a put down … but that was the way he said it. I couldn't have said it … and I wouldn't have said it in the first place.

I was not only sensitive to the white/black thing with Brown, but I also had to deal with the white/black thing from other white people!

Brown would say, "Missa Daviss, look at it this way … you know the hard times the black folks have had over the years and all the hell we're catchin'… but you're the one I feel sorry for. You're catching twice as much as hell as us because they think you're a nigger lover. Now I know you're not a lover of niggers, but the white man, like your neighbors and your friends see you running around hobnobbing with us, and I know, you gotta be catching twice the hell we're catching."

It was true. I've been chased down the streets of Harlem by a guy with a knife saying, "I'm gonna cut you, whitey," and I also found out that some good ol' boys in Georgia were plotting to burn a cross in my front yard and then blow up my house … with me in it! I caught hell from everybody for my relationship with James Brown.

But Brown knew our relationship went beyond race. I had a commitment and a respect for the man, and my job was to do everything to support him … no matter what.

I said, "When times get bad, Mr. Brown, I'll be the last one standing next to you. And whatever it may be, I got your back. And if there ever comes a time you get arrested or go to jail, hell, I'll go to jail with you. I'm not gonna run. I ain't scared of the devil."

Well, maybe I ran my mouth too much bccause Mr. Brown got put in jail for contempt of court, and we couldn't get him out. There was no bond. And I'm hollering at the court and all the lawyers telling them to let him outta jail, and that I, not James Brown, would be responsible for providing the financial data that the court required.

The judge gave me a long strange look. Then he proceeded to put me under the jurisdiction of the court. Legally speaking, it meant that if I couldn't provide the data to prove Mr. Brown's case in court, the judge was going to throw me in jail along with Mr. Brown. The judge announced from the bench, "I will put Mr. Brown back in jail, and Mr. Daviss, I will put you in the cell with him."

James Brown turned around and grinned at me and said, "At least we're gonna be in the same cell." I didn't see the humor.

So, the judge let Brown out of jail, and he went back to relax in his suite at the hotel, and for five straight days, the lawyers grilled me unmercifully on the stand, trying to nail something on Brown … and me. When it was over, they couldn't prove their case and let us go, but after that everybody felt a deeper respect for the white boy … because I came within a gnat's ass of going to jail defending James Brown.

But sometimes it was the smallest things that meant the most. It happened that my two daughters, Kelley and Pepper were about the same age as Brown's daughters, Yamma and Deanna. They'd often get together and play. During the time they were all in grammar school, they had their class pictures made, you know, with those wallet-sized photos.

Kelley and Pepper were so proud of their school pictures that James Brown made a big thing of asking them for copies. He said, "Girls, I'm gonna put these pictures in my wallet right next to my personal photos."

And it tickled them to death 'cause they went to school and told everybody that James Brown carried their pictures in his wallet. Apparently, he said something to Yamma and Deanna, so next time I was at his house, they came up to me squealing, "Mr. Daviss, Mr. Daviss, we got our pictures for you."

And I looked at James Brown and winked, and I said, "Girls, y'all are so pretty. I'm gonna put these pictures in my wallet, and your Daddy's got Kelley and Pepper's pictures in his wallet."

And Deanna said to me, "Daddy loves your daughters."

And I said, "I love y'all, too."

I had kinda forgotten about all that until one night, somewhere on the road, when Brown and I got a little melancholy, and I asked, "Mr. Brown, you still have those photos?"

And he said, "Yeah, they're gonna be in my wallet forever, Missa Daviss. Do you still have my girls in your wallet?"

I said, "Yessir!"

He said, "Missa Daviss, you and I have always talked about being family, but you know, this confirms it and kinda documents it that when it comes down to carrying our girls' pictures in our wallet, that I can be braggin' on you and braggin' on your girls and pulling my wallet out and showing it to somebody, even if you're not there … this is a helluva thing. We didn't realize how important it was when we first put them in the wallet, and now, there ain't no way in hell they're comin' outta my wallet."

That meant a lot to me. We were definitely family. Got nothing to do with color. Got nothing to do with how famous he was or how important he was. When you get to become friends with somebody, and you love 'em and you're with 'em that much, you forget how famous they are—and the prestige they have—and all the money they have—until you walk outside the hotel, and there's a big mob of fans waiting for them. And then it comes on you in a different way.

James Brown told me one time, he said, "You know, Missa Daviss, I love you more than anybody I could think of right now. I love you as much as my wife, but in a different way, I love you as much as my Daddy or my kids, but in a different way. It's a *man respect* thing. And I love you. I know you're loyal to me, and I know you don't bullshit me, and you're not trying to ride my coattails … you're honest, and you love me, too."

There have been a lot of books and film documentaries written about James Brown. None of them were written by people who had a deep, first-hand insight of the man … only the legend. They were just re-telling stories. But what I'm telling you is the real thing. It's The Honest Truth.

James Brown tried to set the record straight by writing several autobiographies. They were very factual, but *not really honest*. You know what I mean? They were sanitized, cleaned up … and he simply forgot to mention a lot of details to the writers … the kind of details that make a person real … that makes him come alive.

So don't be too quick to criticize or form an opinion about James Brown or me. It was a complex relationship in a turbulent social time, and it's unfair to judge the past by today's standards. But what I want you to know is how much I loved James Brown and how much he loved me. There's a lot in this book that on the surface that may look racist, but if you read the whole thing, you'll know the truth. And the truth is almost unbelievable.

* * *

It is *unbelievable* that somebody like me would be swept up into something so big, so outrageous and so socially and culturally foreign as working for Mr. James Brown. First, you've got to consider my roots. I grew up in middle Georgia, and by middle I mean, if you stuck a thumbtack dead center on a map of Georgia, you'd get close to my hometown.

The other thing was the time in which I grew up … I graduated from high school in '58, a turbulent time of segregation … when it was a white man's world of privilege … even though there was a bland cultural sameness to our lives. The only thing to listen to back then was big band music and a lot of country stations, but I didn't care for that hillbilly stuff … too much crying in your beer. Then, later on, when I was in junior high, the kids started to listen to black music and slipping into the black clubs, looking for *the new sound* … wild, untamed sexual music, which naturally appealed to young men. And that's why Elvis sounded like a black man-because it was the black man's music. Same way with Jerry Lee Lewis.

All my friends and I would listen to the early black artists: the Drifters; The Coasters; Lavern Baker; Little Willie John; Bo Diddley and of course, James Brown. Then, when we started driving, we were able to listen to the radio in the privacy of our car, but when we pulled up in front of the filling station, a guy would come out to your car to pump the gas. That's when we had to cut the damn radio down … otherwise he'd be tellin' on my ass to my Daddy that, "Fred's been listening to that nigger music again."

There was so much black culture around, not just on the radio, but in Macon and the surrounding area. Ray Charles was born in Albany … Little Richard was from Macon … early in his career, James Brown also lived in Macon … Ma Rainey "The Mother of the Blues" and Big Mama Thornton lived close by … and Otis Redding grew up in Macon where he was managed by a teenaged Phil Walden who later cultivated The Allman Brothers into a great success. There must have been something in the local water supply!

It was great for me 'cause I lived close enough to Macon so that I could catch the local bus and go to the shows at the old City Auditorium, where for only about $3.50, I could see Little Willie John, James Brown, the Drifters and the Coasters. But since this was a time before civil rights … that meant that the auditorium had a balcony.

In a reversal of segregation, the white guests were forced to sit in the balcony while the "colored people" (as they were called then) had the run of the auditorium. That way, they got to dance on the floor, and raise hell. We were so jealous. And we'd hang over the balcony and talk to the guys down below us. Soon, we got to know each other by name, and they would say how sorry they felt about us white boys who couldn't get down from the balcony.

A lotta things may seem strange to us now, but I really believe that I had a very normal childhood in the very best times of times. Like, we never locked the house—in fact, I don't think we even owned a house key! We'd go outta town every year on vacation and didn't lock the house. Plus, we never took the key outta the car. It stayed in there all the time. You'd pull up in the yard and get out, the next morning you'd go out and crank it up. You didn't have to hunt your keys.

Even when you went to town, you'd never take the key outta the car. Nobody bothered your car. You could go shopping and be in the store for an hour or two. You'd leave the packages or pocketbook on the seat, come back, and everything would still be there. Those were the times we came up in … a very unreal, and sheltered existence … and boy, was I naïve!

When I grew up, most of the roads were unpaved, and we had to make our own fun. I spent my spare time playing baseball, shooting marbles or playing mumbly peg with my pocketknife. But even so, every day was an adventure … like the time when a friend and I caught a bunch of deadly cottonmouths and planned to build a snake farm in my backyard. When my mother found out about our plans, she just about had a damn fit! She told me to rid of 'em, so we stuffed the snakes in a cardboard box and dumped them underneath our neighbor's house ... you know, houses in the south back then were up on brick piers, about three feet high. I never figured out where the snakes crawled off to ... but later on, my friend and I ordered a baby alligator from an ad in the back of a *Popular Mechanics* magazine. Cost us $3.95.

It came in a box, delivered by the U.S. Mail. It's funny they would send stuff like that in the mail. We thought about ordering a monkey, but figured an alligator would be easier to keep from our parents. Each day, we would take the gator from its secret hideaway and let it spend the day in my friend's bathtub while his parents were at work. Unfortunately, his father came home from work early and apparently took his clothes off to take a shower. He stuck his arm past the shower curtain to turn on the hot water, and when he pulled the shower curtain back and saw the alligator snapping at his toes, he snatched the shower curtain down and ran out of the house and into the front yard ... a nekked man, wrapped only in a shower curtain staggering around in his front yard, screaming bloody murder.

They made us get rid of our little pet, so we threw it into some nearby woods ... so today, there's probably a 12-foot alligator lurking around in the creeks of Macon, Georgia. I admit it ... I did a lot of stupid kid stunts, however, I was a good student, graduating in the top 10 of my class. I was fortunate to get accepted at Georgia Tech where I was planning to be an aeronautical engineer. But I quickly found out that I didn't want to build planes, I wanted to fly them. Being an engineer was not my cup of tea.

In the meantime, I got married to a girl named June and transferred to Georgia State to pursue a degree in finance. It was a busy time because I was working fulltime at the First National Bank of Atlanta while going to school at night. I was fulfilling the dream of the ambitious, white, middle-class, suburban professional, including two daughters ... Kelley born in 1962 and Pepper in 1964.

But I wanted more ... *not more kids* ... more money, a better job ... and especially, I wanted to fly! So I started taking flying lessons. Eventually I got my commercial pilot's license and later earned my instrument rating so that I could fly for the airlines and start to make some real money.

During the meantime, the bank transferred me to a branch office at the Atlanta Airport across from the Delta Air Lines check in. The location was designed to service business travelers—because of this, I happened to see a lot of celebrities coming through the airport.

Every Tuesday, Martin Luther King used to come into the bank to get his expense check cashed. And we had this ol' laid back southern boy who worked there. He really hated black people, and especially King, and he always gave him a hard time about one thing or another, but King would just sit through it patiently. I mean, I was embarrassed about it, and I asked Dr. King one time, "Doesn't this kinda thing bother you?"

He replied, "Well, I'm used to it."

I didn't think one way or the other about Martin Luther King. I knew he was out there crusading for the black people, but I had other things on my mind. I was more interested in looking at the sexy, young stewardesses strolling back and forth on the concourse. Hey, I promised that I was going to tell "The Honest Truth" ... maybe not the most "Appropriate Truth" ... but at least I'm honest!

In any case, James Brown came walking in the airport bank one day. He was still flying commercial then—he didn't buy his first Learjet until 1965, so this was in the early '60s, about 1962 or 1963. I saw James Brown in the bank, but he kept his two assistants out in the concourse, hanging on to several large, bulging bags.

This was an unusual situation. James Brown didn't have an account at the bank, and he was just trying to cash a little $300 Western Union money order somebody had given him. He was trying to get it okayed by the good ol' boy who continued asking him for some identification. Brown had already checked his luggage, and his outfit didn't have any pockets ... so he couldn't produce any identification.

As the little drama played out at the good ol' boy's desk, I was standing there thinking, *Damn, that's James Brown. I used to go to his concerts when I was in high school.* Of course I was used to seeing movie stars at the airport … but James Brown was different. In any case, he continued to get a rude treatment from the good ol' boy.

Brown continued to tell him he didn't have any identification, and said, "But I'm James Brown!"

But the guy replied, "I don't care … if you don't have any i.d., I'm not going to okay the check."

That's when Brown started grandstanding in front of the other customers. He threw his hands up and said, "But I'm James Brown! You don't know me?"

The guy ignored him, but Brown persisted.

"I was just on TV, and my picture's been on a bunch of magazines!" Brown looked at him like, *Where the hell have you been?* It was ironic that outside the door, his two guys were guarding at least a million dollars of cash in those bulging suitcases, but Brown couldn't even negotiate a little $300 money order in the bank.

He didn't get mad, and kinda laughed the whole thing off, but as he turned to walk out, I stood up at my desk and interjected, "Mr. Brown, I know who you are."

He took another step or two and froze. Slowly, he turned around and looked at me with a big smile full of white teeth. And at that very moment, a pivotal point in my life took place, for as soon as our eyes locked, I felt something powerful. And he turned to look at the people working in the bank, and he must have been thinking to himself, *Why can't y'all be like him? Here's a cat that's current. He knows what's goin' on.*

I was kinda embarrassed at that moment, and kinda nervously laughed as I told him that I would okay his check. Afterward, he signed an autograph for me. I was so excited to meet "The James Brown!" I was also thinking that I'd like to sit down and talk with him, because I'd never been that close to someone famous before. To keep the conversation going, I told him that he needed to open an account with the bank.

And he said, "I'll do that the next time I come in. I'll be back."

But when he walked out that day, I thought cynically, *Yeah, you'll be back. You'll forget who I am.* I was just another fan to him, but sure enough, about a week later, he comes walking back and came straight to my desk. He didn't stop.

He said, "I got another one of those checks that I need you to okay." But I hardly looked at the check as I okayed it while reminding him that he promised to open an account. He said he remembered the conversation.

He said, "I'm a man of my word, Missa Daviss. How much money does it take?" I told him that he could open an account for $5 … back then you could. But then he pulled a wad of hundreds outta his boot and said, "Make it $1,000." Then he quickly turned his back and said to me, "You need to count that."

As he turned his back and was talking to one of his guys, I counted the money. It was $1100.

Immediately I said, "Mr. Brown you gave me too much." And he turned around again … smiling. I realized later that he was waiting to see if I was going to notice the $100 difference and try to pocket the cash. He tried me from the very first time we did business … it was an honesty test … a street hustle.

He would constantly bait people. I've seen him stuff $800 to $1200 down into the crevice of his airplane seat. Then he'd walk off and leave his pilots alone in the plane. As he stood nearby, making sure nobody else got on the plane, he'd wait a while before asking the pilot to fetch something he left on his seat. He was testing them to see if they would pocket the money. I've also seen him leave money on the plane overnight to see if his pilots would steal from him. It was his own little game.

Our banking relationship quickly blossomed. Within six weeks, he had deposited over $250,000, and in a matter of three or four months, he put about six million dollars in a checking account. Things grew and grew, and he would come through the bank at least once a week, sometimes twice a week, and we'd sit and talk. I got to know him, and he was calling me almost daily for something. In a few years, it got to the point where I had become "his banker." And every once in a while, he would invite me to some place like Las Vegas. He'd put my wife and me in a fabulous suite, and I tell ya, I'd never seen that kind of money and glamour … or prestige. When we checked into the hotel with Mr. Brown, people just kissed his ass … and they would kiss my ass, too! Brown was baiting me. Another time, he gave my family first class airline tickets and put us up in the penthouse suite of the Eden Rock Hotel in Miami. Had a rental car and told me to charge anything I wanted at the hotel … just sign my name. Gave me $1000 spending money. Just laid it on.

I was real impressed by all this! I was livin' like a rock star … but I was still working at the bank and trying real hard to complete my commercial pilot's license. Finally, in 1969, I got all my ratings and got hired by Eastern Air Lines. I turned in my resignation at the bank and told Mr. Brown about my plans, but that's when he got real serious and asked me why in the world I wanted to be an airline pilot. I gave him two reasons … I would be earning a much better salary and that I simply loved to fly. I just couldn't image anybody paying me to fly an airplane!

He exhaled with a lot of frustration, "Missa Daviss … Mis-ter Daviss … " as he walked around me a couple of times shaking his head. "I tell you what, since you've already turned in your resignation, why don't you go to work for me? Forget about the job with the airlines! You go to work for me, and I'll pay you more from the first day than you'd be making when you retire from the airlines. I'll make you a rich man." And he thought for a minute. "Let's see … that takes care of the money end of it … what's the other reason? Oh yeah, you 'love to fly'? Missa Daviss, if you come to work for me, you'll make so much money, you'll be able to buy your own airplane!"

Well, I couldn't turn down an argument like that! I said, "Yes" … and when I told my wife what I'd done, I thought she was gonna divorce me! However, I took the job, and a week later on Monday morning, I flew to Baltimore. My mission was to straighten out the financial chaos at his radio station. He gave me the order, "Missa Daviss, I want you to get in there, and I want you to clean those niggers out. You get in there and bust some ass. I want you to look out for my money." And that was the start of the Fred Daviss/James Brown journey … the story of an educated, but naïve middle-class white boy who happened to open his mouth and say, "I know you Mr. Brown. I know you." Pretty unbelievable, isn't it?

CHAPTER 2

JAMES BROWN—THE ONE AND ONLY

Most things about Mr. Brown were unusual ... his musical talent, his personal ambition, his business sense and his ability to reach into people's minds and separate the truth from deception. At times he was spooky, and I dare say supernatural. He had the psychic ability to read the future. It was powerful ... and I could feel it from the first time I met him. It was almost like an aura around him ... a charisma that you just don't get from most people, and it was so strong you could feel it in the air coming from his soul. James Brown had a sixth sense about him. It was so strong that you couldn't lie to him. He was so intimidating. When he'd look you face-to-face, all you could see was your reflection in his eyes ... which seemed like a bottomless black pit. They were the coldest eyes you've ever seen, and he always knew if you were lying.

I'm not the only one who felt that way. When I was in Augusta, I knew an old colored lady who used to sit on her porch with a bandana wrapped around her head. She'd tell stories about James Brown growing up. And she would say, "Lawd Missa Fred, that James Brown, when he was a little boy ... he was a pisser. He was a mean little shit. He was so arrogant and hard-headed that I remember one time, I came over there, and he had been shining shoes ... and he didn't even have any drawers on. And he was living down there in a whorehouse on the levee ... just James and Missa Glenn, his cousin."

She said when he was just a little child, James bought some chicken feed but somehow was holding on to it in order to bargain for some sort of favor. They were all standing on the levee and she said, "James, give me that damn chicken feed or I'm fixin' to whup your ass right here." He said "No" … not until he got his way. It came down to a standoff, and rather than back down, she said, "The little shit poured the chicken feed right in the damn levee and wasted it right there." And then he just stood there, defiantly, with a look on his face like, *Now what are you gonna do?* Well, she whupped his ass all over the yard—whupped Willie Glenn, his cousin, too.

But the old lady knew that James Brown was special, even in little raggedy-ass clothes. And she knew that there was something different about James … that he was going to be someone special. And she told me, "That James Brown is what we call "The Chosen Child."

I mentioned this story to James Brown one night. We were sitting in a hotel suite about 3 o'clock in the morning. He had gotten a little melancholy, and he was just sitting there, and I asked him what the old lady meant about being "The Chosen Child." I could see his mind working. And he stuttered around, and said that he had never really thought about it till that moment, but he started telling me this story, trying to make sense of all the things that had happened in his life.

He started to speak in a soft voice, full of vivid thoughts and memories. "Back in the days in Augusta, that's when it happened … when my Daddy used to change tires at the old fillin' station." Then he explained how poor they were, just his Daddy and him. He wasn't barefooted, but had on these old kinda like tennis shoes. And no socks. Old broken laces, short britches with no drawers. He told me he didn't have any store-bought underwear until he was seven.

He said, one day they were down in the shed where you pulled the cars in to work on them. It had a dirt floor with an old air compressor back in the corner. The ground was kinda soggy 'cause the filling station was built right next to a levee. And he was just a kid, running around in the station doing something, and there was a bunch of old white guys sitting around on the Co-Cola crates talking. And he stopped and leaned up against the air compressor to listen to these white men shooting the breeze when he said, "My hand grounded out on something with this air compressor, and I swung around by reflex and grabbed it with the other hand, and it got a hold of my ass, and it stuck." That was because he was standing in soggy, wet mud creating an electrical ground. He said, "I stood there and shook, and that electricity was going through my body, and it grabbed me to the point where I couldn't turn it loose, and everybody was jumping around kicking the Co-Cola crates back.

After about 20 seconds of this current going through my body, I was looking down, and I was snatching and jerking in a spasm, and I could see my damn shoes frying, and the water started bubbling down around my feet. I know you think I'm exaggerating about the length of time, but I stayed hooked up on this thing for at least three-and-a-half to four minutes … enough to kill anybody. But you know, after about 20 to 30 seconds, it started feeling good, and all of a sudden, I didn't care if I turned it loose or not. I felt something building in my body. It was a powerful force, and it felt like there was a balloon being slowly blown up inside me, and it started swelling somewhere down in my gut. And it swelled and swelled and swelled and the longer I was hooked up to this power, the stronger I got. I felt like Superman. It was pumping a supernatural power into my body … just like filling up a gas tank.

Them white boys couldn't believe it didn't kill me. My ears were ringing, and I could smell my hair sizzling. There was damn smoke coming outta my ears, and the smoke was even coming out from around my tennis shoes—and my feet were burning.

Finally, somebody shut the power down, and I was just as calm, but I was still smoking. And they set me down on some Co-Cola cases, and they couldn't believe that I was still alive. And my tongue had this funny taste to it."

He told me that they tried to get his tennis shoes off, but they had melted on to his feet. At that point, he slipped off his bedroom shoes and stuck the bottom of his feet up and he says, "Here, look at my feet … see how hard this skin is."

Then he said, "From that day forward, even back then at six years old, I was a legend." And as he put his hand on my knee and leaned up into my face he said, "Missa Daviss … *I was different.* I knew deep down in my gut that I was different. It was a powerful feeling in me. I knew I was special because it didn't kill me. And I guarandamntee you I was hooked up to that thing being electrocuted for four minutes. And after that I was the talk of the town. From that day on, I acted different, and I wasn't scared of nobody. I wasn't scared of nothing. I always knew that I was going to be somebody. I knew that the world was going to recognize me one day … I didn't know how … I didn't know where it was gonna come from, but I knew that the world was going to know me one day. It wasn't an ego thing. I just knew the world was going to say 'That's James Brown.'"

* * *

Although he denied having an ego, he was wrong. His ego was so large that you just accepted it. It was like the air around you. It surrounded you, you breathed it in, it was a part of your existence, and he made a point of proving that everything he had was better than what you had. His dog was more pedigreed than your dog—his wife was better looking than your wife—and she could cook better, too … in other words, anything that Brown had was a notch up on what you had. And then he could somehow manipulate it into *I've got the best of everything.*

One night we were driving back to Chicago from a big music festival in Milwaukee. It featured Woody Herman, one of Mr. Brown's idols. It was about 3 o'clock in the morning, and I was dressed in a tuxedo riding in the back of a stretch limo with Brown's entourage … including his hairdresser, bodyguards and maybe a poor ol' soul from the band. When Brown gave a band member "the privilege" of riding in his limo or jet, it was only because he wanted to have a little talk with him, one-to-one-like being sent to the principal's office or something.

As we were coming down the highway, all I could think of was getting back to the hotel. I was leaning back on my briefcase, and getting a little shuteye, but Brown was laughing and having his little bull session with the other guys—must have been six or seven other people in the limo. I was the only white guy.

They were all laughing, cuttin' up and having a good time. And of course, everybody would laugh on cue along with Brown. He was orchestrating the whole thing. But suddenly, everything got real quiet. I was half asleep, but in the low light of the limo, I could hear Mr. Brown in the midst of a conversation as he leaned into the group.

He said, "Fellas, I got to tell ya fellas … you take Missa Daviss … y'all think you know him, but Missa Daviss is not-a-lover-of-niggers." And then he laughed.

Let me describe the James Brown laugh. It was not a "ha ha" laugh, or a chuckle, in fact, it wasn't really a laugh at all … it was more like some sort of attack—like he was suffering spasmodic convulsions. His arms would draw up with an inhuman reflex looking like a bug, a praying mantis … and his fingers would contort like a person with palsy, and he always threw his head back, squinting his eyes. And then he would stand on one leg, shaking, as the other leg drew up toward his body—he frequently fell to the floor and rolled around as he continued to laugh. And his laugh, well, it sounded like a small animal caught in a trap … choking and in pain, and sometimes it went on for a long time. In any case, it was obvious that something was humorous.

So there I was, in the limo, with James Brown laughing, *Awawawaw!!!* And as he and the other guys were laughing on cue, I was thinking, *What in the hell is gonna come outta this conversation?*

And then Brown repeated, "I tell ya fellas. Do you hear me? Do you hear me? Missa Daviss is not-a-lover-of-niggers." *Awawawaw!!!*

And I was thinkin', *Oh my gawd!*

And finally they got calmed down from the laughing and Brown leans over real serious like and puts his hand on my knee. Then he got up in my face. I kinda cracked one eye, like he just woke me up. He then leans up even closer and in a deadly serious tone said, "Missa Daviss, you don't like niggers, do you?"

That's when I really started to think. Even though I was half asleep, I knew that you always had to keep one step ahead of Brown. You don't want to get in a conversation where he's gonna beat you down or back you in a corner. And I was thinking, *How in the hell am I gonna answer that?* I know I'm not gonna say, *Oh yeah, Mr. Brown, I just love niggers!* That would be an obvious insult to him, so I'm thinking, *How in the hell do I answer this question?* Whatever I say is gonna be taken the wrong way.

So it popped in my mind the fact that in every town, there's always a ghetto—a black section. In Augusta, there was a place on 9th Street that Brown knew real well. If I told a story about 9th Street, then maybe he could relate to it. So I gathered some courage and said, "Well Mr. Brown, let me put it to you this way … No, I don't like none of them niggers down on 9th Street."

And he was still looking at me with that cold gaze, and everybody is sitting there real quiet wanting to see what his response is to me, and I continued, "No, not those kind of niggers … but y'all are alright … y'all are different. Y'all are my friends, and hell, I work with you every day!" And everything was quiet enough to drop a pin … and this silence goes on for like 30 seconds … and I'm staring at him with my one open eye. And Brown is still right up in my face, still with his hand on my knee. And the seconds slowly tick by … then 30 seconds later, he just explodes in laughter … *Awawawaw!!! Awawawaw!!!,* and he was shaking his leg, and *Awawawaw!!!,* with his shoulders drawn up in that typical James Brown laugh, *Awawawaw!!!,* and everybody is laughing and everybody is kinda letting out this sigh of relief like, *This conversation was getting a little too tense.*

As the laughter died down, Brown tried to tell them something. He said, "Now fellas, the point I'm trying to make is that y'all all know that Missa Daviss is a nice man, and y'all think you're getting tight with him."

I knew what he was doing. Brown always wanted to keep his workers alienated from one another. He didn't want them to get tight, because if they get tight, they'll gang up on him. So, if he could keep everybody apart, he could control things better. That was the point of this whole little educational exercise.

So he continued, "Don't get too tight with Missa Daviss. Now I know behind my back he'll lend you money, because he's a nice guy, and you'll give him the old sob stories ... but I'm hip enough to know better. Missa Daviss will loan you money ... he will come out of his coat if you're in a tight place ... and y'all think that Missa Daviss is your friend, but he's just an ol' southern white boy. The point I'm trying to make is, don't get pulled off on this path where you think that y'all will be buddies, because you're not. Missa Daviss is just a nice man, but don't think that you can ever socialize with him."

After making his point, Brown leaned back, took a breath, and said, "Let me tell you fellas something ... our relationship is different. I love Missa Daviss, and he loves me. We're that close ... and we're like family. But the point I'm trying to make to you fellas is that you'll never get that way with him. The reason we're that way is that... I'm a different kind of nigger."

CHAPTER 3

Confidence

The relationship I had with James Brown was based on confidence … a lengthy trial requiring eight years from the time I first met him until I went on his payroll. All during that time, he was testing me, but also building his confidence in my ability to manage his financial empire.

I knew Brown was buttering me up. Occasionally he'd have to sign some papers—I could have mailed them to him but he'd say, "Missa Daviss, why don't you fly to Las Vegas with your ol' lady this weekend?" And he'd send me first class tickets and put me in a nice suite. Oh man, this was a glamorous life! I had never lived this way … I'm just an ol' southern boy!

One trip was unique … I'd even say it was historic in the world of show business. On this occasion, he flew June and me to Las Vegas with first class tickets. A limo picked us up at the airport, and Brown put us up in a nice suite at the International Hotel, now the Las Vegas Hilton. He had been performing there for several days, and as the limo pulled up to the front door, I could see "James Brown" up on the marquee in huge letters. Very impressive!

Brown didn't like to play Vegas, even though it was good money. To me, it seemed like the perfect fantasy with its luxurious hotels and non-stop gambling. But he said, "You can get old playing here … you're singing to the same corner of the room every night for a week. I like a new place, a new audience, a different town, and I don't like to play any place more than two nights. I like the one-nighters because you're not staring at the same corner all the time."

When I began to work for him, I wish he had played Vegas more. It was hard moving a small army of people every day … day in and day out. Hell, I wish he would stay weeks or months in Vegas … it would have made my life a whole lot easier!

This was an exciting time in Las Vegas. The International Hotel had opened several months before when Elvis played over 50 historic performances. It was a big deal. Now, James Brown was booked for about two weeks … he was closing on Saturday night, and Elvis was coming in to take his place at the International the next day.

I had flown out there on Friday and was able to catch Brown's act. On Saturday night, I saw it again … so I was having a big time. When Elvis arrived on Saturday night, there was a big buzz all through the hotel like, *Elvis is here!*

On Sunday afternoon, I was laying around in my suite, taking it easy, because I had been up all night gambling. Brown called me and asked me very abruptly, "Missa Daviss, how'd you like to meet Elvis Presley?"

And I said, "What?"

"You want to meet Elvis? Not many people get to meet Elvis."

And I got all excited and said, "Hell yeah, I want to meet Elvis!" But then I had to stop myself … I thought, maybe I was a bit too enthusiastic, so I quickly had to back off from what I said like, *Hey Elvis is big, but they don't come any bigger than you Mr. Brown!* After all, Brown had flown me out there, so I attempted to push the idea that, *You're the star here Mr. Brown, sure, I'll go meet Elvis … I don't have anything else to do.*

So I got ready and ran up the hallway to Mr. Brown's suite. I don't know why my wife didn't go, she probably would have wanted to fix her hair and stuff like that. But I got to Brown's suite as fast as I could and his little entourage, his hairdresser, his bodyguard (maybe three or four of us, Danny Ray, his emcee, Willie Glenn, his cousin, and Henry Stallings) took the elevator up to Elvis's suite.

Elvis's people met us at the elevator and here comes Elvis busting out of the main suite door, and James and Elvis started hugging in the hall. I was in awe, I mean, my knees got weak, and I was thinking to myself, *Damn! I'm gonna talk to Elvis Presley!* Then we went on into the suite, and they got to talking and hugging and playing grab ass with each other and carrying on like long lost friends.

Finally, Brown got around to saying, "I want you to meet Missa Daviss. This is my banker." Once again, Brown started his street hustle, one-upping Elvis, like, *Elvis, you need to get you a banker.* Brown would look down his nose at almost everybody … always giving advice, like, *This poor boy, Elvis—I'll have to teach him how to be successful like me.* Brown always had to have the best of everything … like, *My banker is better than your banker.*

Elvis had a baby grand piano in his suite, and we were all sitting around talking. Then he ordered some sandwiches and coffee, and we were all having a big time. And I was just in awe, listening to all these personal conversations between Brown and Elvis. Then, Elvis slid over and sat at the piano and asked James if he remembered a certain gospel tune. Elvis would run his hands across the keys and sing a few bars as Brown would throw his head up to the ceiling, and do his own little musical rendition of the song. Then, Elvis would nod and come up with another gospel song for Brown.

After a while, Elvis really got cranked up, and he got to bouncing up and down on the bench and banging away at the keyboard. And then they'd both join in, having a good time going back and forth, testing each other's musical knowledge.

Then they got to talking about how they each grew up in the church and how many gospel tunes they knew. Elvis would say, "Yeah, I know all these tunes … I grew up in the church," and he would play a little tune on the piano.

But Brown kept on like, *Well, I know more church music than you do.*

And Elvis would say, "No, you don't, I grew up in the church … and I also came up in the black neighborhood, so don't tell me you know more than I do." And it just kept on with all this stuff, back and forth until Elvis finally said, "James, come on over here—come sit over here on the bench with me."

And Brown looked at me with a bit of anxiety, kinda like, *I don't want to loosen up too much around this guy.* It might have forced him to reveal himself, but I also know he was busting a gut to play with Elvis, like, *Hey, we'll never be able to do this again!*

Years later, I realized that I had been blessed to be part of an exclusive audience to see them together like that. The stars must have been aligned that day to have these two guys in the same city and same hotel at the same time! And I sat there for at least two hours as they played gospel music. They had the best time together. It should have been recorded.

But I got real embarrassed about it, too. Brown was telling Elvis, "I know you're having a hard time now. Your records aren't selling, and you're struggling. I just wish you could get back up there like me. Elvis, I don't know why these guys are trying to blackball you. I don't know why they would put you on behind me. Your show shoulda played first because everybody knows … nobody can follow me."

Oh man … Brown was really putting him down, but he was right. James Brown was a hard act to follow, and nobody wanted to play behind him because he would suck all the damn juice outta the audience. There was nothing left for the next act.

But it was a helluva thing to witness … the Godfather talking down to the King like that. In many ways, Brown was right, but Elvis showed a lot of class. In any case, I was a witness to a once-in-a-lifetime, private musical performance between two great musical legends. It began with James Brown setting out to show me the glamour of show business, and he did … but I also knew that nobody, not even James Brown, could ever top this!

* * *

About that time, I went to work for Mr. Brown, taking care of his various financial duties and running his day-to-day business. In my spare time, I managed his three radio stations and several publishing and production companies. Occasionally, I would tour with the band, and once I went with him to Europe and the British Isles. After doing a concert in Manchester, we had planned to drive back to London that night. The promoters had lined up Mr. Brown to ride in a real exotic 1930s limo … I believe it was a Rolls-Royce, and it had the mahogany interior and the leather seats. And the chauffeur pampered the car like it was his child.

So, after the concert, we were driving through the countryside with James Brown, his hairdresser, and Willie Glenn and a couple of other people, just laughing and talking. We were out in the middle of nowhere. Nothing but cow pastures on both sides on this two-lane road—out in the damn country. But it was colder than hell. It was snowing and there was about an inch or two of snow on the ground, but it was a pretty sight because the moon was out. It was pretty bright.

The driver had mentioned to me two or three times, that he had just had the car tuned up that day. He wanted everything to be just right for Mr. Brown. Despite that, all of a sudden the limousine stops. It just goes dead.

So we were on the side of the road, and Brown was always bragging about how I could fix anything. I knew that I was a pretty good mechanic—when I was young I used to build up car engines.

The driver just didn't know what to do, so he cranks and cranks on it. And I said, "Hey man, you're running the battery down on it. It's not firing." I remembered that the chauffeur had mentioned about the tune up, so I had a feeling that the distributor points had closed up on it.

The guy had a flashlight, a pair of pliers, a screwdriver and a crescent wrench in the trunk, or the *boot*, as he called it. I was wearing a tuxedo, with no overcoat, so I rolled my sleeves up and started to look under the hood. James Brown was encouraging me by saying to the group, "Missa Daviss can fix it." But I didn't have that much faith in myself … all I knew was that I had to do something. I looked at it—it had one of those straight six cylinder engines in it and side draft carburetors with big metal air filters. So as the driver is holding a light on it, I'm just taking off these filters and throwing them out on the ground. The chauffer is just about to shit—he thinks I'm tearing his car into pieces. Finally, I got down to the distributor, and I get the distributor cap off. The points looked closed, and I got him to bump the starter a few times so that I could eyeball the clearance on the points. Then I got the distributor cap back on after setting the points with my frozen hands.

About that time, a car full of young fans from the show stopped and offered James Brown a ride. Hell, he was fixin' to leave our ass out there when I said, "Let's try to start it again." So the chauffeur got back in, and he hit the starter, and *Pow!* … it cranked right up.

I didn't even put the damn air filters back on, I threw 'em in the boot, or the *trunk* as I call it, and told the driver to get moving—and turn the damn heater on! We were still about 50 miles outta London, it was about three in the morning, we hadn't had dinner, and it was freezing cold. But James Brown was impressed with me. I had saved the day … one of many countless times. Brown was braggin' on me and said, "Missa Daviss saved our life … we would have froze to death out there. I told y'all that he could fix anything … Missa Daviss is a genius."

CHAPTER 4

"He's Okay… He's One of Us"

Even though I was a genius … it was very obvious—I was so out of place. Unlike anybody else in his organization, I had a formal education … I had eight years of work experience in a large bank, and I was a *soon-to-be-pilot* for a major airline. However, I was not at all street smart.

I was so uncool, and I was jealous of the white boys like Bob Patton and Alan Leeds. Bob was a former DJ, and he was Mr. Brown's advance man in charge of promotions. Alan also worked with Bob to set up the venues. They were so hip in everything they said. I'd say, "How about the concert up in Nashville?" But it was not a "concert" it was a "gig"—"we're going to the gig." The words didn't come off of my tongue the same. And Bob and Alan dressed hip, and they talked hip … and here I was, an ol' straight guy that came out of the bank with a crew cut, white socks and a J.C. Penney suit. I quickly learned that I had to get a crash course in being hip.

I hadn't traveled around the country much, you know, I had been to a few places, but I hadn't seen any of the big cities or been to New York. But I was doing my best to act cool, and I was practicing the soul handshakes and the slapping of the palms—the "give me five" gesture.

I was doing my best to assimilate what I had learned, whenever I could. One day, a bunch of us were riding along the New Jersey turnpike.

Normally, James Brown would ride in a limo, but every once and a while, he'd let his hair down and drive himself. On this day, he rented a Cadillac Eldorado, and he had Danny Ray, and maybe Leon Austin, and somebody else in the back. I was sitting in the front seat, leaning on my briefcase as the guys in the backseat were talking and laughing … and Brown was running down the expressway at 90 to 100 miles an hour.

Somewhere along the way, I had drifted off in my own thoughts and had lost the gist of their conversation. I didn't know what in the hell they were talking about, but James Brown turns to me and mumbles something, and then he stuck his hand out across the console of the car with his palm up. I saw this as an opportunity to practice my cool, so I said, "Yeah, Mr. Brown—right on!" and I slapped his hand and gave him five.

And he looked at me and laughed, I was thinking that I was real cool. But the conversation went on, and I'm looking like I know what he was saying. And he turned around again and said something right to my face and stuck his hand out. And I decided to be really cool so I kinda cocked my shoulder around with my left hand backwards and gave him five. Like, *Yeah, Bro'.*

All of a sudden, I realized that I had not understood half of what they're saying … plus, I got a feeling that everybody in the car was laughing at me. About the third time, Brown mumbled something at me, and I wanted to back him up, so I said, "Yeah, Mr. Brown! That's right!"

But when the Eldorado immediately started to slow down, I'm thinking, *Aw damn, something's wrong.* There had to be a problem, and I probably had something to do with it. It was just before we reached the tollbooth, when he slowed the car down so that I could hear him better.

And in his clearest voice he said, "Mr. Daviss, do-you-have-a-quarter?"

All along, that's what he was saying! He wanted a quarter to pay the tollbooth! Well, I gave him the quarter and felt a little stupid 'cause I couldn't understand him … but at least I had mastered the "give me five" gesture that day.

* * *

It took a long time for me to be accepted by Brown's entourage. Mr. Brown and I spent eight years getting to know each other, but to everyone else, I was still an outsider. That's why I was in awe of how guys like Bob Patton and Alan Leeds could step into their roles so easily. In fact, Alan met with Mr. Brown backstage after a concert and within the hour, Brown had hired him and was flying him to the next venue in the Learjet. After Alan's career with Brown, he moved on to work with Prince and then Chris Rock ... so he's done pretty good for himself.

But back in the 60s and early 70s, Alan Leeds was a skinny-looking guy with coarse, kinky, dark red hair and real fair skin. Alan looked like he'd never seen a ray of sun. And at that time, I had never seen a white boy with an Afro. I mean, it was as big as a basketball! ... all kinky, but it was perfectly symmetrical.

One time I was in Richmond, Virginia, and had to go to meet Alan at his hotel. I found him sunning himself out by the pool with Buddy Nolan, a black guy who was his sidekick at the time. It was really ironic that here was Alan, a guy I had never seen in a bathing suit, and next to him was Buddy Nolan, sitting in the hot sun wearing a suit and tie.

I kept thinking about how Alan was gonna blister because of his fair skin, but apparently he got a little hot in his lounge chair and was fixin' to take a dip in the pool. Then, all a sudden, it hit me! ... Alan's enormous Afro looked like a big sponge, ready to suck up gallons of water, and if he got wet, he wouldn't be able to swim outta the pool. Worst of all, I was gonna have to dive in and pull his ass out ... and I'm wearing a suit and tie! But Alan went ahead and dived in ... and when he surfaced, it was just amazing to see all this water run out of his hair. It was still in place, and he just shook it a little bit, and it was all still standing up in perfect shape. Now I knew about Afros—even though I've never had one.

Another thing was that Alan dated nothing but black chicks—and he eventually married one. This did not escape the attention of James Brown. He used to make remarks to me about Alan's hairdo and his preference for black girls and the black mannerisms he used. He summed it up when he said, "Missa Daviss, I think Mr. Leeds had done forgot that he's a white boy."

That became pretty evident one night in Augusta. We had been in the recording studio, and it was probably 1:30 or 2:00 o'clock in the morning. Alan Leeds and I were the only two white guys along with about eight black members of Mr. Brown's group … his hairdressers and bodyguards, and a couple of guys in the band. We were looking for a place to eat, so we stopped at a Ramada Inn, which was one of the few places that was open. It was so late that they had closed down most of the dining room tables so the 10 of us had to sit at the counter. I was on the very end, and Alan Leeds was sitting next to me. When the waitress, a little white girl, brought a tray of glasses, she went down the line, setting the water in front of everybody. But after she got to Alan Leeds, she ran out of glasses.

And I'm sitting there grinning, and thought to make a little joke about it and I said, "What's the matter, you're not gonna give the white boy some water?"

And she turned away from me and said, "I'm fixin' to get your water, honey."

Alan Leeds realized what I had said but apparently didn't pick up on my subtle sense of irony. He quickly turned around to the waitress as he pointed to me and said, "That's okay, give him some water … he's one of us."

Apparently, Alan thought I was the only white boy there! Later on, I told this story to Brown, and he kinda laughed, shook his head, and said, "Yeah, Missa Leeds thinks he's a brother."

* * *

It was obvious that I would never become a black person. I was white, but more than that, I was from the south … which opened me up for a lot of discrimination. I'm not trying to get your sympathy, but it's a fact—white people from the south are considered second-class citizens by the rest of the country. Or at least in New York.

When James Brown lived in St. Albans, Queens, I caught a cab ride to his home on many occasions. I finally discovered that it was about a $3 ride, and I had been paying $15 to $20 simply because when the cabby heard my southern accent, he'd charge me extra. I didn't know any better.

I was always traveling somewhere to meet Mr. Brown. Every Saturday night, no matter where he was, I would deliver the paperwork, catch up on contracts, and do his payroll … no matter if he was in Tokyo, South America or Europe. Once I arrived, we ended up doing most of our business after the show, and I knew I'd be up until 3 or 4 in the morning. But before the concert, Brown wanted to see me before he hit the stage, simply to know I had arrived at the venue. So I would plan my schedule to be backstage about 30 minutes before the opening … I really hated hanging around … waiting and waiting.

James Brown had played the Apollo many times before I began to work for him, but when my first "gig" at the Apollo came, I wanted to plan my movements very efficiently and timely. I had arrived too late at the hotel to grab the limo to the Apollo, so I asked the doorman at the hotel how much the cab fare would be. (I didn't want to get ripped off again.)

And he said, "Oh, you're going to the Apollo Theater on 125th Street in Harlem? You don't need to pay a cab fare … not in this kinda traffic at this time of day. You need to get up there kinda quick. See the subway sign across the street over there? What you do is get on the train and get off at the 125th Street station."

Sounded pretty simple to me. Hell, I'd never been on a subway, and I had been wanting to ride one anyway … plus it was a lovely summer evening—wasn't quite dark yet. And the best part was that it would only cost about 50 cents. The doorman was very helpful and told me to get off at the 125th Street station, and when I came up the stairs, to go two blocks down the street until I saw the big Apollo sign. Quick, easy and cheap.

So I started on my way. I had my banker's suit on with its late-60s flared pants, a light blue shirt and my Gucci briefcase. I went down into the subway, put my money in, went through the turnstile and got on the train. Nothing to it. And soon I was in awe of the whole thing, and I watched all the sights go by until I got to the 125th Street station. *Man, this didn't take long at all! I'm gonna get there early, too!*

When I got off the subway and the early evening sunlight hit my eyes, I could see the long line of people underneath the Apollo sign. *Man, this is something!* And then I started walking down the street, and I was kinda whistling and swinging my briefcase-real carefree, but I had only gone about 50 yards when I heard footsteps about six to eight feet behind me … two young black guys. When I looked over my shoulder, one guy's holding an open switchblade, and he's pitching it back and forth from one hand to the other. It's not a good sign when both guys had big grins on their faces. And as we continue walking, in a step-for-step cadence, the guy with the knife leans in toward me and said in a deceptively innocent voice, kinda sing-songy, "Hey, whitey … Hey, whiteyyy… "

He was just messin' with me, but I picked up the pace—just kept walking. I turned around again for another glance, when he said in strong, serious tone, "Hey, whitey. I'm fixin' to cut your ass. I'm gonna cut your ass, boy."

I didn't say a word, but I'm thinking, *Oh, shit! I'm fixin' to get my ass cut.* But I'm getting closer and closer to the box office, but he's still pitching his knife back and forth … and they're beginning to laugh … they're tormenting me now.

"I'm gonna cut your ass, whitey."

But I just kept walking, never breaking my stride, and I'm thinking, *Maybe I should break into a run now.* I was trying to judge the distance between us and wondered if I could make it to the box office before he cuts me. But then I started thinking that the best thing is to keep walking and don't let him know I'm scared. But then, I'm thinking that there's two of them, and I really don't see any white people anywhere … hell, I don't even see any police cars … and no taxicabs either! I'm thinking, *Damn! What in hell have I got myself into?*

These guys were serious. They weren't just playing. They were ready to cut me. But I eventually got near the theater, and there were all these people gathered up around the box office. I got caught up in the crowd of all the people waiting to get in, but I pushed my way up to the theater door.

The doorman said, "You can't come in here without a ticket. You've gotta go down this alley and go to the stage door." And he peeked around the corner and said, "See the stage door down there?" And there were people milling all up and down the alley … including the two guys, and they're still grinning and pitching the knife back and forth.

But I told him, "Naw, I'm coming through the front door. Look buddy, I'm the one who's paying you tonight. I'm the moneyman. I handle the money."

And he said, "I don't care who you are. If you don't have a ticket you can't come through the front door."

Fortunately, at that very moment, Henry Stallings and Danny Ray come to my rescue and told the doorman, "Hey, back off. This is Mr. Daviss—he be the man. Get outta his way."

Then we got in and headed for the dressing room where they started to laugh and told Mr. Brown about my adventure. Brown got to laughing, too, *Awawawaw!!* And then he said, "Missa Daviss! Missa Daviss!! You mean you rode the subway over here?" And he shook his head like, *Lawd, I thought you had more sense than that.* He continued talking to his dressing room entourage, "That's Missa Daviss—always trying to save money—riding the damn subway over here. Missa Daviss, you shoulda come in a limo."

But I said, "Mr. Brown, the doorman said to catch the subway."

And he continued to laugh and asked, "Weren't you scared, Missa Daviss?"

And I said, "Hell yeah, I was scared!"

Then Brown started to look introspective, and he said, "But you didn't run, did you? If you hada run, they woulda cut you before you even got to half speed. That's what they were waiting on … they wanted to see how bad they could scare you before they cut you. And I'm gonna tell you something else, you better be glad you got a blue shirt on. If you had your white dress shirt on, they woulda cut your ass right away. The blue shirt saved you … the blue shirt made you a little bit hipper than if you had the white shirt on. They would have still cut your ass and taken your briefcase … your money … even your shoes. I know they really liked those kangaroo skin boots you're wearing."

So I had to stand there and listen to his philosophy. He wouldn't let go of it. He said, "Missa Daviss, you need to stay outta them white shirts. Wear blue shirts, and wear a tan shirt when you wear a tan suit. You don't need to wear them white shirts unless you got a tuxedo on."

I usually didn't understand half the shit he was tellin' me, but I suppose, for my own survival, he was just trying to school me to be a little more street smart.

* * *

It seemed like my whole existence was based on Brown giving me an education on the realities of life. Another lesson came about one day when we were all gathered on the sidewalks of New York—I believe it was outside Polydor Records at 1700 Broadway. We had just finished up some business there, and we were standing outside Mr. Brown's limo shooting the breeze. As usual, I was wearing my banker's suit and holding my Gucci briefcase. Two or three feet away, Mr. Brown was talking with Reverend Al Sharpton, a guy who latched on to Brown like a son, eventually got on his payroll, and moved to Augusta, Georgia. This was about the time that "Rev" formed the National Youth Movement.

I call him "Rev" as a term of endearment. He really is a cool guy, and I've been knowing him a lot of years … and he really is an articulate, funny guy if you know him personally. I've got his number on my cell phone, and I recently told him to come visit me next time he was in Georgia, and that he could stay at my house. But he said, "No thanks, if your neighbors found out, they'd burn down the house." Well … maybe not …

But anyway, we were standing around with Rev who was with these young guys in the National Youth Movement. I don't know if they were his bodyguards or what. There were probably 10 or 12 of them, and they were gazing out into space. Real militant looking. And they were all dressed the same, with these National Youth Movement t-shirts on. Plus, they wore these little tams, combat boots and fatigues. They were all standing at semi-attention, spread along the wall of the building … apparently waiting on Rev to finish his business.

As part of my education, James Brown was always trying to make sure that I developed a little street smarts. He was concerned about me being so naïve that I would get into trouble and not even know it. So every once and while, he tried to caution me about things and try to head off any problems before they started.

Brown looked at the militant young men and said, "Missa Daviss, come here I wanna tell you something." And he points to the guys and said, "Missa Daviss, you see those cats over there?"

And I said reluctantly, "Yessir." Oh man! I could see that I was gonna be in for some more education. A class called, "Basic Streetwise 101."

And he said, "Missa Daviss, you see those cats over there? They're some badass niggers. They're baaaadddd!"

And I could see that Brown was groping for a term. He stuttered, "You know why they're bad, because they know how to use dat … dat … uh … uh … "

One member of our entourage, Al Garner, a smooth, radio-voiced whiteboy, overheard him and said, "Karate, Mr. Brown. They know karate."

Brown said, "Yeah! They know that kung fu karate stuff. Man, those cats are fast Missa Daviss … you don't want to tangle with a cat like that. They be so fast, they can kill you with one karate chop. One or two blows at the most. They faaaasssst! Do you understand what I'm talkin' about, Missa Daviss, they faaasssst!"

And then he started to laugh, *Awawawaw!!* … you know, standing on one leg … and everybody was laughing along with him on cue.

And I said very solemnly, "Yessir, Mr. Brown, I understand, 'They're fast'."

But he went on and said, "Missa Daviss, do you really understand what I'm saying? They-are-fast! They can kill you with one lick … fast!"

After a moment, everybody calmed down so that I could get a word in. And as I was looking very closely at the young guys, I'm pondering over the whole thing, and I got to thinking. I had a license for a .38 Smith & Wesson, a little magnesium snub nose I kept in my briefcase. Brown knew I had it, even though I wasn't supposed to have it in New York. But as all the laughter died down, I said, "Mr. Brown, let me ask you something. You talk about how fast they are with this karate chop … are any one of those cats fast enough to karate chop a bullet?"

Everything got real quiet—real quick. And Brown got up in my face and was staring at me real quiet. Thirty seconds go by. And suddenly Brown laughs, *Awawawaw!!* "I know Missa Daviss … he'd just shoot the nigger!"

And I said, "You got that right, Mr. Brown, I know better than to tangle with a guy like that. I know they're fast, but are they as fast as Superman? You know, Superman can stop a speeding bullet … but can these guys do that? Before he gets within six feet of me, I'm gonna get my gun out, and I'm gonna shoot him. Let's see if he can karate a bullet!"

The whole time, Rev was standing there next to Brown, and I could see that he was a little shocked by what I was saying. But I realized what Mr. Brown's intentions were. He knew I was hot tempered and that I'd swing on somebody in a heartbeat without thinking. So Brown was looking out for me … telling me not to mix it up with these type guys. I'm not a crazy man, but Brown knew that I would take on somebody no matter how big the guy was or whether he had a gun, or knife, or even if there were 12 of them. And more importantly, Mr. Brown knew that if he was ever in trouble, I would defend him with my life. He knew that for a fact.

Mr. Brown taught me something that day … but I also proved to him that I would stand up for him … no matter what—no matter how—no matter when.

CHAPTER 5

THE REWARDS OF FAME

James Brown was a superstar in the United States, but few of us knew what a following he had overseas … especially in Africa. At that time, there were two people known around the world … Muhammad Ali and James Brown, and on my first trip to Africa with Mr. Brown, it was simply unbelievable … you'd thought that Jesus had landed … uh, that's probably not a good way to put it. However, I'm sure that Brown thought he was bigger than the Pope.

I was sitting up in the first class section of a Pan Am 747 flight. Even though we were on a concert tour of Africa, we shared the huge plane with a variety of unsuspecting passengers. Eventually, the plane was scheduled to land for a brief stopover in Senegal—mainly to disembark a few passengers and board a few others. However, word had eventually gotten out that James Brown was on the plane.

This became real apparent the moment we landed, as a sea of black people surrounded the outer areas of the airport. They piled up behind this big ol' fence around the runway and in the bush on both sides of this dilapidated-looking airport. Next thing I know, the crowd had flattened the fence and had overrun the tarmac. We were in a swarming pool of African people!

They were up under the plane and hanging on to the landing gear, and they just seemed to keep on coming outta the bush. There weren't nearly enough policemen to control the crowd, and as they were swinging their billy sticks, it was like spitting in the wind. One guy even shot his gun off three or four times, but the crowd just laughed at him. To put it simply, it was just a damn riot! But James Brown nonchalantly looked out his window and said, "Yep, somebody done let 'em know I was here."

I'm sure the other passengers on the plane—the ones who didn't know James Brown was a fellow passenger—might have been frightened, but when the crowd started chanting, "James Brown, James Brown, James Brown," it became obvious what they wanted.

It was the biggest damn mess you have ever seen. Finally, some local officials pushed up a rolling staircase and came on the airplane. They tried to speak to the pilot, but he started raising hell. "Man, we gotta get outta here. They're gonna fuck up my airplane!" At the same time, the stewardesses were running around in a panic until the police finally came up to Mr. Brown, trying to figure out what we were gonna do.

Brown, very confidently, told them, "I can disperse the crowd," like it was not a big deal. "Y'all don't understand how to handle these people. I'll speak to them and tell them what the situation is, and they'll clear back. First of all, you're going about it the wrong way. You can't do it with billy clubs."

The police listened to Mr. Brown, and it was agreed that he would address the crowd and help to clear them away from the plane. But it wouldn't be easy.

The first thing to do was obvious—hair and makeup. In such a short time, it couldn't be a professional job, but Mr. Brown got a mirror out of his girlfriend's purse and started teasing his hair … puffing it up and getting it all fixed like he was going on stage or TV.

Finally, he made his grand entrance at the doorway of the plane and stepped out on the top of the staircase. There was a deafening wave of noise that ran over the crowd as people hollered and screamed and fainted. It was unbelievable.

The airport crew had rigged up a public address system with four huge speakers on it, and James Brown began by telling everybody how glad he was to see them and how much he loved them. He said that he had come back home to Africa to see *his people* and mentioned, "Don't forget, I will be back soon and perform in Senegal."

He spoke for about four minutes—five minutes at the most—and then he did his little dance. I think he might have done a split up there on the top of the steps and hollered, *Yowww! Yowww! Goodgawd!* and of course, that made them even more crazy. Finally, he said, "Look, I know y'all love me, but we have other people on the plane. We've got 350 people, and they're trying to get home to their families, and trying to get to their business, and they're just like y'all … they've got to be there to make their connections. So please, be ladies and gentlemen. Clear off the runway. Please step back … give us some room, because I don't want y'all to get hurt under the plane. So please move back beyond the barriers."

And magically, they started spreading away from the plane. And he smiled and said, "Thank you, thank you. Brother to brother, brother to sister … I need to be on my way. I got to take care of the world's business—to make your life better."

The mass of people started backing away from the plane, but with so many people packed together, it was scary. He added, "I will be back … and I'll do a free concert here. Just please keep moving back from the plane."

Then he steps back inside the plane, and the crowd started to part just like Moses and the Red Sea. They finally got everybody out from under the plane, and then they pushed the staircase back from the fuselage. All the time, Brown was up in the window smiling and waving, and he turned around to me and said, "Missa Daviss, wave at 'em … wave at 'em."

It was an extraordinary sight, and all 350 people on the plane had their noses pressed to the windows as the plane revved up and turned around, spraying kerosene exhaust all over the crowd. As we were taxiing down the runway, everybody on the plane was applauding James Brown, so he undid his seat belt and did a little bow in the middle of the aisle. He said, "Now that's the way to take care of business."

And as we built up speed going down the runway, the whole plane kept applauding, and we could see masses of people on both sides of the airport. In the press, they estimated 80,000 people had shown up … without the benefit of any promotion.

I was just in awe at that kind of power … just like when he stopped the riots in Boston and all over the country when Dr. King was assassinated. He had this kind of influence on people, and to this day, it still amazes me. People just loved and adored him … but sometimes it got crazy. I've been in crowds in the States and overseas when things got scary—even dangerous. I've had sleeves ripped off my suit as fans tried to push past me, trying to get to him. They were out of control, but they didn't know what they were doing.

One time I was in a crowd trying to get into Brown's limo. I was three-deep back in this damn sea of people so the driver let the limo window down, and I kinda body surfed on top of the crowd. The guys in the limo grabbed me by my wrists and pulled me over the top of the people through the window of the limo while the crowd was damn near pulling my britches off. Then the fans would be all over the hood of the car like flies, and laying over the windows so that it was totally dark inside the limo. What a mess.

And one time we were in Africa going down a river in a flat bottom boat. There were all these people jumping into the damn river along with the crocodiles and the piranha fish, grabbing the boat, trying to get in. And when they swam along side, the people who were acting as our guides were beating them with paddles so they couldn't turn the damn boat over. Now that's scary!

As all this was going on, I asked James Brown if he could swim. He said he could, but I got to thinking, "I bet he's lying. I ain't never seen him swim." But one day, the both of us swam around in his pool at home. He didn't like the water very much … but I've seen him part the Red Sea.

* * *

James Brown was on tour in France, but I had gotten separated from the entourage doing some business with a publisher in Belgium. Then I picked up some money, went to Geneva, back to Brussels and finally on to a music festival in Paris where Brown was scheduled to perform.

I arrived in Paris by train, but since the festival was so massive, I had to take a helicopter to the venue. I hadn't expected it to be so big!—bigger than Woodstock!—and they had about 20 giant TV screens set up like the world's biggest drive in theater. Just a sea of people! I finally worked my way through the crowd and got to Brown's trailer. He was expecting me, and I walked into his dressing room with several of the news media. Brown was holding court for about a dozen TV people as he put the last finishing touches on his appearance. As he teased his hair in front of the mirror, I talked to his back, even though we had eye contact from the mirror. It was all for the benefit of the press.

I said, "Mr. Brown, there are so damn many people out there I had to get a helicopter just to get in."

"Whatttt???" The he kinda paused, and said, "Really? … a lot of people out there, huh? How many people you think there are?"

"A promoter told me that there were a little over two million people! Two point two million to be exact!

"Whatttt??? Whatttt???"

"Yeah, Mr. Brown … that's more people than the Pope draws."

Then Brown got real quiet, put his comb down and stared at me in the mirror. He slowly turned around so that we were face to face, and in a quiet voice said, "Missa Daviss, you said a helluva thing there. A bigger crowd than the Pope could draw?" He looked around at everybody in the room to get a consensus and said, "Fellas, we can't let this get outta the room … we could cause a world conflict. We-cannot-let-thi s-get-outta-the-room!"

I said, "That's right, I've never seen a bigger crowd."

Then he turned around to the mirror and went back to teasing his hair. I could see him think, and he took a deep breath as a smile came over his face. Then he looked over at me and said, "Yup, Missa Daviss … I reckon I'm bigger than the Pope."

To him, he was. He was bigger than the Pope … he was bigger than Elvis … he was bigger than life itself.

* * *

As big as James Brown was, he was never too big for the home folk. And Brown had a real love for the University of Georgia Bulldogs. I guess we all got swept up in the frenzy of the 1980 season when the Dawgs, along with Herschel Walker, won the college national football championship.

During that time, Mr. Brown had a music/dance TV show on Ted Turner's local Atlanta station, WTCG Channel 17. It was called "Future Shock," and a sports commentator named Happy Howard introduced Brown to Vince Dooley, coach of the Bulldogs. After Dooley was a guest on the TV show, Brown and Dooley really clicked, and Brown started showing up on the sidelines at the football games and giving pep talks to the players … and since Athens was just an 80-mile ride from Augusta, it wasn't a big thing to take the limo over there for the day.

All the Bulldog fans were in a razzle dazzle frenzy about the team. Herschel picked up yardage every time he got the ball. They won, game after game, and somebody swiped some lyrics from a Jim Croce song, "meaner than a junkyard dog," from "Bad, Bad Leroy Brown" and started using it. That's how the Bulldogs became the "Junkyard Dogs!"

Soon afterwards, Happy Howard wrote down some lyrics to "Dooley's Junkyard Dogs" on a legal pad, and Brown agreed to record the song. That's when we gathered in an Augusta recording studio with this young house band of white boys to cut the record. Before we started, Brown stood there and hummed a tune, and more-or-less adapted one of his songs, "Jam 1980," for the melody.

Brown looked at the legal pad and read the words. Then, he cocked his head and started looking up at the ceiling and humming … then he started snapping his fingers and shuffling his feet while rapping the lyrics to "Dooley's Junkyard Dogs." The guys sitting there, young white boys, started picking out the guitar part, and the guy on the drums jumped in with the beat. Twenty minutes later, they had cut the tune, and the song became a big hit on the radio … but they never really released the single. Brown could have made a lot of money off of the tune, but he didn't. It was kind of a gift to the University of Georgia Bulldogs. It was a blessing … a very, unselfish gift that helped to built school spirit. Ya know, he could have rewarded them with a check for a million dollars, but he decided to give them something more valuable … pride.

* * *

Fame is a very contagious thing … and it tends to wear off on the people around you. I got caught up in it, and eventually so did my Daddy. James Brown and I were a lot alike when it came to our fathers. He was very close to his father. He called him "Pop," but James Brown also had the same feelings about my Daddy … and he would call him, "Pop," too.

Sometimes my Daddy would tag along with Mr. Brown and me as we traveled from one venue to the next … and there were times when we'd all be at the airport at 4 o'clock in the morning, and my Daddy would be leaning up on the wing of James Brown's jet just talking away, and I would get impatient with my Daddy and say, "Mr. Brown, you're a busy man. You need to be going … you got all these people waitin' on you."

But Brown would snap back, "I can go when I want to. Let 'em wait … Pop and I are in a heavy conversation here." Brown would do that … make Daddy feel like he was the most important person out there. Like, *This is your time, Pop.*

One reason I was so close to my Daddy is that my mother died at an early age, and since he had plenty of annual leave, there were times when I could take him to experience the jet set life. He loved it.

On one occasion, I carried him to Baltimore for a concert. Brown had a radio station there, WEBB, plus he also bought a hotel where we all used to stay. I'd put Daddy up there in the bridal suite all the time. The first time the suite was already booked, we had to put Daddy in another suite, he got his mouth stuck out … he thought it was his own personal suite.

James Brown really spoiled my Daddy. He said, "Pop, you make yourself at home at the hotel. Anything you need, you just sign a ticket for it, and Missa Daviss will take care of it and okay it with the hotel manager. We've got a restaurant, a drug store, coffee shop, valet service, a bar … anything at the hotel—just make yourself at home, sign the ticket, and Missa Daviss will take care of it. And Pop … have a good time!" Sure enough, Daddy was living the good life.

One night, I was busy, so I left Daddy on his own. He wanted to go in the bar and chase some women. The next morning, Daddy and I were sitting there eating breakfast when the young, hotel manager leaned over my shoulder and asked if I could okay some hotel charges. I was going through them and found various receipts where Daddy had ordered room service and bought some film in the drug store, but when I came to the bar bill … I looked at it and thought I was seeing double. I had to wipe my eyes … the tab was $780!

I said, "Gawdamighty! Damn, Daddy, how can you drink $780 worth of liquor?"

But Daddy just folded his arms and rears back with his mouth stuck out and said, "Well hell, James told me to just sign the tickets for whatever I needed."

I said, "But Daddy, there's no need to abuse his generosity!" All the time the manager is standing there anxiously waiting for me to sign the tickets, but I kept on. "Daddy, how were you able to run up a bill like this?"

Daddy said, "Well, I was sitting there, and got to talking with people and I told them that my son worked for James Brown … and we owned the hotel. So I bought a few drinks for this nice couple from California … and for another couple on the other side, we got to talking, and they wanted to know if I knew James Brown and I said, 'Hell yeah, I know James Brown! … my son works for him'. And then there was this other couple … I bought them a drink … and there was another guy sitting at the table, and he was talking about the Atlanta Braves and Georgia football … and hell, I bought him a few drinks … and as a matter of fact, after a while, I set the whole damn bar up!"

So that's the story! Daddy was in the bar bragging like he owned the hotel … like he was Donald Trump or somebody. And I said, "Damn, Daddy!"

And about that time, James Brown walks up, and he could tell that I was irritated with my Daddy about something, and he said, "Pop, how are you doing this morning?"

Daddy said, "Fine."

And James saw the frown on my face and the receipts in my hand and said, "Missa Daviss, what's wrong?"

I said, "Aw Mr. Brown, I'm just getting on my Daddy here. He run up a pretty good sized bar bill, but it's too much … I'll take care of it myself out of my pocket."

He said, "What are you talking about?" And then he looked at the tickets, and he saw the $780, and said, "Well, what's the problem, Missa Daviss?"

I said, "The problem is, this is outrageous. Daddy knows better than this."

And James Brown said, "I told Pop that he could have anything he wanted. He's having a good time. You leave your Daddy alone. Pop, you can have anything you want in the hotel. Missa Daviss, okay those tickets and give them to the manager, and let's have breakfast." Then he put his arm around Daddy and sat down and said, "I'm glad to see you having a good time, Pop. Missa Daviss, you leave your Daddy alone. He's having a good time."

And I said, "Hell, Mr. Brown, the next thing you know he'll be wanting to borrow your jet."

And Daddy added, "You know that's not a bad idea! I'd like to take another ride on it without having to ride with all them other people."

I couldn't believe it. I got real sarcastic and said, "Yeah, he'd be wanting to take it off to the Bahamas or somewhere."

James said, "Pop, you just sign any tickets you want."

So Daddy's sitting there, and he cut his eyes at me and had his mouth stuck out, and he looks at me with this old "F You" look. If I was the one who was running up the bar bill, James Brown would have blown his stack. Like, *Who do you think you are … giving away money?*

It's funny that James Brown would let my Daddy get away with murder. I'd do the same thing for his Daddy, too. I suppose no matter who you are, whether you're rich or famous, it's always a great feeling to be a hero to somebody … not to a whole sea of people, but just to one special person.

* * *

Working for James Brown, I discovered the power of fame and how it'll open doors for you. And I also learned that when you're famous, or even if people *think you're famous*, you become a much more interesting person.

This all became evident when I was doing a lot of work in Baltimore at WEBB. I spent a lot of time with Al Garner, the other token white boy, and the black station manager, Jim Sears, who called himself, "Diamond Jim Sears—God's Gift To The World." Al and Jim were a real pair … and they could pull off more stunts than you could ever imagine. Jim Sears could even sell you a sack of sand in the desert.

A couple of times a week, I commuted back and forth, from Atlanta to Baltimore. I'd fly up in the morning, and return on the 5:20 or 7:20 flight. And if I missed those, I could fly out around 8:30 from Washington. Anything to get out of Baltimore.

I hated to spend the night in Baltimore. I didn't like the city … I didn't like anything about it. I went there, did my business, and wanted to get back home for dinner. I knew the flight departure times so I could schedule my travel schedule down to the minute. But one time on the Wednesday before Thanksgiving, Al and Jim kept me late in meetings. I had already missed the 5:20 plane, but my ticket was good as a standby for the 7:20 flight. But Jim kept reassuring me, "Oh yeah you're gonna make the plane" … but this was the day before Thanksgiving!

All I had was my briefcase … I didn't have an overnight bag, because I didn't plan on spending the night. I kept telling Al and Jim to take me to the airport, so to pacify me, they gave me one of the frozen turkeys they had been giving away at the radio station. Finally, I got a little bit pissed off and said, "We gotta go. Now get in the damn car, and take me to the airport!"

I was looking at my watch—I knew we were going to miss the plane. And when we got to the airport, there were two agents working the ticket podium … and the place was elbow-to-elbow with holiday travelers. My standby ticket was almost at the bottom of the stack, but Jim Sears kept telling me that everything was okay. "Oh I'm gonna take care of you, Babe … we're gonna make it … I'm gonna get you on that plane."

And I'm said, "Jim, you're full of shit, man! I've had enough of y'all." And I've got my mouth stuck out, and I was stomping around there in the middle of all the people milling around, but Jim was working on a plan.

He kinda sidles up … moseys up … to the two agents, and they're busy with their heads down working on their little paperwork on the counter … and Jim asked one of the agents, "Hey Bro' … am I gonna be able to get on this plane?"

And he said, "I don't know. What's your name?"

"Fred Daviss … "

And the guy said, "Let's see Daviss … Daviss" … as he was thumbing through the standby tickets, and then he said, "Naw, there's no way you're gonna get on this plane. You see all these people here?"

That's when Jim, a big black athletic-looking guy, started to go through the motions. So he leaned back and kinda looked important, and he kinda stared off into space. Then he eased over to the guy and said with a lot of urgency, "Hey Bro' … I've GOT TO GET TO ATLANTA!"

"Yeah, everybody else has got to get to Atlanta, too. I'm sorry."

But Jim persisted, "Yeah, but you don't understand—I'm Fred Daviss with the Atlanta Braves. I play ball for the Atlanta Braves." And the guy kinda lifts his head up from his work as Jim continues, "I've got to be in Atlanta in the morning. I've got to sign contracts. Man, I have got to be in Atlanta … you know how they treat us niggers down south. I got to be there."

And the guy really brightened up and said, "Hey man, you play ball?"

This is when the power of suggestion kicked in. People in the crowd picked up on the conversation and started to whisper, "Hey that's Fred Daviss with the Atlanta Braves." And Jim's standing there, kinda boasting with his head up in the air, looking around … a typical ball player.

And then the ticket agent said, "Yeah … yeah, I remember you last season … I believe it was you who went up on that fence and snagged that damn ball outta the air … "

Jim said, "Yup … that was me."

That's when the ticket agent turned to his co-worker and gushed, "Yeah! Fred Daviss with the Atlanta Braves!"

Jim repeated, "Yeah that was me, so you see, y'all gotta get me home. Y'all got any boys at home that play ball?" The ticket again said he had two sons and Jim said, "Well write their names down here. I can get them autographed baseballs from the whole team. Write your name and address down, and I'll be sure to get an autographed baseball."

"Would you do that man?"

Jim said, "Yeah, yeah … I like the kids."

And as Jim was talking all this mess, several hundred people were whispering, standing there in awe, and they're pointing at Jim saying, "Hey man, that's Fred Daviss with the Atlanta Braves" … and the next thing you know, they were asking Jim for autographs. So Jim is autographing my name on every scrap of paper shoved at him when it comes time to board the standbys … two coach seats and one first class.

Without looking down at the tickets, the ticket agent gets on the PA system and announces the standby passengers. He says, "Daviss. F. Daviss." Then Jim reaches across the counter to grab his ticket as one of the agents says, "You have a good flight Mr. Daviss … and be sure to send me those baseballs."

Jim says, "I'm gonna take care of you, Bro'," as he walked past the velvet ropes to board the jet way. Now, all the people who are elbow-to-elbow in the passenger area are looking and pointing at Jim as he walks up to me, pretending that we're business associates. I don't look like a professional athlete … I got my briefcase in one hand and a dripping turkey under my other arm. Al comes up to me with a big grin and says, "Babe, I told you I'd get you on the plane." And with our backs turned to the ticket agents, Jim slips the boarding pass into my hand.

I said, "Jim you son-of-a-bitch!"

I looked over my shoulder at the agents, and they're still giddy, like, *Man, I just met Fred Daviss with the Atlanta Braves!* As we walked together in the passenger line, we came to the end of the velvet rope … I turned to go down the jet way, but Al kept walking straight for the concourse exit, saying, "See you later, Bro'." And as I was heading up to the door on the plane, I got a glimpse of the ticket agents with a puzzled look on their face … the little wheels are turning in their mind like, *Damn … something ain't right here.*

Even as I cinched the seat belt in my first class seat, I kinda felt like the stewardesses were going to pull me off the plane. But they never did. And as the plane lifted off for Atlanta, I told the passenger next to me about my brief career as a left fielder for the Atlanta Braves. Which only proves, no matter who you are … even if you have a soggy turkey under your arm … if people think you're famous, you're gonna get a break.

CHAPTER 6

Touching Stars

Through my work with James Brown, I got to meet a lot of famous people. A lot of times, I'd meet entertainers backstage at a talk show, or at concerts or at awards ceremonies. It's not hard to meet celebrities that way … the trick is getting backstage in the first place. But when you're with somebody like James Brown, the doors would always open.

When Brown and I used to have meetings in Los Angeles, we'd go to a suite hotel … the Beverly Comstock. It was about four stories tall, California style, and just a really neat place. They had this Italian restaurant on the second floor called Derek's, and it was a hangout for the pretty people around there. In fact, we had dinner there with a lot of TV personalities like Bob Barker and Ed McMahon.

One time I went there without Mr. Brown, and I was unsure of the dress code, because every time I had been there, I'd be with James Brown, and I had to wear a coat and tie as part of my business attire. I also wanted to know if I needed reservations, because James Brown didn't need reservations. We'd just walk in, and they found us a table, no matter what. So after just stepping out of the shower, I called down to the restaurant as I cradled the phone on my shoulder. I spoke with the maitre d' … a short, little fat guy named Richard Simmons. Yeah, the same guy.

He was so sissy on the phone, and he said, "Oh yes, Freddy … Freddy Daviss! … Where's Mr. Brown tonight?"

"Well I'm not with Mr. Brown. Do I need reservations?"

"Oh no, no, *you* don't need reservations. I'll have a table ready."

"What do I have to wear? Do I have to wear a tie?"

"Well Freddy, what do you have on now?"

And I kinda chuckled, and I said, "Right now, I'm standing here nekked, drying off, I just got outta the shower."

Then he said very suggestively, "Ooohhh! Just come the way you are!"

And I was thinking, "That little sonofabitch"! And when I got down there, Richard Simmons was dancing and flitting around the restaurant, and before I knew it, he was sitting on my knee … then, a second later; he kissed me on the forehead. Before I could react, he had gone to somebody else's table. But I was still fuming, like, *What is this son-of-a-bitch doing kissing me? I'll whup his ass!*

That's the thing about fame … even the hired help can become famous. But fame is a powerful thing, and a lot of people can't handle it. Coincidentally, the Beverly Comstock is where Freddie Prinze killed himself. He checked in but never checked out. As a matter of fact, I had stayed in that same suite. I learned that *after* I had checked out! From then on, I always got a room at the other end of the hotel … the whole thing gave me the heebie-jeebies.

But I still went back to the hotel many times and had some good times there, and I'll always remember having dinner with Ed McMahon. The ironic thing about it was several weeks later I was driving back from Augusta to my home in Riverdale, just south of the Atlanta airport. It was about 11 o'clock at night when I decided to drop into the Waffle House and get a quick bite. If you're not familiar with Waffle House, I'll have to describe it. It's a small, short order restaurant usually situated on off ramps or along busy intersections. They're open 24 hours a day … they have great coffee … and you can meet a cross section of America… muddy construction workers, prom queens, families with kids, and late-night party-goers trying to sober up. It's a great place.

So as I walked into the Waffle House, lo and behold, it was Ed McMahon sitting in a booth by himself! He was as surprised to see me, as I was surprised to see him! I couldn't believe it. I said, "Hey Ed, this sure is a long shot from the Italian restaurant at the Beverly Comstock."

He said, "Yeah it is, but hell … I like the Waffle House!"

And I said, "I do, too," and as we sat there, drinking our coffee, it dawned on me that fame is just an illusion. If you take a celebrity and put them in another environment, you can actually see them for what they are … without all the glitter.

People are just people, no matter who they are … and spending so much time with James Brown, I eventually saw him as a person, too. But even as an ordinary person without the glitter, he was still unique.

* * *

I guess what I'm trying to say is, "Celebrities are people, and you don't have to be a celebrity to have an attitude." I know about "attitude", believe me.

I told you about James Brown and his relationship with the University of Georgia football team. Well, one Saturday, Mr. Brown wanted to take my wife June and me to a game in Athens. We took his bullet-proof, Mafia limo to the Athens Ramada Inn for a pre-game breakfast. There were about 500 people crammed in there, and we were meeting a lot of old friends, including Happy Howard. We even ran into the actor/singer, Jerry Reed, a guy I had befriended through the years. Jerry was surrounded by all these Bulldog fans, and of course, everybody had their eyes locked on him, as he was deeply involved in the telling of a story.

To begin with, my wife June was in a foul mood … she was pissed off because she was going to have to waste a whole day hanging out with James Brown at a football game. At this point, I've got to mention this: June, my wife, hated to be called "Jean." When people called her "Jean," she used to blame me for slurring my words and introducing her as "Jean" instead of "June." It would piss her off to no end.

It was funny … June never called me "Fred" … it was always "Daviss," like she didn't want us to get too intimate or something … I'm just grateful she didn't call me "Mr. Daviss."

When June and I walked into the Ramada Inn dining room, Jerry Reed stopped his storytelling, jumped up out of his chair and hugged my neck. June just stood there in her fur coat and diamond rings and got her nose in the air like she smelled something, and I said "Jerry, I want you to meet my wife, June."

Since Jerry was deep into telling his story, he hurriedly said, "Well hello, *Jean* … how are you doing? It's nice to meet you." Then he quickly turned to a group of people and continued with his story while she's standing at his left shoulder. But she's obviously pissed off … got her nose in the air. So she grabs his shirtsleeve and snatches it to get his attention.

She says, "Hey! Hey! My name is *June!*" So he turns to see who's tugging at his sleeve but he keeps talking. In a moment, she snatches his shirt real hard, and he turns around again, but this time, he makes this hard eye contact with her.

And she gives him a look that would make you draw your ass up between your legs … and as she was grinding down on her teeth, she says, "My name is *June. Not Jean!*"

She finally had Jerry's attention … plus the attention of the 500 people sitting there having breakfast, but Jerry instantly turned into "Jerry Reed, The Comic Actor" just like you've seen in the movies, you know, the funny way he acts. So he turns around like he was going to make a big joke out of it … and for the benefit of all these people, he drops down on his knees in front of her and puts his hands together in a prayer position. Then he looks up at her with this pleading look on his face and says in a very loud, theatrical voice, "Please forgive me Miss June. I'm very sorry. I didn't mean to call you Jean. Please forgive me."

And the whole place was deadly quiet … everybody was shocked, but Jerry knew that it was a big joke … he was just smiling up at her … but June looked down at him, then she looked around and sized up the room thinking that she was the target of all this embarrassment. Then she looks back down at Jerry (the poor guy's still smiling) but June had a murderous look in her eyes and says, "Get up offa your knees … you fool!"

Jerry Reed was speechless … and you could hear a pin drop in the restaurant … even with carpet … and as everybody tried to get past the moment, June went over to our table to give her order to the waitress. So I was standing there alone with Jerry, and as he got up off his knees, he leaned over on my shoulder and whispered in my ear. He said, "Fred, you've got a cold wife."

I said, "Jerry, you don't know the half of it."

* * *

Whether you're famous or not, it seems like most of us men end up with female problems. James had his, I had mine … and while he was married to Deedee, his second wife, I was married to June—not Jean. Mr. Brown and I shared a lot of the same challenges … Deedee didn't like me, and my wife didn't like James Brown. And I believe it all came down to competition … Deedee had to compete against me for Mr. Brown's time, and June had to compete for my time against Mr. Brown.

Some wives would have taken it in stride, but not June. She was very no-nonsense—very straightforward. If she didn't like you, she didn't make any bones about it. She would let you know real fast that, *I really don't like you, and I've got no time to go through this bullshit trying to be tactful with your conversation … we've got nothing in common.*

James Brown tried to help the situation by keeping June involved in my career. After a concert, usually about one or two o'clock in the morning, Brown would get excited about something and suggested we call June and tell her about it. He'd usually call her "Sis", like sister, or Miz Daviss … never "June."

On a frequent basis, Brown would make me call June to tell her something. I'd call from a hotel or a dressing room, and when she answered, she'd say, "Why in the hell are you waking me up at two in the morning? I don't want to talk to James Brown! … even at a decent time, I do not want to talk to him—do you understand?"

But I say, "June calm down. This is my boss," but it was all she could do to keep from cussing out both of us.

There was no getting around it … no matter what interesting observation on life James Brown had in the middle of the night, nothing seemed to impress my wife, especially anything involving show business … except she thought Mac Davis and Tom Jones were cute. Coincidentally, we were planning to go to London for the production of a TV special with Tom Jones, and she was dying to meet him. I knew the trip would be a good way to spend more time with June because it always seemed that I was on the road. I would constantly commute back and forth to New York … leave in the morning and come back in the evening just to see my girls cheerleading at a ball game … or to see a movie … or just to have dinner together with my family.

Once on a concert tour in Chicago, I realized that June was getting mad at my continued absence from home. I was in the dressing room when somebody called and said that Tom Jones was at the box office, trying to get into the concert. James Brown sent me down to fetch him, but first I had to make sure it was Tom Jones and not somebody pulling a prank. So I went to the box office to check him out. I was surprised at first … he seemed shorter than he did on TV, and he had pockmarks on his face … a rough-looking guy with greasy hair and tight britches. But I checked his identification and sure 'nuff … it was Tom Jones, so I brought him back to the dressing room.

There, I explained to Tom Jones in front of James Brown, that, "You know I'm in the doghouse with my wife about coming up here to Chicago … and you know, Tom, my wife has been dying to meet you, and she'd be real disappointed to know that I met you and she didn't."

James Brown started laughing, and he says to me, "I didn't know you were in the doghouse! … why don't you call Miz Daviss … call Sis up right now, and let her talk to Tom. Tom, you talk to Miz Daviss and smooth it over."

I said, "I don't know if this is a good idea. I know she wants to meet Tom … but I know we're probably gonna piss her off."

James Brown said, "Naw, naw … call Miz Daviss … she'll love talking to Tom!"

And now it's about 1:30 or 2:00 in Atlanta, and as I dialed the phone and heard June answer, I got my ass drawn up, and I took a deep breath and said, "Hey June, guess what?"

"Daviss, what are you doing? Don't you know that it's two o'clock in the morning?"

I said, "June I've got somebody here who wants to talk with you."

And as she's talking through her clenched teeth, she said, "Daviss, it's two o'clock in the morning … and I don't want to talk to that son-of-a-bitch, James Brown!" And I'm trying to shift the phone from one ear to the other so they can't hear … but I know it's obvious to them that she is really pissed.

I said, "No baby, you don't understand. I've got somebody you've been wanting to meet."

"I don't want to meet anybody at two o'clock in the morning."

"No baby … it's Tom Jones."

"Tom who?"

"Tom Jones the singer. Tom Jones!"

And all of a sudden, she changed her whole attitude, and she said, "Oh my god! Tom Jones? You mean you have Tom Jones there?"

"Yeah baby. He sitting right here, and he wants to talk to you. He wants to meet you, too … and he wants to invite you to London and get you some front row seats for the taping."

She said, "Oh my god! Daviss, I can't talk to him … I've got my hair in curlers!" Whatta thing to say! … like Tom Jones could see her over the phone. Anyway, Tom got on the phone with her, and he calmed her down, and she was floating on a cloud after that. And I'm very thankful to him for getting my ass out of the doghouse … but then later, she was real pissed when her plans to go to the TV special fell through.

* * *

In show business, you never know who you're going to meet. I'm sure June never dreamed that Tom Jones would wake her up in the middle of the night just to chat. And I never figured that John Belushi and Dan Aykroyd would come outta the blue to offer Brown a role in *The Blues Brothers* movie. Strange things happen, and that's how I got involved working with a couple of movie contracts. After the film had been shot, I went to a New York recording studio with Mr. Brown to make some final changes in the soundtrack. That's when I found out what big fans John and Dan were.

When Brown and I arrived at the studio, John Belushi was just hanging around, simply waiting to see James Brown again. He was like a little kid … and not just because he was wearing some ol' beat up tennis shoes with knotted-up laces. I mean, I was the same way when I was a kid … the laces would break and I'd always tie a little knot in them, and they'd break again and I'd keep tying another knot until I didn't have enough to tie … finally I'd have to buy some new shoe strings. John Belushi's shoes were knotted up this way.

Usually when we'd go into a recording studio, there were always one or two gofers who would run down the street to get coffee and sandwiches. But the first time we went into the studio, John Belushi came running up to hug James Brown … excited as any little kid, and John said, "James, James, do you need coffee … sandwiches … what do you guys need?"

And James Brown said, "Yeah, I believe I will have a little coffee," thinking that John Belushi was going to send somebody to get it. But here was John, taking all the orders and writing them down with a pen on the palm of his hand. When he got all the orders for coffee and sandwiches he said, "I'll be back in a few minutes," and he ran out the door, and sure enough, he ran back a little while later with a sack full of coffee and food.

John Belushi was so down to earth that he never thought about sending anybody out to get coffee. Hell, he thought it was a big honor to get coffee for James Brown. He'd say, "How many sugars … how many sugars you need, James? … I gotcha some cream, some real cream for your coffee." But that's the kind of guy he was … even at the movie's premiere in New York.

Universal Studio really went all out for this movie, not only in the production but also for the premiere. They put us up at the Pierre Hotel and had limousines lined-up on 24-hour call in front of the hotel. They were there just for the exclusive use of James Brown and his entourage which included James Brown, his bodyguards, hairdressers, Miss Ella the maid, his young-uns and even his dogs. We stayed about three days, and Universal covered all the expenses for this small army of people.

On the night of the premiere, I put on my tuxedo. James Brown wore a modified tux with a short, black jacket with some sequins on it, and it had big, wide lapels. The jacket came down to his waist, and it fit real tight. And he wore tight, black pants along with his trademark black boots with those little thin soles … his dancing boots. Oh yeah … his wife was dressed nice, too.

So we were all decked out, and they were getting the limousines lined up outside to take us to the theater when Dan Aykroyd walked up, wearing some dark slacks and a short leather jacket. I was wondering where John Belushi was at, but while we were standing out in front of the hotel under the awning, I was distracted out of the corner of my eye by some homeless guy … looked like he was picking through a trash can or something. New York is like that.

The guy didn't drift away, as they usually do, but as I focused more on him, he turned out to be John Belushi! Gawdamighty! He was wearing those old tennis shoes with the broken shoelaces, some ragged-ass jeans and a flannel shirt with his sleeves rolled up to the elbows over some long handle underwear coming down to his wrists.

I wanted to say, *John, have you even had a bath recently?* But he was comfortable, and James Brown never said a word. Nobody said a word. Hell, if I had shown up with just my tie loose, James Brown would have probably fired me! But all of this didn't matter at the premiere, where we whooped and hollered like a bunch of kids at a Saturday afternoon matinee, eating popcorn and candy bars. We had a great time.

The Blues Brothers was a big success, but when Universal came to producing *Doctor Detroit,* they had tightened up the purse strings. They wanted James Brown to perform in the film, but they didn't want to pay for his band and entourage … they just wanted to use some local house band. This was unacceptable, and as we were on the phone, we told the movie producer that James Brown would never perform in the movie without his own band. He would just pull out of the project. It was really coming down to the brass tacks … and we had James Brown, the producer and everybody else on the phone, talking at the same time. That's when Dan Aykroyd jumped on the phone and said to the producer, "Don't worry about it. I'll take care of the cost personally."

When Dan said that, James Brown said, "No, I can't let you do that. Let's split it." In the end, I don't know who eventually paid for the band … I know James Brown didn't pay for any of it … but the band did get paid … and they're in the movie.

James Brown was really indebted to Dan and John for helping him get his career back on track, and it was reassuring for Brown to know that he had some devoted fans who hadn't forgotten him. Unfortunately, not everybody loved James Brown.

* * *

During the darkest days with the IRS and the FCC, Brown thought that he was so big that he could simply pick up the phone and call the President and ask for a favor … man to man … and there was no chit-chat, no bullshit about it. Brown would say, "The damn IRS is on my ass, and you need to do something about this. Hey, I'm the good guy! I pay my taxes!"

In reality, he didn't pay any taxes and only paid a portion of the withholding. I believe he was fooling himself by thinking that was enough. And he always thought he was above the law, especially when it came to something as trivial as owning radio stations.

At that time, it was hard for anyone to buy a radio station. Normally these licenses would pass through the family from one generation to the next … from the granddaddy, to the daddy, and then the son. It was a closed society, like a country club, and station ownership was something that was traditionally bestowed to the owner.

The ironic thing was that by acquiring radio stations, Brown was supposed to be joining this elite little clique of people who had their own little rules about how the game was played. But he thought, "The hell with the rest of y'all. I'm gonna play what I want to, and y'all can all kiss my ass. This is my radio station."

But there were rules that you had to follow. Actually, they were laws … and when you broke those laws, there were fines to pay. One real important rule involved the power and direction of the signal and having the antenna in the proper phase. This was something he learned about when his Baltimore station blew all the Washington stations off the air. Suddenly, Brown was the most talked about man in town … talked about, but not in a nice way. And when the FCC started coming after him, his response was like, *Hey, don't mess with me.*

The IRS also had an ongoing investigation that was just getting cranked up. They were after him for criminal charges, and they were out to put him in jail for things he did … not just owing money. So, that's what precipitated the meeting with Nixon.

Brown needed some backup, so I went to the White House to clarify some things that his radio engineer flunkies couldn't digest. Fortunately, Brown had met Nixon before and so we weren't going in blind, but we had great expectations. He told me, "You just don't know what this man has done. Missa Daviss, did you know he's put 168 black people in positions they never had in the administration?"

Apparently, Nixon had pulled out some documentation about how he had put all these blacks in powerful positions. And Brown was very impressed with this, and said, "This man, he's out to help the black people. He's no racist, and he's a smart man, Missa Daviss."

My role in the Oval Office meeting was rather minor. Brown briefly introduced me, and we had coffee as Brown and Nixon, hunched up on their knees, huddled over a coffee table. The President listened intently and acted like he had all the time in the world for us, and his sincerity was genuine, because right after our meeting, he took the heat off us.

It was kinda strange … all of a sudden, the criminal investigation about his taxes turned into a civil matter, and I could tell that Nixon wanted to help James Brown with the FCC. He knew that James Brown didn't know how to conform to all those FCC rules, and he didn't understand the IRS system either.

About three months later, I was in New York on business. Let me just say it ... I hated New York! I hated the cold, the slick people, the IRS, the record companies and the battles with the Madison Avenue lawyers. So many things were negative to me. And I'd be physically sick at my stomach ... I always had a headache. I hated it. Later on, I learned how to go with the flow and got to make friends in New York and Chicago, so it took me a while to see past all the negatives.

At that time, I was still not a fan of the Big Apple. I had spent the day arguing with lawyers at Polydor Records over money and contracting, and it was one of those typical wintry days in New York where it starts to get dark at 5:30. It was nothing but traffic jams, spitting snow and rain-and it was colder than hell. The Polydor offices were at 1700 Broadway, and I did a little dogleg turn up to the Avenue of the Americas to my hotel. There I was, I had my head down fighting the cold, trudging across the sludge with my usual New York headache, and all I could think of was to getting to my room, having dinner and taking a nice, hot bath. I was in a foul mood. I got to crossing the street, and I look up and I thought the damn hotel must be on fire. They had this barricade down the street and the policemen on the horses were keeping the crowd back. Then I notice this line of limos, and a cop said that the President was at the hotel for a function.

When I finally got through the security, and walked into the hotel lobby, Richard Nixon was standing there in front of a lot of microphones taking questions from the press. And as bad as I felt with my headache, I figured I should take a look at the President ... I just met him two or three months ago. While I was standing there, dripping wet in a crowd about three deep, Nixon was up there talking to the TV cameras when all of a sudden, he locks eyes with me. And then, he just stopped in the middle of a sentence, and he kinda cocked his head, and yelled out, "Fred!!"

And I'm turning around looking over my shoulders like everybody else trying to find out who he's talking to. But then, people were all turning to look at me! ... like, *Who's this guy?*

Nixon motioned for me to come up to him ... and I'm thinking, *Damn! This is weird.* So I pushed through the crowd, still dripping wet, and I was so shocked when he threw his arm around me and said, "Hey, Fred!" Now, everybody was really looking at me!

All of a sudden, my New York headache went away, in fact, the misery of the whole day just disappeared as the President of the United States was squeezing the wet, soggy shoulder of my raincoat and asking me, "Fred, how ya doin' buddy?"

I said, "I'm fine." I didn't know what to call him. He was calling me "Fred"—was I supposed to call him "Dick?" And everybody was breathless listening to what I was saying ... or stuttering. "I'm fine, uh, uh, uh, Mr. President."

And then it hit me like a ton of bricks ... this man knows me! He knows my name! I had only been introduced to him once by Brown as "Fred Daviss, my *Money Man*," but Nixon somehow had remembered my name! And now he was so friendly and so genuinely glad to see me. But he could also see how uncomfortable I was. And as he turned from the TV cameras and faced me, things got real quiet. He asked, "How's James doin'?"

I said, "He's fine."

Then he asked me what I was doing in New York, and I told him that I was fighting with the record company and going through all this mess with James Brown. He said he could help.

About that time, one of the Secret Service tactfully leaned over and whispered that the President was behind schedule. Nixon gave him a hard look and uttered something in my ear like, *son-of-a-bitch* in his gruff voice. His attention was elsewhere, and he could see a coffee shop through the window of the hotel.

He got right up to me and said, "Ya know, I wish we could just walk across the street and sit down and have a cup of coffee and shoot the shit."

And I said, "I do, too."

But by that time, the Secret Service guy was about to wet his pants, and Nixon leaned over to me again and said, "This is a shitty job."

I said, "I can imagine."

As they were hustling him out of the lobby, Nixon asked me if I was ever in Washington, and I told him, rather bitterly, that I was usually in Washington once a week. I said, "You know, the FCC has got a whole damn wing set up on us. They ride our ass like you wouldn't believe, and they're trying to put us outta business."

He said, "Really? James didn't tell me about that. Fred, tell James I'll take care of it." And he grabbed a business card from one of the agents and wrote down a telephone number and said, "When you're in Washington, give me a call and let's talk." I probably saved the card somewhere ... I used to keep it in my wallet all the time.

He was a man of his word ... he took care of the FCC, and just a few days later, I could see the change. The heat got off us all of a sudden, and people weren't threatening us anymore. They used to give us ultimatums and deadlines, and now, they were "going to work with us." But it was one thing for Richard Nixon to remember me ... but I'm sure the FCC will always remember James Brown. I bet I could walk into the FCC office right now and mention James Brown's name, and they would all just shudder with repulsion. I mean, he was like a damn hound dog throwing fleas all up and down the neighborhood, and they'd be squawking, "This man is ruining the radio business! He's destroying it. We've got to get him outta here!"

After seeing Nixon in New York, I got to know him better in meetings at the White House and through telephone calls. The first time he called the house was about 1972, and my daughters were having a spend-the-night party with about 10 little girls ... must have been a Friday. I just flew in from New York and flopped down in my favorite chair when the telephone rang. My daughter, Pepper, answered the phone as I read the paper, and I could hear her stuttering, "Yes sir. Yes sir, oh, yes sir. He's right here—he just got back from the airport. Yes, sir, yes sir."

And she peeped into the room, her hand was cupped over the phone, and she had a wild look in her eyes. She said, "Diddy, Diddy", not "Daddy." She was so breathless, she could hardly speak, and she began pointing at the phone and whispering, "The President ... the President!"

When I got on the phone with Nixon, he just wanted to ask me something about James Brown … he needed some details, and we talked for about 20 minutes. And I kept thinking what his motive was, because he was taking his personal time, on a Friday night, to do some detail work that was usually an assistant's job.

And as we were talking, I could see 10 little heads sticking out from the corner in the hall. During the following week, 10 different families had apparently spread the story, helping me to become a celebrity in the village of Riverdale. And parents would comment to my wife, "I didn't know that your husband was friends with the President." I suppose they were in awe … but they also didn't know I had the Godfather of Soul call me on the phone, *every night!*

It was the same ol' thing … I'd have to listen to Brown pissin' and moanin' about something or just chit chatting like I had all the damn time in the world to talk to him. All the while, I'm thinking I had to get up the next morning and do his business while he goes back to sleep.

I even had to have a separate phone line. This was before call waiting, and when he called me, I better damn well answer the phone. So, one time, about two in the morning, I was talking to him on the phone, and the other telephone rings.

Brown said, "Who's callin' you this time of night?" He was curious, and always suspicious, figuring it was somebody who was plotting against him. But I answered the phone and it was Richard Nixon. I mentioned to him that I was on the other phone with Mr. Brown.

Nixon was shocked and made some comment about Brown calling me "this time of night!"

I supposed I was tired and frustrated, but I came back to Nixon by asking, "Well then, what the hell are you doin' calling me at 'this time of night?'"

Brown was on the other line, and he got real quiet and said, "What does he want?" I could hear the jealousy come out. But Nixon only said that he was sorry to disturb me, and that he was still up doing paper-work … he simply wanted to pass along some contact information and phone numbers.

Mr. Nixon continued to call me on the phone, and frequently he would bring up his problems … mainly about the people who pissed him off. So I asked if it ever bothered him, and he said, "Hell yeah, it bothers me. I'm really a good guy!"

And of course, I agreed with him. He was a good guy … he was helping James Brown and me. I just wish I could have returned the favor, because I knew he had a lot on his plate. And it really hit home one time at the White House when we were standing there, and he made some comment about the news and how he thought he was being misunderstood. He said, "Fred, you know, I realize that everybody thinks I'm a son-of-a-bitch," and he turned around and looked me in the eye with this real serious look and said, "But you know, it takes a son-of-a-bitch to run this office." And that was the best way he could put it. He really cared that people misunderstood him, and apparently, it really bothered him.

* * *

I guess everybody remembers where they were when they heard Elvis had died … just like when John Kennedy was shot. I heard about Elvis on the radio driving from Augusta back home to Atlanta. Then once I got home, James Brown stayed on the phone with me half the night talking 'bout about how "poor Elvis is dead."

James said we needed to go Memphis and pay our respects because the Presley family wasn't going to give Elvis any respect, like *they were just glad to get him in the ground and spend his money.* Even when we were at Graceland, James said to me, "Poor Elvis, they done put him in this little ol' $200 suit. Like they'd gone to J.C. Penney's."

The truth was, Elvis had a nice suit on, but James Brown was trying to say, "They don't respect him," and they shoulda done this and done that. James Brown had his own opinions about things … he was always putting things down like that.

At that time, James Brown flew a Hawker Siddely DH125, but it was in Montreal having some work done on it, so we tried to get a commercial flight into Memphis. They were full, and we might not have been able to go when we wanted to go.

Brown knew I had a commercial pilot's license, and I offered the use of my own twin Comanche in Atlanta, but he said, "Oh no, Missa Daviss. I'm not riding on a propeller airplane."

He just didn't want to be seen in it … like Elvis would have been ashamed if James Brown flew to his funeral in a propeller plane … kinda like it was beneath him. In the meantime, I had been off and on the phone with Bob Patton who worked as a promoter for Brown. Bob was friends with George Klein and all of the Memphis Mafia so he had the connections to get into Graceland. Even so, it was hard getting a call to the house … I think they changed the telephone number three different times that day, but we finally arranged our arrival so that it was compatible with their schedule.

I was able to charter a Learjet out of Charlie Brown airport in Atlanta. I left my car there, and we flew into Augusta to pick up Mr. Brown. It was getting toward 9 o'clock, and fortunately at that time of night, I had enough cash on me to charter a jet.

As soon as we got to Augusta, I told Mr. Brown that I needed to be reimbursed. But Mr. Brown was notorious for getting amnesia about a bill, and he hemmed and hawed around until I said, "Mr. Brown, I need my money … now!" He reluctantly pulled the money outta his boot, and we got on our way. We were also taking Willie Glenn, one of James Brown's cousins who worked for him and Danny Ray, his emcee and the guy who put the cape on Mr. Brown at the end of his performance.

It was a 55 minute flight from Augusta to Memphis, and since they're an hour behind us, we got there five minutes before we left. It was around 10 o'clock at night, and it had already been a full day. We had been on the phone all day, and then we had to wait for Brown to get dressed and take care of all his little business. And I thought, "This is a helluva time to go pay our respects. It's the middle of the night!" But Brown had no concept of time, except when he had to get to a concert.

Once we got to Memphis, we had three police cars meet us at the airport. Instead of getting a limousine, we figured riding in the police cars would work better because we had to get through the crowd … thousands of people peeping into the windows. We were moving so slow, it actually took longer to drive from the airport to Graceland, than it did to fly from Augusta to Memphis.

I had never been to Graceland … I don't think James Brown had been there either. But I remember we didn't go through the main gate … we went through a side gate at the end of the fence. By then it was almost 11 o'clock, and we went down this little road into the backyard. They had floodlights on, and there were a good many people scattered around the back … sitting in rocking chairs on the back porch and sitting on the fence. We went in the back door and through the Jungle Room, up that tight little staircase through the kitchen and into the dining room. There was hardly anybody in the house … a couple of policeman came in with us, but they immediately turned around and went back out. They must have hung around in the backyard for the four hours we were there, or either they left and they called 'em back.

The casket was laid out at the end of the living room. The living room didn't have any furniture in it except for a big piece of furniture, kinda like an armoire, too big too move. And there was a wing-type chair and four or five folding chairs. The casket was at the end of the room with some sheer curtains behind it that went into the music room. His head was to the left, and his feet were pointing toward the front of the house, and they had the bottom half of the casket closed from his waist up … his hands crossed.

When we first walked up to the casket, Danny Ray had his sunglasses on … I don't know why, I reckon to look cool … so we stood there, Danny to my right and James on my left. As we were staring down in the casket, James Brown cried a little bit, hung his head and then he patted Elvis on the chest. Then he really surprised me when he started talking to Elvis … "You rat. You rat. I'm not Number Two no more. Elvis, you've gone and made me Number One now."

And I'm standing there thinking, *What in the hell is he talking about?* And I turned and looked at Danny Ray, and he's peeping into the casket at this big diamond ring that Elvis has on. From what I read later, it was like 11-carats. It was really big, and Danny can't get his eyes off it. And he raised his sunglasses and leaned into the casket and said, "Lawd!" Then he got up in my ear and whispered, "Missa Daviss, that's a heapa ring Elvis got on."

And Danny is looking over both sides of his shoulder, checking to see who's standing around behind him, and I'm thinking that Danny is gonna reach over there and get it, 'cause it was almost too tempting. I stared at him real stern for a moment and said, "Danny, you better leave that ring alone!"

But I couldn't worry about Danny, I was so focused at looking at Elvis … I couldn't believe that he was dead. He was just so young, and I think Brown could sense my anxiety, so he leaned into me and said, "Missa Daviss, you need to touch Elvis."

I said, "What?"

That's when Brown patted Elvis on the chest again as a way of showing me what he meant. Then he said, "Now, you need to touch him."

"I don't know Mr. Brown, I don't care about touching dead people."

"But Missa Daviss, if you touch him, it won't bother you no mo'."

"Whatta ya mean, it's not bothering me now!" But finally, just to pacify him, I reached over and touched Elvis on the chest and patted him on the hand. That seemed to satisfy Mr. Brown.

And he asked, "Don't you feel better?"

I replied, "Yessir."

Touching Elvis was a little difficult, not only emotionally but also physically, because I had my right hand in a cast. Several weeks earlier, James Brown was visiting my house in Atlanta and riding go-carts when I had a wreck … and I was in the hospital for a week where they had to sew my thumb back on. Now, every time I look at that scar on my thumb, I relate it to the time when Elvis died.

A lot of things went through my head while we stood there. One thing was, I never realized the size of Elvis's head. I guess it was because he was laying down rather than standing up. I thought, *I've never realized his head was that big.* This man had a big head on him! … and with his poofed-up hair it seemed even bigger. Also, he didn't look as fat in the casket or as swollen. He kinda went down or deflated somewhat … he looked more like the young Elvis.

The reason I noticed his features so much was that when I was young, my mother owned a hair salon, and she had a lot of little blue haired ladies come in to get their hair teased. They had a bluish tint in their hair, and you could actually see a little bit of pink scalp through their fine hair. It was the same way with Elvis. Even though Elvis still had a head full of hair, if you stood there for four hours like I did, glancing down there looking at little details, you're bound to notice things.

His hair was thin, it had been teased, and I could actually look down through his hair and see his scalp. Kinda pink looking, just like the little blue haired ladies. Later, my dad asked, "Are you sure that was Elvis?"

And I said, "Hell yeah, it was Elvis! That was him!" I saw little details that you usually never focused on, like a little blackhead or a little bump on his face, but when he's lying there, and not moving, you could really focus on him. So in my mind, there was no doubt that it was Elvis … and not a wax dummy.

A year or two later, Bill Bixby had a TV special about why Elvis could still be alive. They put these clues together with pictures, and threw in stories about why they had faked his death. Ridiculous! And one day I was coming up the road listening to a radio talk show, and I couldn't help but call in and tell them that I was tired of hearing all this bullshit. I told them who I was, and I said, "Y'all want to hear the real story?" And they put me on the air so I could talk with their "expert."

She asked me with a lot of authority, "So, you really think Elvis is dead?"

I said, "Well let me put it to you this way … I didn't see any of those eyewitnesses at Graceland that night … none of these so-called experts who are trying to prove that he's alive. They weren't in the house. I was in the house. I saw his body. And I guarandamntee you, Elvis is dead. I touched him."

While we were at Graceland, a lot of things were going through my mind … about life, about death, about friends, and we stood around and talked for a long time. And after you've stood there for an hour or so, you're gonna prop up against the wall ... or lean on something. I don't know what happened to snap me back to reality, but suddenly I realized that we were all havin' such a big ol' time that we didn't notice we were hanging on to the casket like it was some jukebox in a bar. Brown had even backed up to the casket and got his elbows down in it. It was almost sacrilegious, and I whispered, "Mr. Brown, we're leaning all over this man's casket!"

He stepped back, gave a quick look and jumped in horror. "Goodgawd!" he uttered. Then he leaned into the casket and quietly said, "I'm sorry, Elvis."

I needed a break after that. So I had gone back into the kitchen and made me a ham sandwich from some cold cuts. Everything was so plain in the kitchen. There was a washer and dryer and some newspapers were scattered around. I only saw two or three people in the house. The maid was a black lady, and a little ol' lady came through with bedroom shoes on. She had a bandana on her head like she was ready for bed.

Later, Lisa Marie came down, and I guess she must have been about nine at the time. She came down to the foot of the stairs, and she sat down on this round hassock. She was real quiet and curious about who these people were in her living room. She sat there sucking her finger, and I squatted down and talked to her for a minute. I asked if she wanted something from the kitchen, but she was real shy and didn't say much.

Then, Priscilla came down, and she was talking to James Brown. As she was standing next to him, she kept glancing over to me like, *Who's the white boy?* She was also noticing the cast on my hand. I guess Brown picked up on Priscilla's curiosity and said, "This is Missa Daviss ... "

Priscilla's face lit up, and she threw her hands out and gushed, "Fred!"

Well, I was real surprised ... I had never even met her, and she hugged my neck and wouldn't let go. And James Brown was standing there like, *What the hell is goin' on?*

As she continued to hold on to me, she leaned back and looked me in the face. She was half way crying when she said, "Fred, I've known you for years. We've just never met."

Then she told a little story about the times that Elvis and I would talk on the phone. She would usually be in the next room with the door cracked, sometimes putting her hair in curlers, as she enjoyed listening to Elvis and me swapping stories. She ended the story by saying, "Fred, Elvis really loved you."

And I said, "I really appreciate that."

She said, "Naw … he *loved* ya."

I was a little embarrassed and said, "Yeah, I guess that's because I didn't have to 'yes' him … I wasn't on his payroll."

She got the joke and continued with a bit of sarcasm by asking, "What, like James?"

We kind of laughed about that … but Brown chuckled out of courtesy, and he kept standing there wondering, *What in the hell was Missa Daviss talking to Elvis all these times when he was supposed to be working for me?*

But Priscilla was real nice to me … and I couldn't ignore that she was really a good-looking and sexy woman … you know, she just reeked with it. She put out an aura around her that her pictures just didn't do justice. Then she asked me about my hand, and I told her the mini-bike story. Of course, Brown jumped in and took credit for taking me to the hospital and saving my thumb. He didn't mention that he damn near wrecked the car pulling up to the emergency room.

Then Priscilla led me over to sign the guest register. She leaned over and helped me write, and as her hand awkwardly guided mine, we both began to laugh. I thought it was pretty cool.

We left Graceland about three in the morning in the police cars and went back through the crowds. Somebody in the press requested an interview so we stopped at a local TV studio for a while. By that time, the sun was coming up as we left Memphis and flew to Augusta. I continued on to Atlanta and then drove my car back home. And as people were driving to work in rush hour traffic, I was ending my day … a very memorable and surreal day.

I realize that a lot of people would love Elvis to still be alive. But that's the whole thing about it. When you're gone, you're gone. Just like

James Brown. A lot of times, I think of something I want to tell him, and I pick up the phone and remember that he's not there anymore. And I've had many dreams about Mr. Brown, particularly in the first few weeks after he died … almost every night. Same thing with Mr. Bobbit, his personal manager … we'd laugh about it like, *Damn, he used to keep us up all night when he was alive, and now, he's still keeping us up all night! He's doing it from the grave!*

I've had some dreams that were so real that, I swear, I felt like he was in the room with me. I still can hardly believe that he's dead. I really can't come to grips with it. Sometimes I'll get to talking, like I'm talking about him in the present, rather than the past. When I was at James Brown's funeral, just before they closed the casket for the last time, I walked up there and I got Mr. Brown by the hand, and I was crying because I knew that would be the last time I'd see him. And I could see people close by in the front pew, straining to hear what I was saying. I said, "Mr. Brown, remember that night we were at Elvis' house, I just wanted to tell you … 'You rat! You rat!'"

I almost expected him to smile … maybe wink his eye at me. I didn't have anything to do with the funeral arrangements, but what I didn't like was, they had put gloves on him. While I was standing there, I knew that this was the last time I'd ever see Mr. Brown. And I remembered Brown wanting me to touch Elvis, so I leaned in and patted James Brown, but I was thinking, *I'm touching you Mr. Brown, just like you wanted … but they put some damn gloves on you.*

That was right before they closed the casket up. And I've thought about that many times, and I wondered that since James Brown had died, who is Number One now? Well, as far as I'm concerned, nobody could ever take his place. No one.

CHAPTER 7

Didn't See That One Comin'

Every day I worked for James Brown was like some sort of damn drama. It was never *business as usual* … and if things got too routine, Mr. Brown would do something to stir up the pot. But stuff would happen all the time … stuff that you never saw comin' … just like the time when Porter Wagoner called and invited James Brown to appear on the Grand Ole Opry.

Now Mr. Brown wasn't the only black person to have ever played on the show. Charlie Pride had been on there but he was kinda in a category of his own … but I could never get over hearing this black guy singing along with this old country twang. In any case, Bonnie Raitt found out about James Brown, and she started raising hell about having this damn wild man setting foot on the famous Grand Ole Opry stage. But Porter Wagoner had his way, and they rolled out the red carpet for us and put us up in the best suites at the new Opryland Hotel.

When it came time to do the show, Brown was more distressed about his appearance than any of the Opry people. They welcomed him with open arms, but Brown didn't know what to think of it. The thing about James Brown was … he was a very private person, and his dressing room had all sorts of security around it. In fact, you were a privileged person to be able to come into the dressing room to get an audience with James Brown. Nobody could just walk in … I don't care if you were the President of the United States!

But at the Opry, it was a tradition to leave your dressing room door open so that everybody could walk right in and give you a hug. And that's what happened, and James Brown was in awe of this genuinely warm camaraderie. And it really never ceased to amaze me that James Brown could mellow out sometimes and actually change. So that night, James Brown kept his dressing room door open (except when he was putting his pants on) so that all these people like Barbara Mandrell, Tom T. Hall, Mel Tillis and Porter Wagoner could just walk right in. It was real folksy, and these stars were just family, you know, talking and gossiping and so forth, and they'd even walk in while Brown would be sitting at this dressing table trying to fix his hair.

Between all these people coming and going, Brown was getting a little anxious about his performance—his interpretation of an old favorite, *The Tennessee Waltz*. The whole time backstage, James Brown would be nervously humming the song like he was going on an audition or something. It was so out of character. And he starts mumbling the words, "I was dancing with my darling to the Tennessee Waltz … " but he'd get to a certain place and would lose it … couldn't remember the next three or four words. It was stage fright—something I had never seen. James Brown never got nervous going on stage. His performances were always cut and dried because he was well rehearsed, and he owned the stage.

But this night, he was wandering around backstage, and during every free minute he would lean over into my ear and say, "I was dancing with my darling … " but he'd lose it and he would snap his fingers and say, "Missa Daviss, I hope I don't forget those lines." And of course, I knew the song so I kept feeding him the words he couldn't remember. But I was thinking, *What have we come to when I'm telling James Brown the words to a song? It's just not right! I'm the one supposed to be handling the money … not the lyrics.*

That's because Mr. Brown used to say, "Missa Daviss, I'll take care of the show business—you take care of the bucks." That's why it was so ass backwards. Even right up to the time he went on stage, he was standing there peeping out from behind the curtains and still humming in my ear. "Missa Daviss … 'I was dancing with my darling'", and then he'd repeat the words over and over.

Finally I said to him, "Could you please shut up! I'm tired of hearing that damn song. If you can't remember the words, do you want me to get out there and sing it for you? If you want, I can go out there on stage with you!"

But when it came time to go on stage, the audience was applauding when they introduced him, and he starts to sing *The Tennessee Waltz*, and I was listening very closely, and sure enough, when he got past the first line, he lost it. But he was so smooth and professional that he just hummed through that part like it was supposed to be that way … his personal rendition. Then he went right back to the words and nobody in the audience ever realized that he couldn't remember the words.

After the show, Porter Wagoner gave a big party for Brown and presented him with a real expensive watch for his birthday, which was about that time. The watch was engraved, "From the Grand Ole Opry—Porter Wagoner." Mr. Brown accepted the gift with a lot of gratitude and expressed his appreciation to Porter Wagoner for allowing him to perform on the show, but later on, Brown just threw it into a shoebox with a bunch of other watches. He was not sentimental about stuff. I'm sure people thought he was gonna show off all his watches in his trophy case. But it meant nothing to him.

Later on, I'd bring up the story about the Opry to him, and we would laugh about it. I'd brag on him, and I'd say, "Mr. Brown, you were cool. You dropped the words, but you just picked right up on it, and never missed a beat." Of course, with his ego, he'd just eat it up, but the whole time I was thinking to myself, *Why in the hell didn't he write the words on his hand or at least have a little cheat sheet?* But I suppose he'd never been in a situation where he couldn't remember the words … and one thing I'm certain about … the Grand Ole Opry was the only place he ever got stage fright.

* * *

Early in my career with Mr. Brown, I'd often meet him at the Apollo Theater, and I kept running into this group of kids hanging around backstage like they were fans. It was my understanding that a guy named

Baby James Pearson, who worked for James Brown as a gofer, was trying to get a music contract for this struggling family singing group with Mr. Brown—he tried to sell the group's contract for $500. I'll tell you more about Baby James later, but he was a big tall guy with a gap between his teeth … and he had hands that could wrap around a basketball. He was a pretty intimidating character and had to duck his head going through a door.

Baby James had some sort of contract with these kids, and they were so young, but they had their father with them all the time. The father was Joe Jackson … and the kids were called the Jackson 5 … and I just remember how violent and how mean Joe was to the kids, and it seemed to me like he would stay on Michael worse than the rest of the kids. One time I walked out of the dressing room and Joe picked up Michael, had him swinging by one arm three feet off the floor, just beating the hell out him with his other hand.

I didn't want to butt in, but I said to Joe, "Joe, you're gonna hurt that child."

And he told me, "Mister Daviss, you need to mind your own business. He needs an ass whuppin'."

But by the way he was snatching him around and holding him in the air by one arm, I said, "You're gonna snatch his arm out of his socket and dislocate his shoulder."

Joe said, "Well, if I snatch his arm out, then we'll take him to the hospital."

And I said, "I don't care … you're abusing that child."

It really bothered me to see him beating on Michael like that, but they soon quit hanging around after Mr. Brown confronted Joe in the dressing room. Brown reportedly told him that he needed to keep the kids in school and that they didn't need to be out on the road, regardless of how much talent they had. Brown also said that he would consider auditioning them again after they had finished their schooling.

Mr. Brown had taken other performers under his wing, like Marva Whitney and Viki Anderson, but it seemed like he always had to control their creativity. Marva and Viki could have been successful with a different producer, but James Brown kept them too tight with his show and tried to mold them in *James Brown-style* rather than in their own style.

So, the Jacksons went their own way and made a big hit in the music industry. Not too many years later, I met the Jacksons in Los Angeles at the American Music Awards. It was the first big awards show I had gone to, and it was a helluva thing to see. There was so many people there backstage, and they had these big buffet tables laid out with everything from carved roast beef to lobster … just about anything you wanted to eat. And I saw Olivia Newton-John, John Denver, Tony Orlando, Glen Campbell, The Captain and Tennille and Dinah Shore. It was the first time I had met that many stars under one roof.

Plus, I saw the backstage stuff that the TV audience never sees … all the egos and the politicking and the vulgarity and obscenities … people hollering and screaming at each other. In particular, John Denver, who was in an argument with somebody and was spewing obscenities. I just couldn't believe it. And I couldn't believe how Olivia Newton-John had these beautiful purple eyes … maybe because she was wearing a lavender dress, I don't know. I also remember how many freckles Toni Tennille had on her back … you never see that kinda stuff on TV.

I couldn't resist the buffet, and as I was chowing down on all this great food, I saw Michael Jackson standing up against the wall by himself with this little tuxedo on. I had to squat down to talk to him, and he was looking so sad, just staring at the floor. He wouldn't make eye contact with anybody.

"Michael, don't you want something to eat … aren't you hungry?"

"Nawwsuh. Nawwsuh."

"Don't you want some chicken or a sandwich or a piece of cake … some fruit?"

"Nawwsuh. Nawwsuh, I'm not hungry." And he wouldn't eat anything, but I will never forget him standing there with his little spic and span tuxedo on all by himself … and it seemed like that was the last place he wanted to be. It was a pretty unforgettable night, and because James Brown was a presenter that night, I got to sit on the front row … right next to Dinah Shore.

But that night, looking at how Michael Jackson had matured into a great performer, I remembered how James Brown told me that the biggest mistake he had made in his career was not signing the Jackson 5 to a contract. But it's probably for the best … if he had signed them, he would have probably taken Michael Jackson down another musical path. We would have never heard the Michael Jackson we know today, but it would have been a helluva deal. We'll just never know.

One thing I do know is that James Brown was jealous of Michael Jackson. That's no big deal … James Brown was jealous of everybody. But when Michael started to develop into a superstar, he was no longer a cute little innocent kid … he was competition.

I remember one time Michael Jackson got on stage during one of Brown's concerts and started dancing. I'm sure Michael idolized Brown and even stole some of his dance moves from him, but Mr. Brown did not see any honor with Michael crashing the stage. James Brown sure nuff got his ass drawed up, and I could see the real anger in his eyes toward Michael. Crashing James Brown's stage just wasn't allowed … even though it was okay for him to do it to other performers.

James Brown had to always be the center of attention. He had to control everything.

* * *

James Brown didn't leave too much up to fate. If he wanted something, he went after it. Somewhere along the way, he decided that he wanted to produce a TV dance show … like American Bandstand, but with a little different twist-a soul version. He named the show *Future Shock*, after Alvin Toffler's book, but I don't know if he ever put the two together at the time—he just liked the name.

We produced the first two shows at a TV studio in North Augusta, South Carolina, but Brown quickly got paranoid and thought that they were going to steal this great show concept so we connected with Ted Turner who had a little UHF station in Atlanta—WTCG Channel 17.

This was before he created CNN, but it was in the works, and we were all impressed that he was going to spend $4 million dollars on a satellite!

We made a deal with Ted to shoot *Future Shock* at his little TV studio on West Peachtree. I guess he needed the money. At that time, Ted drove an old Toyota, and he put a sign next to a parking space by the front door that read, "Don't even think about parking here." That was Ted Turner's parking place, and everybody knew it.

We came up with a production format … James Brown was the host, and all he needed to do was a little on-camera opening and closing segment. Other than that, we featured a different musical guest each week, and there was a lot of dancing during the rest of the show.

Eventually, we got the production down to a predictable routine … like going to church on Sunday. Each Wednesday, we'd all congregate at the studio for a pre-production meeting, followed by an audition of the dancers for the show at 5 o'clock. Then we'd finish shooting the show about 10:30 or 11:00 and then edit it until about 1:30 to 3:00 in the morning. After that, we'd go down to the International House Of Pancakes on Spring or Peachtree or Ponce de Leon … wherever it was. I usually got home about 5:00 in the morning, and then I'd have to get up on Thursday and do my regular work … maybe hop a plane and go somewhere else.

One night, I drove Brown's Excalibur to the show … we were going to use it as a prop during the production. The yellow and black car was an exotic replica of a 1929 Mercedes with a 327 Chevrolet engine, headers, a Hurst shifter and big exhaust pipes coming out from the long hood. And man, it ran like a scalded dog! After we wrapped the show, four of us headed for the IHOP … me, my cohort Al Garner, a producer named Pooch and the show's director. As we left the studio, I decided to take the Excalibur on a little spin through Atlanta on the downtown connector near the Varsity drive-in on North Avenue. I wanted the guys to see how fast it would go so I ran it up to about 140 before I backed it down. Everybody had their ass drawed up, and I'm sure James Brown would have had a damn fit if he found out.

Despite the long hours, I really enjoyed doing the show and meeting a lot of legendary entertainers, but the coolest guy was Ted Turner. One night Ted brought his wife to the studio … she reminded me a lot of my wife, June. Enough said. Ted was drunk as a skunk and was tripping, falling and stumbling on the coaxial cables on the studio floor. He had obviously been at some social function … he was wearing a tuxedo, and she had on a full-length fur coat, and she was holding Ted up by one arm and somebody else had him by the other arm … and he was chewing Clorets, or some breath mints, apparently to get the liquor off his breath, but he had this green foam running down his chin, and his wife kept wiping it off. He was very charismatic, even when he was drunk.

They finally got Ted into the control room, and when Mr. Brown walked in, Ted threw his hands up and said, "James, you son-of-a-bitch! How the hell are ya?" It was so funny. Ted Turner was such a charming guy, he could get away with murder, and he was so disarming that he could even call Mr. Brown by his first name!

I knew Ted had an ego, but he was different than anyone I had ever met. One day we were having a business meeting in his tiny little office. I mean, it was small! … his desk took up most of the room with just enough room to squeeze beside it … and we had about four or five of us huddled around in chairs.

We were talking business when it came time to leave the studio for a lunch break. Ted had on his business suit and tie and had an overcoat hanging on the coat rack in the corner. While he was still discussing business, he said, "It's cold out. I'll need a coat." So as we stood up to leave the room, Ted became extremely focused on getting his overcoat. His eyes were riveted on the coat rack, but rather than walking around his desk, he stepped his long legs up on the desk and begins to waddle across the desk like a duck until he stepped off and grabbed his overcoat. I suppose in his mind, that was the shortest route to the coat rack. What makes it strange is that he didn't do it to show off … he just didn't realize what he had done.

During the run of the *Future Shock* show, I met a lot of fascinating people … like Dick Clark. Brown had made a trade-off deal with Dick

… if Dick would be a guest on *Future Shock*, Mr. Brown would be one of the presenters on the *American Music Awards*—a program that Dick Clark created and owned.

I don't know if Dick Clark knew what he was up against by having James Brown on his show. During rehearsal, Dick insisted that Brown read the cue cards, but he declined saying, "Dick, I'm a professional. I don't need cue cards."

A heated discussion followed and Dick Clark yelled out, "James, you crazy son-of-a-bitch!" Dick Clark is known to the public as a real nice guy … in fact, he is, but he's also a no-nonsense businessman with a salty tongue.

In the end, Mr. Brown had his way. As he entered the stage, he winked at me, and didn't read a one of the cue cards. Dick Clark said he was "a loose cannon."

Another example of being a loose cannon was at the Letterman show. James Brown performed a couple of tunes on the show and drove the audience crazy. When it came time for a commercial, Brown and Letterman were standing on the stage talking as Paul Shaffer led his band to the commercial break. But when the show came back on, Brown and Letterman were still talking on the stage. There were several more guests scheduled for the show, but Brown didn't want to give up the stage. The audience was still revved up for Brown shouting that they wanted more … he had the audience eating out of his hand, and this was something that he couldn't resist, so he yelled out to Paul Shaffer, "Hit it!"

The band struck up again as James Brown took over the whole show and performed for the rest of the show. The other guests never appeared.

After the show, Letterman was livid. He was cussing and raising hell and threatened never to have James Brown on the show again. But Brown was cool, and simply replied, "Man, you can't afford to do that … I'm too popular."

So when it came time for Dick's appearance on *Future Shock*, I could only imagine what stunts James Brown might pull. In any case, I went down with a limo to pick up Dick Clark at the Atlanta airport. I had met him several times before, but we had never been close enough to be off by ourselves talking. I knew that he was a real pistol … a very hard-nosed business guy, but when he got around my family, June, Kelley and Pepper, he was very gracious. Plus, Dick didn't let his ego get in the way … when it came time to shoot the program he told James, "I'm at your disposal. Tell me what I've got to do." I must say, Dick Clark added a lot of class to that particular episode.

While he was in the studio, it was up to me to work with him to iron out the details of production. Since the WTCG didn't have any dressing rooms, Dick and I went into one of the offices so that he could change clothes. Everybody had been impressed with how young Dick looked, but none of them had the opportunity to see him strip down to his silk bikini drawers. It wasn't like I was checking him out! I was just sitting there, just the two of us, but I couldn't help notice that his skin looked like a man half his age. No wrinkles, no liver spots, no gray hairs … his toenails, his fingernails, even his bare feet looked like a 20-year-old guy! I couldn't believe how young he looked! Later on, I commented about it to June, and she said with a lot of regret, "I wish you would have called me in there … I would have loved to see how young Dick Clark looked." Oh yeah, I shoulda done that! *Hey June, come in here! You won't believe this … and bring Kelley and Pepper, too … they'd love to see Dick Clark in his drawers!*

Every week, I'd meet some other people on the show. We had many entertainers on, like The Union Gap, The Chi-Lites and The Spinners. And B.B. King was one of the nicest … one of the last gentlemen. He's always been nice to me over the years, and every time I've been with him backstage, he always took the time to talk with me. A very gracious guy.

The strangest guest we had on *Future Shock* was Tiny Tim, and I suppose we caught him during his 15 minutes of fame. To be honest, he was a novelty act. He was this tall, strange-looking guy with long, stringy black hair, and he wore all this raggedy, hippy-type clothes. He had this big ol' nose, played a ukulele and sang in a falsetto voice and acted extremely effeminate … not a typical guest on our show … or on any show!

We had all seen Tiny Tim on Ed Sullivan and Johnny Carson and he even married Miss Vicki on *The Tonight Show*, so we knew what to expect. But when Tiny Tim and Miss Vicki came in from the airport, we took them back in the control room before the show. I looked over at them and saw them sitting there with their fingers laced together, looking like little school kids. I'd have to get his attention every once and a while to go over some production details, and every time he'd respond by blowing me these little air kisses. It was a little sissy mannerism he had.

I also noticed that Tiny Tim had a little brown bag with him, and when it came time to send out for some sandwiches and coffee, he declined … he just wanted a Pepsi. Nothing to eat. That's when Miss Vicki opened his little lunch sack, and pulled out some baloney sandwiches that she had made up. She had even cut the crust off and sliced them in half. And so Tiny Tim proceeded to spread a little napkin out neatly in his lap and eat his little sandwich, with mayonnaise oozing out, as he was dabbing his mouth with the little napkins that Miss Vicki had packed. She also brought some straws so that Tiny Tim could drink Pepsi outta the can, so dainty and feminine, and after eating his sandwich, they'd do a little smooching every once in a while. Tiny Tim was a trip … he was something else, and if he was putting on an act, he never wavered from it for a single minute.

Clarence Carter, the R&B entertainer, was also a guest on the show, and as many times as I had heard him, I never knew he was blind. And when he came into the studio, he had some shades on. Hey, half the time, musicians wear shades anyway—I didn't know he was blind! So while we were standing there, we were commenting on our footwear. Clarence looked down and said, "Those are some pretty good lookin' boots you've got on Mister Daviss."

And I said, "Oh, thank you." And I was real proud, holding them out, looking at them, twisting them around to catch the light, and I said, "Those are kangaroo skins."

And he said, "Yeah, those are some hip-looking boots you've got there."

And everybody around me was laughing, and I was laughing too, not knowing that I was the butt of the joke. When the laughter died down, Al Garner said matter-of-factly, "We don't need any cue cards for Mr. Carter."

But I jumped in and said, "Oh, no. We've already got the cue cards made up for him." And all of a sudden, everybody started laughing at me again. I got defensive and said, "I'm not kiddin' … we got the cue cards right here."

Al said, "He doesn't need the cue cards."

I said, "No, we gotta have the cue cards!"

And then Clarence said very diplomatically, "Okay, we'll use the cue cards if you want to." Finally, somebody called me over in private and told me he was blind. Oh man! I was embarrassed as hell, and I kept apologizing to Clarence half the night. Fortunately, he thought it was funny and laughed every time I mentioned it to him … obviously, it was a big joke to him, too.

By working on *Future Shock*, I learned several valuable lessons about fame:

1. Just 'cause somebody wears sunglasses, doesn't mean it's sunny
2. A lot of famous people try to act weird … some are genuinely weird
3. If somebody is rich and powerful, they can still drive a Toyota and be cool
4. And ultimately… There's no reason for famous people not to be nice.

* * *

A lotta times, fame comes from a simple association with famous people. Like fame wears off on you, and I think that's why people like to hang out with famous people … that way they can become famous, too.

Excuse me as I namedrop a little … as June as I were having dinner with James Brown and Ed McMahon at the Beverly Comstock … June noticed that Monty Hall, host of the TV show *Let's Make a Deal* was sitting at the next table. Oh, she was beside herself … a real celebrity! To

June, Monty Hall was famous! … not James Brown or Ed McMahon. Mr. Brown sensed that June wanted to meet Monty, so as we shared the elevator after dinner, Brown introduced June. She was a typical fan and really started to swoon all over Monty Hall, "Oh, I watch your show everyday!"

Monty was nice about it and asked June, "Are you going to be in town tomorrow? If you are, I'll have you on the show."

Very pessimistically, she said, "Oh I wouldn't win anything … "

"Oh no, we'll make sure you win something."

"Well, I'm not that lucky … "

Then, James Brown started tugging at her saying, "Miz Daviss … Miz Daviss … if he says you're ***gonna win*** … then you're ***gonna win something!*** Don't you know all these shows are fixed?"

I don't know if the games are really fixed, or rigged, or whatever you call it. But what Brown was saying is fundamentally correct … things rarely happen on their own. In most cases, you've got to know somebody, hang out with somebody or have somebody owe you a favor in order to get into show business. However, in my case … it was just a real miracle!

In any case, June never made it on *Let's Make A Deal* … we had to go somewhere the next day.

* * *

"Hanging out" is one of the most successful ways to experience fame … especially if you hang out in the Green Rooms of TV talk shows, like *The Tonight Show* or *Late Night with David Letterman*. Everybody famous will eventually have to wait their turn in the Green Room.

One night, we were in a Green Room, (I think it was the Johnny Carson Show) when James Brown happened to be on the same show with Muhammad Ali. Ali was a guy who liked to joke around and play little tricks on people, and James Brown was just the opposite … a no-nonsense type of guy. And it may sound strange, but Brown was a pretty straight-laced, conservative man. He didn't like his employees to drink or smoke, and he had his moral code about him. He even gave his dog a Christian burial, so when it came to the fact that Cassius Clay had changed his name to Muhammad Ali … well, he just didn't particularly go for all that kinda stuff.

Before the show, we were in the backstage hall and Brown and Ali were walking along as Brown was luring him into some real serious conversation. Ali was just going along, trying to look interested, but he started grinning at me. I knew something was up. So as Brown was walking along, looking down at the floor while he was speaking, Ali would put his hand up around James Brown's neck and bring his fingers right up to his ear. And he'd do this thing by rubbing his fingers so that it sounded like a cricket chirping. So Brown continued walking, but he kept hearing something in his ear. He'd stop and look around, but Ali was quicker. He could drop his hand down before Brown could catch him. Finally, Brown realized what he was doing and got so pissed off at him, and he lit into him and said, "Man, we're not here to play! This is serious! We need to talk about so and so," and he started on a little tirade.

But Ali was grinning and interrupted him by saying, "James you need to chill out a little bit. You're too serious."

Brown said, "No, *you* need to get serious!"

It was a clash of egos, but Ali thought it was funny. I stood there doing my best not to express any facial reaction … I didn't want to get in the middle of this mess. But it was just starting … the next thing you know, Ali got in his boxing stance and started cuttin' up with Mr. Brown. Ali would do his little jab at him, just teasing him, and would come within an inch of James Brown's nose with his signature jab.

Brown was getting hot and said, "Ali cut it out! Cut it out! I'm not playing!"

And Ali said, "Oh c'mon, James, let's spar a little bit."

But Brown was starting to boil over. "I'm not playing! Cut it out! You know I used to be a boxer. And if you keep on, and do that one more time, I'm gonna bust your ass! I will lay you out on the floor! Tell him, Missa Daviss. Tell him that I'll lay him out on the floor. I don't play that stuff. You think you're big … but I will lay you out. We'll do a street fight right here. There won't be no rules like in the ring. I'll lay you down."

Brown was serious. He was a fighter, and I've seen him fight with guys backstage. He'd wrap his arms around you and run you backwards into a wall. He was small, but it was always a fight to the death with him. But Ali was not intimidated … he just looked at Brown like he could snap him like a twig.

Brown cooled off a little bit, and we all went into the Green Room where we settled down into some chairs, when all of a sudden, Ali decides he wants the lights out … he wants to sit in the dark and do some kind of meditation. He had one of his guys reach over and snap the lamp off.

We were all sitting in the dark for a moment when Brown said, "Okay man, I'm not going for this! Cut the damn lights on!"

Ali was real casual and said, "No, we're gonna sit here a few minutes in the dark."

Brown replied, "No! … we're not gonna sit in the dark! Missa Daviss, cut the lights on."

And I was caught in the middle, but Ali was just teasing him with this big grin on his face. So I turned the lights back on, and while Ali continued grinning about it, he would reach back and switch them off.

That really made Brown mad, and he said, "I'm not playing now! I ain't sittin' in the dark with you! You're just like a child! So just cut the damn lights on!"

The more Brown got aggravated, the more Ali was eating it up. He thought it was fun to aggravate *The Great James Brown*. And it was a rare thing that anybody could aggravate Brown, because he always played on his own turf. Part of his intimidation and his control of people was being able to control his environment, but here's James Brown out of his environment having to share space in the Green Room with another superstar. And to make it worse, the other superstar is like, *Hey you put on your britches the same way I do.* So Brown didn't like it one bit. When he got out of his element, he lost control, and he lost power … and that's something he couldn't deal with. Finally, Brown got up out of his chair and walked out. As he was going through the door, his parting shot was, "I'm not staying here with this nigger." As he left, Ali was grinning along with everybody else … we all thought it was hilarious.

* * *

To quote Rodney King, "Why can't we all just get along?" That's right, why can't two people even sit in a room together? And why can't people of differing opinions treat each other with respect?

We're all pretty much the same. People are people, and the one thing famous people have in common is jets. Jets make everyone's world a little bit smaller to the point where entertainment, corporate business and politics are just one big fraternity of the rich and privileged. The only question is … "How can I join?"

James Brown loved his jets. At one time, he had a King Air 90 piloted by Bob Love, a young hotshot pilot who was a real ladies man. But more importantly, Bob was a good pilot, and James Brown really took a liking to him.

But Mr. Brown didn't want to be seen in just any ol' jet … he always had to have his jets customized, painted black, and carry the call number of 123JB. All the air traffic controllers throughout North American and the Caribbean knew James Brown's plane by the tail number and its unusual paint job because Brown wanted the world to know who he was.

After a few years, James Brown traded his King Air in for a Jet Commander that had previously served as a corporate jet for executives at Frito-Lay out of Dallas. You know, the potato chips guys, so it was done up in a very conservative corporate appearance. But when Brown got the plane, he gave it the same treatment as his other jets … he got a black paint job in Oklahoma City, and we spent a million dollars going over the whole interior with this customized, black leather upholstery. It had a real impressive look.

One day, Brown and I were flying along when I happened to look up at the little light fixture over the aisle … and lo and behold, I saw this Frito-Lay logo embossed right into the lens cover. I pointed it out to James Brown, and he looked at me real funny he said, "Oh man … we musta missed it."

I said, "What's this 'we' stuff?"

But Brown's ignored me as his eyes lit up. "Get that damn Frito thing offa that light! ... let's do it right ... let's put a 'JB' on it."

The Jet Commander was different than the King Air, and Bob Love didn't have enough flight time on it to meet the insurance requirements. That meant we had to get a qualified Jet Commander pilot to fill in for a couple of months while Bob accumulated time as his co-pilot. We got a guy out of Atlanta named John Mullins who probably had the most hours in a Jet Commander than any individual in the world ... like 12,000 hours!

This is where it starts to get strange ... after James Brown got rid of his King Air it became George Wallace's plane. Wallace was known as the Alabama Governor who said "segregation now, segregation tomorrow and segregation forever." So it was ironic that the Godfather of Soul's jet fell into the hands of the country's biggest segregationist. Of course, Wallace made some changes to the plane ... he repainted the solid black jet into something a bit more patriotic-a red, white and blue color scheme.

To make this story a little bit more ironic, when George Wallace was traveling all over the country campaigning for President, his staff decided to lease a Jet Commander, and they looked for the best Jet Commander pilot available. Guess who they got? John Mullins ... and John later told me about being at the Laurel, Maryland shopping mall when Wallace got shot. It's very strange that all these things, the plane and pilots, are all tied together making *the jet club* a very small world. Without taking this story down a rabbit trail, Bob Love went on to fly for porno king, Larry Flynt ... but that's probably a whole other book!

For one reason or another, many famous people end up making some weird personal and professional associations. A lot of people don't know that in later years George Wallace became very good friends with James Brown. Wallace even invited him to have dinner with him at the Governor's Mansion in Montgomery. That really surprised me, and I told Mr. Brown, "I can't believe that you're out there hobnobbing with the damn biggest racist in the country."

And it was the same way with Strom Thurmond in South Carolina, a former racist who later backed the MLK holiday. Strom and James Brown became very good friends and even Strom Thurmond's wife, a former Miss South Carolina, became very close with Alfie, James Brown's third wife.

Brown also became good friends with Lester Maddox, a guy who owned a restaurant in downtown Atlanta and refused service to black customers ... then he was elected Governor of Georgia. It's hard to make sense of all this, but it wasn't odd to Brown, and I talked to him about it. He said, "No, Missa Daviss, you don't understand Missa Wallace like I do—he's mellowed now ... and the thing about George Wallace is that he didn't hate blacks so bad ... same way with Lester Maddox ... the thing that made George Wallace so angry during the segregation days is that he didn't like the government telling him how to run his schools. Missa Wallace had a plan, and he said, 'We're gonna keep these black kids over here at this school and keep the white kids here in their schools.' He knew what he was doin'."

Segregation was a complicated thing, and it's hard now to even make sense of it, but back during the days of segregation, it wasn't so much that you didn't want to sit there and have lunch with a black guy. That was not the problem ... it was that you didn't want *your neighbor at the next table* to see you having lunch with a black guy in public. Therefore, you couldn't be caught sitting next to a black person in public, and that was kinda the dilemma I faced when I went to work for James Brown.

Working for Brown created an uncomfortable relationship with my neighbors. I knew, because the way they'd look at me, and they'd refer to me as a "nigger lover." And I've been called a "nigger lover" many times. But on the flip side of that, James Brown wanted to hang out with Strom Thurmond, Lester Maddox and George Wallace. Brown even said to me, "I admire Missa Wallace, and I'm standing up for what he did. But ya know, I don't take any of that racist stuff personally." And that's the plane truth.

* * *

I never knew what each day would bring. It kept things interesting. One day, Al Garner told me about an upcoming TV interview and how we were gonna have to escort the TV crew around town. Apparently, they wanted to do a bio on James Brown and come down to Augusta for a day or so … see his old neighborhoods, his school, the radio station and the bridge where he used to shoot dice. No big deal … in any case, it was always a lotta fun hanging out with Al … especially since he got me drafted as a left fielder for the Atlanta Braves!

As we were getting ready for the TV crew to arrive, Al mentioned that the person interviewing Mr. Brown was Maria Shriver.

I said, "Maria Who?"

"Maria Shriver … she's one of the Kennedys."

I guess I just wasn't that hip, but I got excited about it when we went to the Augusta airport to pick her up. As she and her small crew got off the plane, they gathered up their video equipment, but strangely, I didn't see any luggage.

Maria wanted to stay at a place convenient to our office located at the Interstate West Office Park on the access road leading from Washington Road. The office is still there, but they've remodeled and landscaped the place. We decided to check Maria and her crew into the Holiday Inn, near James Brown Enterprises, right off the corner of Washington Road and Interstate 20. That motel has since been torn down.

After they checked in, we all waited around for James Brown's arrival, but since his day began at 2 o'clock in the afternoon, he hadn't gotten up yet. He was always running late. In any case, we sat there and had a sandwich with her, but the thing I remember most was how aggressive she was and how she was hell bent to "do this and do that" … no friendly chitchat.

And I'm thinking, "Damn, this woman is one of these New Yorkers—a hard nosed, cold woman. She was all business." Like, "When the hell is James Brown going to get up? We gotta meet him … When are we gonna shoot this? … We gotta get a schedule … We want to see where he went to school and meet one of his teachers and go down to the radio station." And she was giving all these orders, and boy, these guys were sucking up to her! And she had her hair pulled back and had these sunglasses up on the top of her head. She had a pretty good suntan, and she was built! … muscular, and firm, stout legs. And she walked with a strong purpose, but it was a sexy walk, too, mainly because of the way she was built.

She was wearing these plain, navy blue pumps and had on this snug dress … kind of a plain dark, navy blue dress with tiny polka dots … silky and clingy. And another thing I couldn't help but notice was that she didn't wear any hose. Most women wear pantyhose with high-heeled pumps, but her legs were smooth and suntanned.

Maria wore very little makeup, but she still had a sexy look to her, and even though you couldn't call her "a pretty woman" … there was something hot about her … maybe because she had a small waist and a big ass which she would swing around when she walked. But she was a no-nonsense, all business-type person who wouldn't sit still—always snapping around giving orders. While we were waiting for Mr. Brown, we tried to make her comfortable, but as we sat there, I discovered we didn't have a whole lot in common to talk about.

By the time James Brown finally had his hair fixed and drove from his home in Beech Island, South Carolina to meet us, it was late in the afternoon. The video crew got some shots, and James Brown had agreed to meet Maria the next day so that they could take a little tour of his childhood hangouts.

The next day, we were running all over town with her. We had breakfast at the Holiday Inn, and then we spent the whole day getting shots until time ran out and she was forced to spend another night. The next morning, we went to pick her up at the hotel, and she called us into her room as she was getting ready. I looked around and noticed that there was no suitcase—just a small tote bag … and so, on our third day together, Maria Shriver was still wearing the same dress.

After three days of hanging out with Maria, Al and I started to see her differently … not as one of the Kennedys … not as a network TV celebrity … not as a guest of Mr. Brown's … but as a woman. And when Al and I were alone together, we'd started to share our observations about the way her silk dress would soak up perspiration and cling to her when she'd be out sweating in the hot sun … and how sexy she looked when she was giving orders to the camera guys … and about the smallest details of this thin, sexy, silk dress she had on. Finally, I said it … "Al, I don't believe she's got any panties on."

And he said, "I've been noticing that. I don't see any panty lines."

At the end of the third day, Mr. Brown, Al and I took Maria to the Green Jacket Restaurant, a famous place named in honor of the green jacket awarded to the winner of the annual Masters Golf Tournament in Augusta. By this time, Maria was looking better and better, and we were getting to know each other. Getting buddy-buddy-like she was one of the guys. She even started to open up to us by saying, "I didn't bring any clothes … I really didn't plan on staying here this long." And she goes on and on about buying some clothes, but all Al and I could do was wonder if that purchase included any undergarments.

As our minds drifted into this trivial speculation, James Brown and Maria got up from the table and started talking to somebody. And as she turned her back to Al and me, her behind was positioned about eye level to us, about three feet away. And we're both just staring at it.

All of a sudden, I zeroed in on her left buttock, and apparently she had backed into one of our cigarettes during the shoot because there was a small cigarette hole about the size of your little pinky finger burned clean through this silk dress.

And I leaned over and whispered, "Al, I'm sure she doesn't have panties!"

"What are you talking about?"

"Look at that little cigarette burn on the dress … you can see skin! I just knew she didn't have any panties on."

And Al and I starting laughing … we tried to keep quiet about it so were really just snickering and giggling like a bunch of kids. That's when Brown turned around and looked over his shoulder and saw us laughing behind his back … naturally, he got paranoid and thought we were laughing at him about something. As usual, in his mind, everything revolved around James Brown … but we didn't have the courage, or the lack of tact, to tell him that Maria Shriver doesn't wear panties.

CHAPTER 8

Dealing With The Family

So far, I've mentioned my Daddy, and how close he was to James Brown. Brown always called his father "Pop", and Pop always called Brown "Junior." But Pop was also like a member of my family … in fact, Pop and I become fond of each other because it seemed like I was always getting him out of trouble. He was a disarming kind of ol' guy who always wore a sweat-stained old felt hat and thick glasses with lenses smudged so much they almost look frosted. And you couldn't help but feel some sort of empathy for Pop … he stuttered so badly it was often hard for him to communicate. I could see his frustration.

Working as *James Brown's Money Man* was a 25-hour-a-day job, and sometimes I think dealing with all his family issues took up more of my time and effort than the music end of the business. One time, Pop had gone to a party in Augusta … somebody had thrown a party at one of the houses and Pop got into a confrontation with some guy from New York. Since Brown was on tour in Africa, it was kinda up to me to find out what happened.

Pop told me that he was in the kitchen, and he got into an argument. I didn't ask, but I presume there must have been a little drinking going on … add firearms into the formula, and you've got a recipe for trouble. It was inevitable. Pop used to carry this big ol' revolver with about a 12-inch barrel, and he used to stick it down in his pants. I've seen him many times walking around town with that pistol sticking out of his pants. And James Brown would get on to him and say, "Pop, you can't be tucking that pistol in your belt. You're gonna end up shooting your pecker off … tell him Missa Daviss," 'cause Pop would listen to me. Brown would always say, "Tell him Missa Daviss … maybe you can talk to him."

So Pop proceeded to tell me about what happened that night in the kitchen when he got in an argument with this "New York nigger." And Pop stuttered, "I tol … I tol … I tol … I told the nigger to shut up. And he picks a knife up outta the kitchen drawer." And when the man came toward Pop, he said, "I told him I was gonna shoot him right between the eyes … and Missa Daviss, he just kept on a coming, and I cocked it, and I told him I was going to shoot him between the eyes, and he come at me with that knife, and I shoots the nigger. I was aiming at his eyes, and the damn gun kicked so hard I had to empty the damn gun on him. They said I hit the nigger four times." Four times at close range! Man! Pop shot him in the neck, the shoulder and the rib cage, but didn't kill him.

One of the black guys at the party called Bill Berry, one of the white engineers down at Brown's radio station about one o'clock in the morning. Bill was a former policeman, so he was about to break the party up and keep anyone from getting arrested by taking care of the police. They swept it under the rug. It was hushed up. So after they got everybody out of there, they carried the New York guy to the hospital and got him patched up. Fortunately, the four bullets didn't hit anything vital, and they taped him up and put his arm in a sling. One bullet busted his collarbone.

Then these ol' redneck boys hauled him to Bush Field in Augusta, bought him a one way ticket to New York on Eastern Air Lines. Their last words of advice were, "Now get your ass back to New York and don't come back to Richmond County again, or we'll finish the job that Pop started."

We knew the Chief of Police, and the police knew all about it. It wasn't a big thing … back then they felt like *it was just a bunch of niggers killing each other … one less problem to deal with.* That's how the good ol' boys felt … and that still continues today. Black on black crime sentences are usually not as long as black on white sentences. I guess you could call it racism.

The police were also looking out for James Brown. In those early days, Brown was well respected in Augusta … he was a novelty, you know, the ol' hometown boy who moved back, and people thought it was a big deal. But later, when they got used to him being around, it wasn't such a big deal after all.

The whole shooting episode died down quickly, and I was able to talk to Brown in Africa and give him all the details. Basically, I told him that Pop had shot this guy and that Bill Berry had cleared things with the police and that there were no charges brought. When Brown returned from Africa through New York, we all went to meet him in at the airport. After he had gone through customs, he was dragging all these African artifacts and souvenirs with him, and as he cleared customs he emerged holding up this big ol' African tribal shield. He came strolling down the ramp, and he was peeping around the shield, acting all scared, and he had his hands up in a *Don't shoot … I surrender!* gesture. I thought it was funny, but Pop just looked at him and said, "You-you-you-you not funny Ju-Ju-Junior."

* * *

Yeah, guns always lead to trouble … sometimes when you least expect it.

One of the least glamorous jobs I had was signing the biweekly paychecks. Just a routine chore, but Brown wanted to involve his second wife, Deedee, into some of the business matters concerning James Brown Enterprises … mostly for one of the radio stations plus a few other companies he had. So he set it up to where she had to co-sign the checks.

On every Friday, I'd have to meet Mrs. Brown wherever she was … at home, at the hairdressers or wherever. Deedee didn't really get along with me that well … kinda like my wife not getting along with James Brown.

The truth was, Deedee was jealous of the bond I had with Mr. Brown ... a bond she could never have. Same thing with my wife—she was jealous of Mr. Brown. And on top of that, both our wives didn't get along with each other. It was a frustrating and ongoing thing, and Mrs. Brown would take every opportunity to make it rough on me by throwing a damn monkey wrench in the middle of things.

We finally got over it, years later after Deedee and Brown got divorced. I ran into her at Bobby and Vicki Byrd's house, and she hugged my neck and she apologized to me for making things so hard for me.

She told me, "Now, looking back ... I knew you were a good guy, and you were probably one of the few honest people that worked with James Brown. But back then, I didn't trust you because of all the rigmarole in this business ... in fact, I couldn't trust anybody ... and since you were white, it made it even more so."

I was really touched by what she was saying, and as she continued, she started to cry, "I'll never forget the time that you put yourself under the jurisdiction of the court in Baltimore ... you could have gone to jail for it. But there was nobody else, not even his family, who would put themselves in that position. You were the only stand-up man who would work for him. I want to tell you, as bad as I hated you, that I really felt sorry for you ... I thought you were going to jail trying to protect Mr. Brown."

I saw Deedee again at James Brown's funeral, and she cried on my shoulder because we both knew that we had a lot in common ... we both had put up with a lot because of Brown, even though we both loved him.

But it took years to reach that level of understanding. Most of the time, we were just slogging away trying to keep things running smooth ... but they rarely did. So one Friday, I was trying to run down Mrs. Brown so that she could sign the checks ... the maid hadn't seen her—nobody had seen her. It was almost as if she had disappeared when all of a sudden Deedee's father, Mr. Jenkins, came to the office. In a real hushed tone he called me back behind closed doors and whispered, "We don't want to let anybody know about this ... but I'm going to have to take you to Mrs. Brown."

And I started wondering to myself, *Why all this cloak and dagger? … What in the hell is going on?*

As I got in the car with Mr. Jenkins all he said was, "I'm going to take you to her." Finally, after a long silence he said, "We didn't want anybody to know … but Deedee is in the hospital."

I said, "Oh no. What's wrong with her?" I thought maybe she was having some type of female surgery that she might be a little shy about mentioning. But that wasn't it, and Mr. Jenkins just kept on hem-hawing around.

About the time we got to the parking lot of the St. Joseph Hospital in Augusta he said, "Now this is not supposed to go any further than us … Deedee had a little accident."

"What happened?"

"Well, we don't want to tell Mr. Brown about this since he's out of town."

"What do you mean … he just left yesterday!"

"Well … it happened just about the time he was leaving."

"So he doesn't know anything about it?"

And he quickly said, "Oh no! … No! … Mr. Brown doesn't know anything about it, but we're going to tell him tonight … he's already called several times wanting to speak to her."

"Okay, so what happened?"

"Well, it seems like she was … I better let her tell you about it. She's got a little minor gunshot wound."

I thought to myself, a *minor gunshot wound?* But as we walked into her room she looked fine except for this bandage on her shoulder. I didn't want to be tacky and try to get into her business … but I just couldn't help myself. So I blurted out, "Mrs. Brown, Mr. Jenkins tells me that you got shot. Where were you shot at?"

She was kinda embarrassed and said, "Oh, right here in the shoulder … "

"My goodness! What in the world happened?"

And she stuttered around and said, "Oh well I … I … " you know, real jittery about it like she had to give me some excuse. "Well, I was sitting on the side of the bed. You know my little pistol I have, I was cleaning my gun, and I dropped it, and it hit the floor, and it went off, and it shot me in the shoulder."

About this time, the nurse came in to change the dressing on it, and I was standing to the side where I could see both the entry and the exit wounds—the bullet went straight in and went straight out the back. I said, "Mrs. Brown, if you were sitting on the side of the bed and dropped the gun on that thick bedroom carpet, how did it go off?"

She didn't respond, but I kept on with more questions … like I was some sort of cheap detective. "How is it that if the gun hit the floor, the bullet would have come up at an angle, and when it hit you, and it would have come out your back at an angle? To me, it looks like it the bullet was level, went straight in and straight out … and what's with these great big blast marks around the entry wound … if that's the case, the gun would have been closer to your shoulder than coming up at you from the carpet."

And she stuttered around and she said, "Well I guess the gun must have bounced against the table and bounced back up, you know, kinda even with my shoulder."

"Uh, okay … then when it hit you on the shoulder, it went off. Is that right, Mrs. Brown?"

I guess I went too far. Very abruptly, she said, "I don't want to talk about it any more Mr. Daviss. Just give me the damn checks and let me sign them."

After that, there wasn't a whole lot of conversation about her "minor gunshot wound." But less than two weeks later, Mr. Jenkins had an accident, too, so I was obliged to ask him about it, so be began to recite his version of the story, "Yeah, it was just like Deedee. I was getting Mr. Brown's laundry down there at the cleaners and getting all them hangers out and the bags outta the car in there and the damn gun fell off of the seat … it hit the concrete driveway and shot me in the leg."

And I asked Pop how Mr. Jenkins was able to shoot himself in the leg just by pulling laundry out of the car and he said, "Huhh! Mr. Jenkins is telling you a damn tale. Ju-Ju-Junior shot-shot-shot Mr. Jenkins."

And I pretended to be shocked, "Really?"

And he said, "Yeah, I think that Mr. Jenkins was try-try-trying to get in his car, and Junior pulled the damn gun outta his coat, and he shot him right in the leg. You outta hear him holl-holl-holler! And he told-told-told him to get his ass outta there. He said 'I'm gonna kill you next time'."

I supposed that sounds pretty irrational to most people. But James Brown was a violent person … that's the way he came up—that's all he really knew … same way with the wife beating, he saw his Pop beat his mother and beat other women, and he just mimicked the behavior … it was a vicious circle.

When I came to know Pop, he was an old man—a lovable kind of guy who was funny with his speech impediment and his stutter. And would always come to me like a little child whenever he got in trouble. I didn't know him when he was young, so I never saw him treat women the way they were treated back then.

I really think James Brown felt guilty about his violence, the way he would lose his temper and get into doing something physical with his wife or his girlfriend … but he never would admit it. He just couldn't help himself.

* * *

I suppose we're all shaped by our environment and our upbringing. As a kid, I grew up listening to the big bands and the 40s music. Then when I became a teenager in the 50s, Elvis Presley came along with this hip new thing called Rock 'n Roll … and it was about the same time that James Brown was becoming famous, and all the kids were listening to the black radio stations and the R&B music. That's what I listened to, because I was probably one of the few kids in the south who didn't like Country and Western music. I just didn't like it. In high school when I first started driving, I used to listen to the R&B stations, but when we went out parking at night with the girls, one of the few clear stations you could get was WLAC out of Gallatin, Tennessee … a station that made the DJs Hoss Allen, John R. and Gene Nobles into national celebrities. Years later, I became friends with most of these fellas, but I would have never dreamed of ever meeting them while I was still in high school listening to their music … even though I never really cared for Country and Western.

While I was still working at the bank, James Brown asked to meet me in his Atlanta hotel suite after work. It was about 5:30 in the afternoon, and as I walked into the room, he was propped up on his knees and huddled up over the coffee table. He was really mesmerized by something on the TV. He cut me off before I could speak, "Shh … shh … shh … Missa Daviss, I'm trying to hear this."

And while I'm standing there, some ol' Country and Western band was twanging out some dreary *cry in your beer-type music.* To me, it was just some worn out honky-tonk ballad but Brown was so wrapped up in it. By the time the program went to a commercial, I said in total awe, "Mr. Brown, I can't believe you're sitting here looking at some ol' honky-tonk Country and Western show on television! Do you really like this kinda stuff?"

And Brown reared back from the coffee table, turned around and said, "Yeah, Missa Daviss, I like all kinds of music … now, I don't really care that much for this kinda music … but those cats have some helluva lyrics!"

And then it started to made sense as he continued, "Missa Daviss, what you don't realize … that's the white man's blues … it's telling a story. You know, a guy's sitting there, crying in his beer, talking about how his wife had done left him for his best friend … even his damn dog run off from him … it's the white man's blues."

I got to thinking about the words to the country music, and Mr. Brown was right … it is the white man's blues—it told a story—and Brown really liked that. He was deep into stuff like that … he surprised me, and I thought I knew him well. It all proves a point … you can never figure anybody out … ya just can't see it comin' sometimes.

* * *

Sometimes when you think you got things figured out, and you try to do the right thing—these are the things that will turn around and bite you, like the time James Brown wanted to surprise Pop with a brand new, dark blue Cadillac Coupe de Ville.

Pop was driving a banged up, beat up ol' Chrysler at the time, and when Brown showed the car to Pop, he was pleased, but he surely didn't want to admit it to Junior. And I think Pop was a little bit insulted like Brown was patronizing like *you don't have to give me no damn car.* The Cadillac was a much better car than the Chrysler … and bigger, too. The only thing Pop could stutter to say was, "It's a damn-damn-damn hog."

As Pop got in the car, Brown said, "Pop be careful." And Pop let the seat back and stretched his legs out and was playing with the window switches and so forth. But he cranked it up and left on out of there. Brown had commented to the Cadillac dealer that Pop would probably have a dent in the new car by the next day.

The next day Pop walked in the office and asked if Junior was in the building, but Brown hadn't gotten there yet, so Pop kinda shyly asked me, "Missa Dav—Dav—Dav—Daviss … what time is Junior coming? I gots some problems. I done bent the damn hog."

"Pop! Did you wreck it?"

Naw, just kinda dented it … "

And as we walked out to the parking lot, I saw that the whole side of it was messed up. I yelled out, "Damn Pop!"

Pop kinda mumbled, "The other side, too … "

So I quietly stepped around to the other side, and it was worse! Both sides looked like they had been sideswiped by a tractor-trailer! Tore all to hell! One of the door handles was dangling off, and one of the taillights was busted. And I said, "What in the hell have you done, Pop?"

And before he could say anything, Brown whipped around the corner in his own new Cadillac. And Pop said, "Oh-oh-oh shit. Here comes Junior."

Brown had seen the car from the road, and when he went past he just turned into the parking lot and stopped the car right in the lane—didn't even park it—just throwed the door open, got out, and stood there with his hands on his hips. I was standing there trying hard to be nonchalant … Pop had his head down like a little boy in trouble.

Brown shook his head and was almost speechless. "Pop! … Pop! … what have you … where have you … what have you done?"

Pop stuttered defensively, "I-got-got-gotcha, Jun-Junior."

Pop decided to exit the scene so he got in the car to leave, but Brown stopped him and said, "Pop! Man, this was a brand new car! What in the hell happened? Missa Daviss, tell me, what happened to the car?"

I said, "I don't know … I just come out here, and Pop said he put 'a dent' in the car."

Brown said, "'*A dent'?* Pop, it looks like you got up between two tractor-trailers or something. You been driving that car out on I-20?"

But Pop shook his head and said, "Ju-Ju-Ju-Junior it was your damn fault. Your fault."

"How is it my fault Pop?"

"You know my gir-gir-girlfriend down there, Suzie off of 9th Street. You know Suzie lives in that damn alley down there … you know that alley place. I wants to drive up in the al-al-alley to Suz-Suz-Suzie's house, and ya know the damn car you bought me Jun-Jun-Junior … it's a damn hog. The damn car is so wide that I gets-gets-gets up in the damn alley, and I never knew the damn alley got narrow. I gets in the damn alley, and can't back the damn thing up, and tore my damn taillight off, the damn door got hanged up in the window of ol' Jimbo … you know Jimbo's apartment over there … and I tore the damn window sill out … but I gets-gets-gets damn stuck. And I got both the damn doors pinned up and co-couldn't get out. I jus-just put it in "L", and I drive that damn car right on out the other damn end. I can't hep it. It tore all the shit off the sides … but it's just a little ol' scratch."

Brown turned to me and said, "What am I gonna do with him?"

"I don't know … he's your Daddy, Mr. Brown."

But Pop wouldn't let it go. He couldn't help but adding, "It's yo—yo—your damn fault Ju—Ju—Junior."

And Brown repeated, "Pop, I just don't know what to do about you."

"I tells ya—I tells ya what you can do. Ju—Ju—Junior you can kiss—kiss—kiss my ass."

* * *

Poor ol' James Brown … even though he was a big celebrity, he was like most American men—always on the line for everybody and everything in the family. Even the little stuff, like the time one cold, winter evening when Deedee had to pick up something from the local 7-11 convenience store. It was just a short trip, so she grabbed the closest car available, a sporty 442 Oldsmobile, and took Miss Ella and Deanna along for the drive. Since it was cold, Deedee just parked the car out in front of the store and kept the car running with the heater on. The car hadn't fully warmed up yet so the automatic choke kept the motor revved up.

As Deedee did her shopping in the store, Miss Ella sat in the passenger seat while Deanna, who was only about five or six years old, sat in the middle … I guess this was back before car seats. As little kids often do, Deanna was fidgeting around and accidentally knocked the floor gear shifter into "Drive" … and since the car was running in a fast idle, the car just shot off like a race car and ran right up, all the way into the store! The car ended up in the middle of the store, and Deanna was sitting up there smiling, like, *What? Did I do that?*

Fortunately, Mr. Brown was out of town, so Deedee believed she could hide the accident from him. So we made some arrangements with the store so that Mrs. Brown could pay several thousand dollars to repair the store without the knowledge of the insurance company or her husband. Soon, Mr. Brown found out about the accident and raised hell, but it could have been worse … 'cause the car almost wiped out a couple of customers in the store. But I think Deedee was more worried about Mr. Brown's reaction to the crash than anything else. So many times, Mr. Brown never knew about the trouble around him … we all tried to spare him—and spare ourselves from his fallout … even from the little funny things that just seem to happen … like the funny things Deanna would do when she was a little girl … she was like my girls … they'd always do these kinda kid things.

* * *

Not only did I have to look out for Mr. Brown's wife and children, I also had to take care of Pop … a guy who had his own set of personal challenges. Pop was dead set on maintaining his independence, and every month when he got his social security check, he felt like he had a little sense of power and independence from Junior. That's when Pop would usually stay up all night and go down around 9th Street to play a card game called Skins.

But one morning he came in, and he was sneaking around the office, shut my office door, and told me he needed some help. That's when he started pulling money out of his pocket—wads of money, and some of looked like it had ol' tobacco spit on it. Nasty, dirty-looking money, but he had it in rolls and wadded up gobs, and he was just dumping it out on my desk … I thought he had robbed a damn bank or something. But what he wanted me to do was straighten it up and count it because he figured that he had so much damn money, he couldn't put it all together.

Pop said, "Fi—fi—fi—fix it up for me like the bank does. And don't tell Ju—Ju—Ju—Junior."

So I took that money and straightened it up, and Pop was so proud. In other words, since I was the *Money Man* and handled millions for Mr. Brown, Pop thought by coming in there to my office, he was just as successful as his son. And as he pulled more money outta his coat pockets and from down in his pants, he said it was "kinda—kinda—kinda like Ju—Ju—Ju—Junior isn't it?" In other words *I got money, too.* It was amazing, but Pop had won about $13,000!

He said, "Missa Da—Da—Da—Daviss … I hits the jackpot."

But that was one of the few times he "hit the jackpot." Mostly he'd come in with a few hundred dollars, but on this morning, Pop wanted to celebrate so he carried me down to the Waffle House to buy my breakfast.

Pop and I had a very good relationship. He knew that he could run around and that I wouldn't tell on him to Mr. Brown. And if Pop got in trouble, I would do anything possible without crossing James Brown. Eventually when Brown found out about me covering for Pop, he got a little pissed off, but deep down he appreciated the fact that I was looking out for his Daddy, and he realized that there was a strong bond between Pop and me for as long as he lived. After they put Pop in the nursing home, Brown said to me, "You know, Pop really loved you, Missa Daviss." And I loved him, too.

* * *

I couldn't help but love his parents, but by the time I knew them, they were both up in their years and were kinda old and sweet. Even though she abandoned her only son when he was just a toddler, Miss Suzie Brown, James' mother, was the nicest little ol' lady … and she couldn't have weighed more than 90 or 100 pounds.

And she was always so polite to me, and when my wife and I came over to the house, she would say to us, "Lawd, Missa Daviss, y'all look like movie stars." She was always commenting on how I dressed and what a sweet boy I was … and she would just stand there, gazing at you over her little glasses, holding both of her hands together in a grandmotherly way. So I got to know her pretty well, and she often rode the bus up from her home in Bamberg, South Carolina … usually staying from three days to a week.

I don't know whether it was because of her age or what, but if you were talking to her she would be as lucid as anybody else … but there were times when I'd be carrying on a conversation with James Brown or whoever, and I'd notice she'd be standing over in the kitchen repeating things. She'd be in her own little world, talking to the wall—she was really a funny little lady, and I'm not saying this to make fun of her—she was just a character, just like Pop Brown was a character. The difference was, James Brown had more involvement with Pop, and even when Miss Suzie was in the house visiting, Brown would still pretty much ignore her.

Miss Ella, the maid, liked to gripe about things—it was her way of getting attention, and she would talk about Miss Suzie, too. And she would say, "Missa Fred, this woman is crazy. She comes over here, just worrying the hell outta me. She will get in the bedroom back there, and she'd be picking these imaginary bedbugs off the bed. Just pickin' 'em—standing there for 30 or 45 minutes just hunched up over the bed just pickin' em real fast like she was getting these little bugs off. And I told her there were no damn bugs on the bed. Then the woman would change the sheets … sometimes six times a day!

For a year or two, Reverend Al Sharpton lived in Augusta and worked out of James Brown's office. He had also fallen in love with Kathy Jordan, a former dancer with Brown's band, and they lived in a two-story townhouse apartment not too far from the office.

When I first moved to Augusta, I was *the new guy in town*, so I was relieved when Al Sharpton, or "Rev" to his friends, became *the new guy.* That meant that Brown had a new best friend and would regularly decide to drop in at 3 o'clock in the morning for a social call. Apparently, he and Alfie would be out gallivanting and decide, "Oh, let's stop by … they'll be tickled to death to see us." And they'd be ringing the damn doorbell at three in the morning wanting to come in and socialize, and Brown and Alfie would stay there half the night talking like, *It's no problem … we don't have to go to work next day.* And because all the restaurants were closed, he'd also want a steak cooked up for him.

After this routine went on for a while, Rev began griping about James Brown and what nonsense he had to put up with on the previous night. One morning, Rev came in real excited and said, "Fred, I swear before God, you ain't gonna believe this story! You know, that Miss Suzie is some kinda woman. Last night, Kathy and I went out with Mr. Brown and Alfie and we went up to The Green Jacket to eat, and we had a good time … at least he didn't come over to my house in the middle of the night! We got through eating, and he decided to invite us back to his house for some coffee. And you're not gonna believe this, Fred!

We were sitting there sipping our coffee, and Miss Suzie wandered into the living room and had set down there around the coffee table on the sofa next to me. She sat there peeping out over her glasses and listening to the conversation, just smiling just as big as life, and I kept noticing how close she was sitting to me.

And Miss Suzie kept inching over and getting closer and closer to me on the sofa. And the next thing I know, I could sense that when I was talking, she was hunched right up over my shoulder just staring at me over her glasses. And finally, right in the middle of our conversation, she was tugging at my shirt sleeve and said, 'Rev, Rev.'

And I stopped right in the middle of our conversation and said, 'Yes, ma'am?' and she was just looking at me with goo-goo eyes.

She said, 'Rev, I like you.'

And I said, 'Well, thank you, Mrs. Brown. I love you, too.' And I could tell during my conversation that she just continued to stare at me. And she goes to tugging again like she's not through talking.

And she says, 'Rev, you know I like you. I like young boys.' And I couldn't figure out where she was going with this conversation … You know, *I like these young boys, Rev. You're so young*. And during the meantime, after inching up close to me, she had her hand on my thigh, and as she talked, she'd squeeze it a little bit. And every time she'd tug at my shirtsleeve, her hand would inch up a little further on my thigh. James Brown wasn't aware of this going on, he was talking and wasn't aware that his mama was almost in my lap with her hand between my legs, squeezing my thigh.

And she tugs at my shirt again and she says, 'Rev, you know why I like these young boys, don't you?'

And I said, 'No ma'am.' And as she's squeezing my thigh and looking down at my crotch with this crazy look, she said, 'Because they've got them big … ' But before she could finish what she was saying, James Brown went to spewing coffee out across the coffee table.

He yelled out, 'Hush, mama!' But she's just sitting there, smiling almost like she was a child, you know, honest and no shame. And you know, that was the only time I've ever seen James Brown at a loss for words.

That's when Mr. Brown jumped up and looked at his watch and said, 'Mama, it's 9:30, I think it's about your bedtime.' So she moseyed off to bed, but first she stopped and looked over her glasses at me one last time, and Fred, that little lady got me so nervous, I felt like a cat on a hot tin roof."

* * *

Ya know, it was always something with Miss Suzie and Pop. And it was impossible to figure out what was going to happen next, so when James Brown asked me to look at his pool pump, I didn't think anything about it. The weird thing was, the pool man had already been there three times, and each time after he left, the pool pump wouldn't work again. Since I had a pool myself, Brown thought I might know something, after all, I was *a genius.*

Brown said to me, "How come the pool man charges me $300 to $400 to fix my pump when you can go out there in five minutes and get it running? I think the pool man is sabotaging my pump, Missa Daviss." He was genuinely paranoid about it.

Come to find out, Pop had been out there screwing with the valves, and pulled the valves, and blew the sand out of the tank and back flushed the damn stuff into the pool. He was just like a child ... messing with everything, and he wanted to mess with anything that would run.

I've seen him do it a dozen times ... he'd stick a screwdriver into a running motor, and the gears or the fan belt would snatch the screwdriver from his hands. I guess his depth perception wasn't so good or maybe he couldn't judge distances very well ... or maybe it was because his glasses were so damn dirty that he couldn't see anything.

He wore these ol' thick horn rimmed glasses and this ol' felt hat, and his glasses were never clean ... they looked like they had little paint specks on them, like he had been hanging over somebody's shoulder while they were spray painting. Just never cleaned his glasses.

In any case, it was dangerous to be around him, and he'd tear up more shit than you'd ever seen ... especially cars. I tell ya, never raise the hood of your car when Pop was standing around! One day he dropped his damn hat into the fan belt, and it tore the damn belt off. It tore his old felt hat up, too, but all he did was beat it back into shape. Whatever it was, you knew that Pop was destined to mess something up. I bet you could even handcuff him, and he would still tear it up!

So when I went to fix the pool pump, and I was squatting down there with a screwdriver and wearing my $400 kangaroo skin boots and my $1500 tailored suit. Pop was leaning over my shoulder to see what I was doing, but Mr. Brown told Pop to go back to the house. He said, "Pop, you're gonna mess it up."

I said, "Yeah, Pop … could you give me a little room to work?"

And Brown repeated, "Go away Pop, let him work," so Pop backed off as Brown squatted down next to me to look at the pump. Pointing to a part on the pump, he asked, "Do you think that's the right one there?"

And as I used the screwdriver to remove the impeller, I felt like I was making progress … but dammit, if Pop didn't hit the power switch and turn on the motor! … and the screwdriver got chewed up in the impeller and tore it all to hell … and as a piece of plastic flew by my head, I jerked back and stood up real fast. What I didn't know was that Pop was hanging onto my shoulder, knocking him backward into the pool. Next thing I knew, Pop was thrashing around in the pool, and James Brown is just standing there in shock. So I dive into the pool, grab Pop, and pull him up to the side of the pool, and he's spewing water out of his mouth and coughing and spitting. And James Brown proudly announces to an unseen audience, "And Missa Daviss is a lifeguard, too!"

I started to laugh, and I said, "Pop, if you need it, I could give you a little CPR."

Pop stammered, "Don—Don—Don—Don't put your mouth on my mouth."

I said, "Don't worry Pop, no kissin' on the mouth." So everything turned out okay. I was able to fish Pop's felt hat out of the pool and reshape it for him, but even better … I got his glasses and dipped them in the pool several times in order to wipe all that gunk off his glasses. He didn't even realize that they were dirty, he was so used to looking at them that way.

And as he put his glasses back on, he said, "Damn! Damn! Missa Daviss, I can see real clear now!"

* * *

As I said, stuff would happen every day in the Brown household. Most things were the mundane part of life, but right below the surface, something was always ready to happen. One day, I had to go over to Brown's house at 3056 Walton Way in Augusta for a business matter. I happened to take a friend of mine, Wilford Thompson, who was also my insurance agent.

This was the first house Brown bought in Augusta, and it was situated on a street full of enormous mansions with manicured lawns. But his house was a rather humble, single-story, 50s ranch with a double garage, protected by five acres of property, a fence and a large, wrought iron gate. James Brown had created a sensation when he moved in the neighborhood. A former Georgia governor lived a few houses away, and each December, Brown would set up these huge Christmas figures in his front yard to both the delight and embarrassment of the public. The big, black Santa figure seemed to get the most attention.

As Wilford and I waited in the den, Brown was still in the bedroom getting ready. He was always late … so Deanna and Yamma, his two daughters, entertained us as they played with their dolls. When Deanna asked us if we wanted to see her dance, I said, "Sure, we'd love to see you dance." She was about six or seven at the time, and just as cute as she could be. The next thing I knew, she ran back into her bedroom to put on her tap shoes and this little short skirt, then she ran into the living room where she set up her little record player on the coffee table. Nobody ever used the living room, so it was kinda bare except for its shiny hardwood floors, which made it perfect for tap dancing.

James Brown preferred wooden floors instead of carpeting. He was germ-phobic and thought that carpets were breeding grounds for dirt and germs so it was not unusual for him to have a bare floor in a room.

As Wilford and I stood there in the living room, Deanna turned the record player on, carefully placing the needle down on a well-used, scratchy 45 single. As the tune began to play at full volume, Deanna went into a frenzy, with this big ol' smile, wildly swinging her hands back and forth as her tap shoes were tearing the hell outta the floor. It was an amazing sight … even more so since her choice of tunes was *Dixie* … you know, "I wish I was in the land of cotton … "

When Deanna finished dancing to the words, "Away down south in Dixie", Wilford and I praised her performance … an event that James Brown had missed. But riding back in the car, Wilford commented to me, "I can't believe it … it was so fun to see this sweet, little child tap dancing. She was so happy … she didn't realize about the music she was playing, but while she was playing it, she might as well have gotten a little rebel flag to wave around while she was dancing."

I don't know where Deanna got the record … that would be an interesting story in itself, but apparently, *Dixie* was the most up-tempo record she had … plus, it's a good tune and easy to dance to.

* * *

I can't explain why Pop Brown was such a funny guy. He's a character you'd never forget. Now I'm not making fun of his speech impediment, it was just part of his character, and he never called his son "James" or "Mr. Brown", it was always "Junior." And he would stutter when he was talking and he'd say, "Jun—Jun—Jun—Junior."

As I mentioned, Pop could mess up anything he touched. He was always getting a screwdriver stuck in things—it was a wonder he didn't get all his fingers cut off. And it got to be a joke. I'd say, "Pop don't even come close to my automobile. Don't even lean on the fender." And James Brown would say stuff like that, too. Pop could destroy a junkyard.

But James Brown thought I was a genius at fixing things. And he'd say "That boy's from Georgia Tech. He'd fix anything. Cars, pool pumps … and the man can fly an airplane, even fix it."

One time Pop had messed up James Brown's riding mower … a small tractor used on his 60-acre estate at Beech Island. It was a nice place. You couldn't see the house from Douglas Drive, but as you'd come along this winding black asphalt driveway, you'd ride up to the house where the gutters and curbing were rolled on the edges to make it all seem very elegant-looking.

Before you got to the house, there was a small pond, and to the right up on the hill there was a set of stables and some ranch type fencing. His house was a contemporary wood and glass design, and his swimming pool was located on the side next to a long pool house.

One evening, the tractor repair shop delivered the mower. They had kept it for a couple of weeks and spent several hundred dollars fixing something that Pop had done … I think he had stuck a screwdriver in the damn fan belt and tore up the timing chain.

As the mower sat in the yard, James Brown started preaching to Pop, but he didn't want to hear any of that mess. Pop had his nose up in the air like he was looking off in space like, "I isn't hearing a damn thing you're saying Jun—Jun—Jun—Junior." Pop just continued griping and mumbling.

But Mr. Brown wouldn't take it. He said, "Pop, you stay away from the mower. Missa Daviss tell him. Stay away from the mower! Stay away from my cars … stay away from my horses … stay away from all of it! Pop, you've got to stop this. We've got yard people who do that work. Tell him Missa Daviss."

And Pop said, "Jun—Jun—Jun—Junior just kiss—kiss—kiss my ass."

So Mr. Brown was real adamant about it. "You stay off that mower. Don't go around it."

So the yardman pulled the mower up to the edge of the yard next to the driveway. Pop was standing there muttering with his hands crammed down in his pockets as James Brown and I went inside the house. About five minutes later, we were sitting in the den, and I heard the mower running. I kinda peeped out the window … and I could see Pop going across the yard headed out there toward the lake. I didn't say anything to Brown, but when Pop turned the mower to full throttle, Brown asked me, "What's that sound?"

"That's the tractor."

He said, "Yeah, I thought I heard something out there."

And he jumped up and looked out the window and yelled, "Damn! Damn Missa Daviss. Pop's on the lawnmower. We've got to stop him. We've got to do something."

And we were standing there looking as Pop runs up on this bank on the side of the lake and I said, "Oh, Mr. Brown … it's too steep."

Brown said, "Good gawdamighty, Missa Daviss!"

And about that time, the mower tilted up and began to flip over. Pop grabbed the top of his head as the mower rolled over about six times down the hill and into the lake. The tractor was still running and the water is steaming and bubbling as it slips totally underwater.

Pop climbs up out of the water, and he's beating his hat against his hip, shaking the water off, and Pop turns around, and he's kinda hunched over like a little child. I could see him looking up at the house and thinking, *Oh shit… I'm in trouble.*

And James Brown ran out the door, and boy, was he pissed off. "Pop, get your ass over here!"

As Brown ran up to him, Pop said, "Jun—Jun—Jun—Junior, I—I—I gotcha."

Brown turned to me and remarked, "What am I going to do with him? What am I going to do with Pop?" But there was nothing you could do … Pop didn't care … Pop wasn't on the payroll.

CHAPTER 9

Money, Money, Money

And that's what it boiled down to … money. I know James Brown is a musical legend, but he didn't dwell on his music. We never really sat down and talked about the impact of his music on the industry. He didn't really have time to think about music … he was always performing. And James Brown wasn't obsessed with chasing women … they just came his way, like turning on a spigot—he didn't have to go lookin' for them, they were just always there. But the one thing that James Brown did dwell on was money. Money, money, money … how to get it—how to make it—how to hold on to it—and how not to let the government get their hands on it. That's why he hired Fred Daviss.

You have to remember Brown's background as a street hustler in Augusta. He never got over it. Everything was a hustle, even when he held all the chips, he still loved the hustle, whether it was hustling his own musicians in a card game or hustling the U.S. Government out of millions of dollars. The first time I met him, he tried to hustle me. It was a big thrill for him. Not like sex, not like performing on stage, but it was always a thrill that he could create anytime, anywhere.

In the late 60s, James Brown was receiving a lot of press about his rising fame and fortune like, *Here's a guy who's making millions of dollars a year … he's selling out his shows … he has a string of hit records … and buying limousines, jet airplanes and all this stuff.* Everybody in the country recognized him as this great black entrepreneur, this important black businessman who was doing all these great things and now moving into radio station ownership. So it seemed to be a perfect fit when The Feldman Group, part of 1360 Broadcasting Inc., wanted to unload their Baltimore radio station on Brown. They were all just tickled to death that they were going to make a deal with James Brown. They thought, *This guy is black, he's got money, and this is going to be a smooth transition with the FCC.* Everyone thought that the FCC would easily grant him a license, and politically, everybody was ready to push for black ownership of radio stations. This is the perfect business scenario.

James Brown had committed to the purchase of the radio station through a telegram. The Feldman Group's attorneys put the deal together and when it came time to deliver the $40,000 down payment, Al Garner, a white boy who managed a radio station in Houston, went to get the check from James Brown.

Brown had a way of getting everybody to wait for him. So here's Al Garner in the hotel at the midnight hour waiting for James Brown to give him the check so that he can close the deal. Brown was taking his time about it—finally he pulled out the nearest checkbook and wrote the $40,000 check. Then Al jumped on a plane, flew to Baltimore and finalized the business. They gave him the keys to the station and overnight Brown moves his own crew in. Or course, he kept some of the on-air disc jockeys like Jim Sears, known as Diamond Jim Sears "God's Gift to the World" and another DJ, Moon Man.

It was a big hullabaloo. Everybody was happy. The FCC was happy, the Feldman Group was happy, and James Brown was sitting back smiling and saying, "I'm in a major market now." So Brown was instantly running the station and playing his music. Back then, the banks moved rather slowly, so it took about 10 days for the shit to hit the fan. All of a sudden, one of the attorneys for the Feldman Group said, "By the way, we've got a problem."

In his real slick radio voice, Al Garner said, "Problem, what kind of problem?"

"Well Mr. Garner, it seems like this check that Mr. Brown gave us was returned for insufficient funds."

"What? There must be some mistake." Al didn't realize the check was no good. Al got them to run the check back through … and it bounced again. After a couple of more weeks, it became a full fledged panic as Brown offered excuse after excuse, stalling them to the point where The Feldman Group was fixin' to void the deal and prosecute him on a variety of criminal offenses.

After several weeks, money began flowing into the radio station … actually it was money that came from the account receivables left over on the books when Brown signed the papers. Basically, Brown took the money owed to Feldman and paid the down payment after writing them a bad check. Whatta hustle! … and Brown probably had more $40,000 in cash stuffed in his underwear drawer the whole time. He just liked to create a little drama for fun. Eventually, we cleared the check up and from that day forward, Brown's relationship in Baltimore snowballed into the biggest nightmare I've ever seen.

Soon, James Brown bought a Baltimore hotel and renamed it the James Brown Motor Inn. He kept the existing manager to run the hotel with guidance from his father … a really smart guy probably with a Harvard MBA.

So now, Brown had a Baltimore radio station and his own hotel, and business was good, even though the radio station was struggling to pay its bills. That was nobody's fault except James Brown … he was using the radio station as a cash cow to subsidize his other operations. He was charging $6,000 to $7,000 phone bills to the station … plus many of his airline tickets and his expenses for his road show operations. Just bleeding the station dry! When I came to work for James Brown, it was my job to clean up his mess … stop "robbing Peter to pay Paul." It wasn't like Brown didn't have the money … Brown just never wanted to spend any money.

As I got into the problem, people like Jim Sears and Al Garner finally had to fess up and tell me about the checks that the station had written to the manager at the James Brown Motor Inn. None of them were good, and the manager had about 12 to 15 checks of various amounts that amounted to probably $6,000. Jim and Al thought that the station would eventually make the checks good, but first, they needed to hide the debts from James Brown. When I found out about this, I knew we had to get this whole mess cleared up. But then I got caught up in it, realizing that this is how the station (and Brown) operated. I decided to get legit later. First, we need to keep all the creditors away and pay the bills.

But I was caught between a rock and the proverbial hard place. The manager needed to keep the knowledge of the bad checks from his father … Al and Jim needed to keep them from Brown. I figured, we needed to buy time.

Al, Jim and I found the manager sitting in the coffee shop, and we started sympathizing with him because he's got a payroll coming up in few days-probably $25,000. And he said he needed another $7,000.

I said, "Hey buddy, we'll help you. We need some money, too … we've got to pay some bills or else they're gonna cut off our telephone service. We'll just float some checks."

He said, "Yeah, but I've already got $7,000 worth of your bad checks."

"Well, let's say you've got $18,000 in the bank and you need another $7,000 to make payroll. Tell you what, let me give you the $7,000 to make your payroll and by the time the check hits, you'll have enough cash flow so you can put it back."

"Yeah, that makes sense … "

"But you need to do something for us. We're in the hole, too. We'll write you this $7,000 check to make your payroll, and we've got $7,000 worth of checks that we need to pick up, let's get all these checks together and we'll give you one check. Tell you what, let me give you a check for $10,000, and I'm gonna give you another check for $7,000, and you give us a check for $17,000 and we'll just swap checks."

The manager's face brightened up. "Yeah, and by the time the checks hit we'll all have enough money to cover expenses. Oh man, if my Daddy found out about the bad checks, he would be all over my ass."

I congratulated him for his insight but added a further incentive. "That's right … you don't want your Daddy on your ass … *or James Brown!*"

So we all swapped checks, and he was so happy. He was gonna put the bad $7,000 check in his safe, deposit the bad $10,000 check into his account while giving me all the bad checks he was holding. So we took his $17,000 check, and he's already got $18,000 of good funds in the bank. When we left the hotel, we went straight to the bank, cashed the check on his good money, and proceeded to pay our bills.

About 10 days later, he gets a little note, and came running to us. "I don't know what in the hell is going on! We got damn payroll checks bouncing everywhere! … the bank has even got their damn lawyer on the phone with me!"

Eventually, we got everything cleared up, but I'm not sure that poor ol' manager ever figured out what had happened. The worst part was, I was a legitimate banker—I knew better. But working for James Brown, I was forced to do things in a situation beyond my control … a situation that was the root of all evil.

* * *

James Brown needed a jet … he really did. He needed to go here and there at his own schedule without waiting in airports and trying to get a ticket. With a jet, you just hop in and you're there. But Brown always had to inject some one-upmanship into every aspect of his life. He started out with a Learjet and upgraded twice until he decided to trade in his current jet for a Hawker Siddeley, a large, expensive, gas-guzzler with plenty of headroom and customized with plush upholstery and nice sofas. It was a hog!

One night, Brown and I were at the Hanger One fixed based operation in New York to close the deal and take possession of the plane. I always liked to hang out at airports—you never knew who you'd run into. In fact, Jackie Onassis once walked right past me as she got on an Olympic Airlines stretched Lear.

On this particular night, we ran into Paul Anka, and he and James Brown were like ol' buddies, hugging necks and everything … plus, Paul Anka was all excited about getting his first jet—a Learjet. When

James Brown heard this, he started laughing and mocking him about what a little jet it was. Brown had no qualms about insulting someone right to their face … never even thinking about being tactful.

And Paul Anka was just kinda standing there, I guess he was confused and shocked, but Brown then invited him to inspect his new plane—the impressive Hawker Siddeley. Paul's Learjet was tied down nearby, and as we walked, he proudly pointed it out to Brown. But Brown just kinda chuckled and said, "Oh that's just a toy … you've got yourself a little toy. Lemme tell ya, I went through that stage years ago. Tell him, Missa Daviss, tell Paul that he needs to get *a real plane.*"

When we finally got around to boarding *a real plane*, Brown pointed out how expansive it was … the big cabin, the nice sofas, the TV, the galley, and the private bathroom with mirrors … no little potty like you have on a Learjet.

About that time, Brown was distracted by someone who wanted to talk business, so as Brown walked off for a promised five minute meeting, Paul Anka and I sat in the low light of the plane and drank a soda.

We talked and talked, and I more or less apologized for Brown's behavior. I said, "Mr. Brown didn't mean to put your plane down, he loved his Learjet … it was his first airplane, too, so don't take it personally."

Paul replied, "I know James … I know how he is with his ego."

But I was so embarrassed and tried to put things in perspective. "Your Learjet is a helluva plane. I'm a pilot myself, so don't let Brown tell you anything about it. The Lear uses a lot less fuel than his plane … that Lear is faster, and it's got a higher ceiling than the airliners. Most commercial jets won't go up but 38,000 or something, but you can carry a Lear up to 41,000 feet … and that Lear has a lotta get up and go. There's nothing to feel bad about with the Learjet."

I went on and on for 45 minutes, but I don't think Paul Anka felt any better. And it wasn't about the planes in the first place. It was about money. James Brown made more money than Paul Anka … James Brown was more famous … James Brown was better.

I sure hope Paul Anka has a healthy self-respect and doesn't see wealth as a personal value. Most entertainers may have thick skin, but

I know there's a lot of soft stuff inside. I've seen James Brown kick the self-respect out of a lotta people—so you had to be strong, inside and out.

Years later, I went to one of Paul Anka's shows in Vegas. Afterward, I gave my business card to one of his stage managers hoping to catch up with him, but the stage manager came back and explained, "Mr. Anka's really tired tonight. He's worn out. He does want to talk to you, Mr. Daviss … but not tonight."

Paul, I'm in the phonebook … you're not still upset about the Learjet thing, are you?

* * *

Whatever he did, no matter what it was, Brown was gonna be the best at it … he was a very competitive person, and he's gonna beat you at whatever you do. One night in Cherry Hill, New Jersey, there was a pool table back in the dressing room area. I had shot a little pool in my day and thought I was pretty good at it. I never imagined James Brown could shoot pool, even though he had hung around pool halls as a kid. He saw my interest in the pool table and asked me if I wanted to shoot a game of 8 ball … for $100! I was still working for the bank … I was just up there to see him on business … and I didn't have any money to speak of, so he said, "I'll bet you $100 to a Coke." I took the bet.

I was very competitive, too! I found out later that *Hey, don't beat Brown too bad … he'll get his mouth stuck out at you.* But I'm not gonna play anybody and them let them beat me! … but I didn't know that at that time.

James Brown was good, and I could see the look in his eye that he was serious about winning that Coke from me. He also saw that I was making some pretty good shots, and he got really impressed with me. He didn't know how good I was … and I didn't realize how good he was either.

It finally got down to the nitty-gritty, and I missed my shot. Brown had gotten all his balls in except the 8 ball, and it was a fairly easy shot. I said to myself, *Hell, I'm beat.* Then Brown bumped the 8 ball into the pocket, and I kinda dropped my head down in defeat. I threw my hands up and I turned away from the table … never looking back.

The next thing I knew, Brown had this real pissed off look on his face. He reached in pocket and pulls out a wad of $100s and slaps a $100 bill on the table. I took it as a challenge and asked, "Do you want to shoot another game?"

He said, "Take your money!"

"You owe me some money?"

"I bet you a $100 on it. You won it fair and square." And I thought he was putting me on, but what I didn't realize was that when I turned around, he scratched on the shot. The cue ball went in the corner pocket after I turned my back!

I thought about it later and I asked him, "If you realized that I wasn't sharp enough to know you had scratched, would you have still paid me the $100?"

"Sure, I'm an honest man, Missa Daviss. I'd pay you."

We'd get competitive on all sort of things. His philosophy in card games was *When you gamble, the guy who had the biggest bankroll, will always beat you if you play long enough.* I've seen it several times in Europe … we'd be on long trips with a band bus in front of us and Brown's limo behind. He'd get the limo driver to toot the horn and pull the bus over. And Brown would say, "I think I'm gonna get on there and play cards with the band," and he would clean their ass out after a few hours of riding up the road, playing Skins. It was a game I never learned. During one six-week tour, there were two or three guys, and after playing cards with James Brown, actually *owed him* a paycheck for the next four weeks! Brown done cleaned 'em out. We'd get back in the limo and I said, "Mr. Brown, you sure are cruel to take them guys' money like that."

He said, "They're grown, they should know better. They'd be glad to take my money when I first got on the bus. They thought they were winning."

"How were you so sure that you would win in the end?"

"The man with the money will always win. If you've got a lot of money, you gonna win at anything. You can beat the other man down.

If you play long enough, you're gonna gradually eat into their money and eventually overtake 'em." And he was right. The only way those guys could save their money would be to get outta the game and quit chasing ghosts. Brown was a helluva man. He was a different kind of man. He was the most different kind of man that I've ever met. The only man I've ever seen with a personality close to James Brown was Richard Nixon.

* * *

It may sound strange to say, but having money can be a real burden-like *Get this stuff outta here!* When we would go to Europe, James Brown always wanted to be paid off in $100 bills—real American dollars. He didn't want to go through the hassle of exchanging foreign currency. One time we got stuck with a lot of foreign money, and when the market fell, we lost several thousand dollars in the exchange. That's why his contract demanded $100 bills.

On one European tour, Brown was booked to do just five or six one-nighters, but once he got over there, he was so hot that he cancelled some of the dates in the States so that he could spend more time in Europe. In all, he did 28 or 30 one-nighters, because it was so much money, he didn't want to turn it down.

I was required to see James Brown every week, no matter where he was, so I flew over to Italy in the middle of the tour to meet the local promoter—Francesco Sanavio. He was the playboy type ... always wore a white suit and had two or three women, and always drove a white Mercedes coupe. Even though Francesco was promoting the shows, somehow or another, in show business, you always get in the middle of the Mafia.

We were in a music festival and since they had not planned on James Brown doing these extra shows, the festival managers had not made preparations to go and get American $100 bills, and I knew that Brown would not accept lire. So I went in search of the festival managers.

Al Garner and I ran into them out behind the dressing room, near these trailers and I said to them, "Hell no! You gotta pay in dollars."

And I was standing there arguing with these three or four guys in their tailored suits. I was getting hot headed.

I said, "Mr. Brown is not going on stage. Fuck you. If you can't come up with the dollars, that's tough." Of course I was bluffing.

One of the guys said something to me in a real stern voice … a big, tough-looking guy. But I was cocky, and I was strutting around like *You don't scare me.* I was just trying to be tough.

But Al was pulling my coattail and saying, "Shut up. Quit arguing with these guys."

"What are you talking about? Fuck these guys."

Al bent his nose with his finger and said, "These are *the boys.*"

I said, "Fuck *the boys.* I don't care."

I was lucky these guys didn't pull out their guns and shoot me. I didn't realize it at the time, but they had these custom-made holsters hanging up under their armpit. But the tough-looking guy looked at me, and he was almost snickering like *This guy doesn't know any better. He doesn't realize that we're the real wise guys.*

I went back raisin' hell in James Brown's dressing room and I said, "Mr. Brown, these guys can't get the money, and I told them you weren't going on stage unless they come up with the $100 bills. They're out there trying to pay us off in damn lire!"

Someone had tipped off Mr. Brown about how I had been messing with *the damn boys* and that Mr. Daviss was gonna have to cool down.

I said, "Why are y'all keep talking about *the boys*?"

James Brown looked and me and kinda whispered, "The Mafioso, Missa Daviss."

"Oh shit! You mean the Mafia?"

"Yeah, the Mafia."

"Oh man!"

Al Garner said, "Fred, I was trying to tell you to shut up."

James Brown said, "Missa Daviss, you gotta back off. You might wanna go out there and apologize."

I quickly realized that we were going to accept the lire. And since there was some sort of holiday going on, it was going to be about four days until the banks open. That meant that we had to accept the currency in small denominations. That's a lotta lire.

Al and I shared a hotel suite with two bedrooms connected to a living room. Night after night, we hauled in truckloads of boxes, stuffed with money. After the third night, we didn't have room to walk. It got to the point where we didn't even count the stuff. We just had all these boxes, and we'd shake em'. "Here's a box worth $10,000 … put it here." It was stacking up so bad that we made little pathways through the room. We had gotten into a damn nightmare!

I was trying to tell James Brown about it, and he said, "Missa Daviss, you're *The Money Man*. Take care of it … when the banks open, you go swap it."

"But we're running outta room!"

"Use your head, Missa Daviss."

We had no place to put the money … we were like a bunch of dope dealers or something. Nowhere to put the money. There was so much money coming in—we just needed more room. That's when we found out about this honeymoon couple who had an adjoining bedroom, so we took over their room and got them a suite—the best suite in the hotel.

Then we had a third bedroom to stack money in, and we had it stacked as high as your shoulders. It was a couple of million dollars … in small denomination lire. When the banks opened, I had to rent two trucks to transport the load. Unbelievable.

Brown had a thing about cash, and there were times when Brown would leave part of the cash in Europe, and bring the rest home. Back then they didn't really have any airport security or check you that close, so I could carry a lot of money on my person. I'd hide $40,000 in this pocket … $40,000 in that pocket … and stuff another $200,000 under my belt and walk right through customs with it. We wouldn't transfer the money by wire … we'd just take the cash with us. Now, I think it's illegal to transport more than $10,000 … it was probably illegal back then, too. Whatta burden.

* * *

Wealth was an ingrained part of James Brown's life. Like breathing in and breathing out. He had money, he made money, he spent money … but only if he had to. And he loved money so much that he probably just wanted to get down on the floor and roll around in it and never let it go.

One night Mr. Brown and Deedee invited our family over to the house in Beech Island. It worked out well since Kelley and Pepper were about the same age as Brown's daughters, Deanna and Yamma … about seven or eight.

As the four adults sat in the den, the four girls had gone off into another part of the house to play. I had tried to keep my eye on them 'cause James Brown was so finicky about different things … he had little rules in his house, and I certainly didn't want the kids to do anything that would offend him (like tap dancing on the hardwood floors).

Every once in a while the girls would run into the den and say something, and then they'd go back playing. And Brown would say to his daughters, "You girls having a good time?"

And they'd say, "Yeah, we're having a good time, Daddy." And they'd go back playing.

Later on when we left, about 10 o'clock or so, we were driving back to the hotel in Augusta and I said, "You girls have a good time?"

And they said, "Oh yeah, Daddy—we had a good time."

Pepper was eating a candy bar, and had her mouth full while talking, and I wanted to get a little more conversation going, so I asked, "Where were y'all at for so long?"

"We were back in the bedroom playing."

"What were y'all playing? You seemed to have such a good time."

And just as nonchalant, she said, "Oh, not much Daddy … we were playing bank."

And I said, "Bank?" And it kinda got my attention, and I looked at my wife and looked back around and said, "What do you mean … 'playing bank'?"

And she said, "We had the money out, and Deanna had this little cash register … but the money wouldn't fit in it."

I said, "Were you playing with Monopoly money—that little play money?"

And Pepper continued eating her candy bar and looking down like she was halfway paying attention to what I was saying, and she said, "Oh no, we were playing with real money."

This struck me kinda funny, so I asked, "Did Deanna have some money y'all were playing with?"

"No … we were playing with Mr. Brown's money."

That really got my attention. I said, "What?! Where did you find the money? Was it laying on the table or something?"

"Oh no, Daddy. It was in some shoeboxes." Then Pepper shoved her little hand from the backseat holding a paper strap. It was the thing that banks use to wrap bundles of bills … a $10,000 strap.

I swallowed hard and asked, "Did this strap come off of the same bundle you were playing with?"

"Oh yeah, they were $100 bills, and Daddy, they were almost all brand new … like they'd just come out of the bank.

"So y'all played with a bundle of $100 bills?"

"Naw, we played with three bundles."

"So, if each bundle held $10,000, do you girls know how much money was in those three packages?"

"Oh, I can count Daddy. It was $30,000."

"Do you realize that you were playing with $30,000?"

"Oh yeah, but we only opened three of them from one shoebox."

"Really? Well how many shoeboxes were there?"

"I don't know … there was a whole chest of drawers stacked full with shoeboxes. We didn't want to mess with it too much because Deanna said her Daddy would get upset … and that we shouldn't tell about it—but we'll tell you. And Daddy, don't tell James Brown 'cause it will get Deanna in trouble. She told us that she wasn't supposed to know about that money. So we played bank with that money, but we only opened two or three packages. They had put it all back, but Deanna said that we'd play with it next time we came over."

I was about to shit ... a chest full of shoeboxes ... and each shoebox was full of $100 bills in $10,000 packages! There was no telling, but there was probably several million dollars there in James Brown's bedroom. But to the Brown family, it was just child's play.

* * *

Money started meaning less and less with me, and eventually I got in a habit of carrying $3,000 to $5,000 in pocket money. I tried to stick to that amount because it wasn't such a big wad that I couldn't fold over and put in my left pocket. Since I always wore a suit, I kept my wallet in my coat pocket along with my credit cards, driver's license and photos of Yamma and Deanna ... of course, I had my two daughters' pictures, too. If the $5,000 wasn't enough, I'd keep at least $30,000 in the trunk of my car.

There were several times on the first cold day of the year when I would grab my overcoat out of the closet only to discover several thousand dollars stuffed in the pockets. I just forgot about the money ... so it was a nice little surprise. And I don't know how many times my suits went to the cleaners with thousands of dollars in the coat pocket. Money didn't mean too much. It wasn't any big deal ... the money just kept on comin' in.

We did everything first class. The only time we ever rode on a coach ticket was when we couldn't get a first class seat ... but we always had the limousines and private jets and I even had my own airplane just for fun. And we always stayed in the best suites. The funny thing about it, when I took my girls, they always reserved a suite-sometimes the penthouse suite. The problem was, they got used to it and in later years, we'd go somewhere as a family and get a regular hotel room, but they got their nose stuck up in the air like *Daddy, this is a little room.*

I'll be honest ... all this money was a damn hassle. There's the well-published story about the promoter Bill Graham trying to get James

Brown to appear at Madison Square Garden with Mick Jagger and the Stones. To show that he was serious about getting Brown to perform, Bill Graham sent him a check for $10,000, but the whole thing became a battle of massive egos … mostly between Bill Graham and Brown. Mick Jagger had already called James Brown and begged him to be on the show, but James Brown told him he wasn't a second act for anybody. He was the main act. Then Mick Jagger suggested that they could share the show billing, but I don't think Brown really wanted to do the show at all. He just kept coming up with more excuses and demanding too many perks, so Brown never did the concert. However, the $10,000 check got pushed off somewhere and years later, I ran across it among some papers. I still have it somewhere, but since it's a personal check, it would be no good.

Brown was always having a falling out with somebody. One time we were at the Beach Music Awards in Myrtle Beach, South Carolina, and Brown got pissed off at the people running the show there. Actually, I think James Brown got real paranoid about the people there, and I think it was because of the stuff he was smoking with his wife, Alfie. So, in the middle of the night, he called me and wanted me to come to his suite. He told me that we needed to go home, but his plane was not there and that it was scheduled to pick him up the next day. He couldn't get a hold of the pilots to pick him up so he decided that I should drive him home in my Seville Elegante. He thought that would be kinda fun at 4 o'clock in the morning!

So, we took off down the road, and Brown sat up in the front seat with me. As we drove across South Carolina, Brown pulled out a joint and lights it up. Then he turns on the radio and twists the knob up and down the channels, looking for some tunes.

He was surprised that I knew some of the songs from the 40s, and I was surprised that he knew the words to the white pop songs, and that he could actually sing along. Then he said, "Missa Daviss, sing along with me and Alfie." I'd got so embarrassed … next thing you know, we were all harmonizing. Can you imagine having James Brown put on a private concert in the front seat of your car?

The weird thing was, we ran across one of James Brown's songs on the radio, and I asked, "How does it feel to be riding around at 4 o'clock in the morning in South Carolina, cut on the radio and hear yourself on the radio?"

And Brown laughed and said that it was a helluva feeling. And as he began to accompany himself on the radio I asked, "I wonder how many people are listening to that song right now ... ya know, truck drivers ... people working the third shift or even people who can't go back to sleep?" He shook his head as he took another toke.

Soon after that, we started talking about a certified check from Island Records. Brown had just gone through a stormy relationship with Chris Blackwell who owned Island Records. They did a one album deal, and Brown made so many demands and caused so many headaches, Chris just got fed up with the whole thing. Toward the end of the relationship, Island Records sent Brown a certified check for $14,000 to cover some per diem expenses. A certified check is actually a check that the bank is certified to accept. It was the old time way of doing a guaranteed check, and I don't know if they still have them, but the bank would punch a hole in the magnetic routing numbers so that when the check hit the bank, it would kick it out to be handled individually. The money that covered the check was actually escrowed at the bank, so whenever a certified check would come through, they'd pull the money out.

After we talked about the check from Island Records, we just laid it on the dash and kinda put the thought aside. Fourteen thousand dollars didn't mean nothing to him, and we never discussed it again—we had bigger issues with Island Records. Years later, I was looking for something under the seat and I happened to find the check down in between the seats and wondered how in the hell the check ever got there. Oh yeah ... we probably got high smoking the joint. That explains it. Stuff happens.

At that time, I was no longer working for James Brown so I stuck the check back in the drawer with the Bill Graham check. Bill Graham was already dead, but I called James Brown, and I knew he'd be happy that I found the check.

But Brown was in one of those moods, the kinda mood where he got paranoid about it. I don't know what went through his mind, but maybe he thought I had deliberately tucked the check back trying to think of a way to negotiate for something. The check was made out to James Brown, and he had endorsed it, so I could have taken it to any bank and cashed it if I had wanted to. He said he didn't want the check back, and after talking to Mr. Bobbitt about it, I realized that he thought there was something fishy about it. I told him that I was not going to cash it, but something made him real paranoid. I was trying to give the man $14,000, but he couldn't care less. I started to say, "Hell, if you don't want it, will you let me cash it, because I can use the money." So, I still have the check, and as far as I know, it's still good.

James Brown had some strange thoughts about money. He got high one night and told me how to hide money in the woods. He started telling me there was a certain way you could cut out a section in a tree and make it weatherproof. He was stoned when he was telling me this, and then he got me smoking with him, and so we're both sitting there giggling, but apparently Brown had done this and put money in trees.

People thought he buried money in places scattered around the county. One of his girlfriends, Estella Johnson, told me that one night they needed some money so they got in his Dodge van and rode out to this rural church near Barnwell, South Carolina. He drove up in the churchyard at 3 o'clock in the morning and got out with a flashlight and left her in the van. He walked past the cemetery, and he was gone about 10 minutes. Then here he comes back with this paper bag with $25,000 in it. He had gone to one of his safes in the woods, and how he kept it weatherproof, I don't know.

Brown always had a stash of money somewhere. He liked to holler and get everybody's attention and say that he was broke. He said, "You come up with the money at the last minute if you need it, but let 'em all think you're broke. And if you tell somebody long enough they'll start believing you."

It's *The Big Lie.* When he had the Flames, he decided to call it the "Famous Flames." The idea is that if you tell people that they're famous long enough, you'll become famous. And the same way with being broke … if you tell somebody you're broke long enough, they're gonna start believing you. Brown was not broke. I don't know what his estate is worth now but one time I heard it was over $200 million dollars. His money was just so diluted and spread out and diversified in so many different ways that he couldn't even remember where he put it all.

* * *

Before I worked for James Brown, I was hired by Eastern Airlines as a pilot, and even though I had abandoned that career path, I still had the desire to fly. I loved it, and with the healthy salary I was making, I was able to buy my own plane—in fact, four different aircraft during the time I was working for Brown. At one time, I had a Twin Comanche, and the last plane I had was a Super 21 Mooney, which was a pretty hot, little 200 mph aircraft.

From time to time, Brown's radio stations would sponsor a concert for other artists, like B.B. King or Wilson Pickett, and I would fly to these concerts when it was convenient, but most of the time I was too tired. WRDW in Augusta booked Jackie Wilson so I went down to handle the money, and I decided to take an old friend, Don Estes, with me to the concert. It was a successful show, and since it was getting late I tried to settle up the money. So we were both counting money and trying to reconcile the books, but I needed to get back to Atlanta because I had to go to New York the next day.

Finally, I said, "To hell with this, I'll finish counting it tomorrow." So I took the last of the money and rather than bundle it up, I raked the loose cash off the table and into a brown paper bag … like a Kroger sack from the grocery store. In total, the bundles and the loose bills amounted to about 80 grand.

I had my plane at Daniel Field, a small airport right in the middle of town just off of Wrightsboro Road. It was more convenient to land there and get to the auditorium rather than to fly into Bush Field which was further away.

When we got to the plane, it was about 3 o'clock in the morning and the airport was quiet—nobody there. As Don climbed in the plane, I set the bag of money in the back seat of the plane and did my pre-flight, and in a few short minutes, I pushed the throttle to the firewall and was heading down the runway. As we got about 50 feet off the ground, all of a sudden Don's door popped open. It made a helluva racket! The door was barely cracked open, but I had the little vent window open on my side so the air current rushed through the plane, sucking the loose money outta the Kroger sack. We were just trying to grab at all this money flying around the cockpit, and Don's eyes were just bugging out as this money was sucked out the door. You may not know, but you can't shut the door on a plane unless your speed is low enough to close the latch. About that time, we had just cleared the end of the runway, and Don is looking at all this money fluttering, and raining down over the airport. I'm cussing and carrying on, so I did a steep turn and went around the neighborhood nearly at treetop level, probably waking everybody up. I circled the airport and touched down on the runway at about 50 mph, and Don's eyes are as big as saucers, because it's still raining money, and I screamed out, "Shut the door, Don. Lock the door!"

He expected me to stop, because we were gonna go out there and pick up the money, but I said, "I'm ready to go home." And Don just couldn't believe it. I hit the throttle, and we came out over the houses. Don got real quiet as he was looking out the window … the money was still floating down—real pretty, like falling leaves in autumn.

During those days, we made so much money that it didn't worry me much … it just wasn't that important to me, and we still had to get to Atlanta, and when we got there, I just threw the grocery sack on the kitchen table and went to bed. The next morning, I counted the money, but the best I remember, it was just a shade over $3800 had blown out … which wasn't bad out of $80,000.

The fortunate part of the story was that it happened at Daniel Field and not Bush Field where Brown parked his jet. It was a secret that only Don and I shared because if it had happened at Bush Field, everyone in the flying community would have known that Fred Daviss was spewing James Brown's corporate money outta his plane at three in the morning.

A couple of weeks later, I had pretty much forgotten about the whole thing when I flew into Augusta and was talking to some guys gassing up my plane. One of the guys said, "Mr. Fred, weren't you here about two week ago? You'll never believe what happened. We came to work about 7 o'clock in the morning, and man, there was money all over the field. I was out there, and it was like picking watermelons. I got $1280 and another guy got $860 and another got $940 dollars, and we spent a half a day picking up money."

I said, "Really? Wonder where all that money came from? It must have been a drug dealer down here in the middle of the night."

Thank goodness that nobody realized that it came outta my plane, because it would have gotten back to James Brown, and he would have raised hell about it. But there's always some good in every negative story—some of those poor guys hadn't seen that much money in two or three paychecks, and it really saved their ass because they were able to pay some bills with that money. And it made me feel good to hear about their good luck ... and James Brown never missed a penny of the $3800.

* * *

I wasn't the only one to treat money so casually. I'm sure there are many other secrets out there that never got back to Brown. Here's such a story.

It was my job to meet James Brown to do the payroll every Saturday night ... no matter where he was at—Asia, South America or Europe. That's where I was.

James Brown played at the famous Apollo Theater every so often, so that Saturday night, I was in New York. Mr. Bobbit, Brown's personal manager, had the job of running back and forth to the box office picking up the money. That was a job in itself, considering that there were often two shows a day. After he got all the money, I'd take it plus all the taxi cab receipts from the entourage, the lobby tickets and hotel receipts and any other receipts from cash payments to back-up things for the IRS. Mr. Brown insisted that everybody had a receipt for everything.

Then, I'd take all the receipts and the cash in old brown paper grocery sacks back to my hotel suite to make an account of the concert. Earlier that night, they handed me three or four sacks of receipts and I had laid them on a counter in an empty dressing room for an hour or two before the show. I was just waiting for Brown to wrap up the concert when here comes Mr. Bobbit … and he's sweating like a pig.

I said, "What's your problem, Mr. Bobbit?"

"I lost the damn $27,000."

"You what?"

"I picked the money up at the box office, and I was running over here, and I can't find the money … and Mr. Brown's coming off the stage in a minute, and he wants to see this money!"

I said, "Mr. Bobbit, where were you? Can you backtrack your movements?" But his armpits were sopping wet, and he's scratching his head, and he's acting crazy."

I said, "Just calm down, Mr. Bobbit," but I really felt so sorry for him because at that particular junction, he was responsible for that money until it passed to me. It was like passing the football—and he only had 10 minutes before Brown came off the stage.

He said, "James Brown is gonna kill me."

"Just calm down, we're gonna find it."

"But what am I gonna do, I had it right here." He was in a tizzy, and we've got six or eight people going through the whole building, and the place is packed, and the music is blaring, and we were running all over the place. I knew he must have set it down somewhere and walked off or left it on the corner of a desk or in the office. It could be anywhere! And I'm walking backstage so I went into this empty dressing room to gather my thoughts. I put my briefcase down, leaned back and lit me a cigarette, trying to retrace his steps. I glance over in the corner where I had put those sacks of receipts, and I wondered … *Naw.* Anyway, I peeked in one of the bags, and I could see all this cash in the bag. *Oh shit …* it had been laying up there for an hour or so in an empty dressing room with all sorts of musicians and crew people walking by. But I grabbed this money and stopped Mr. Bobbit who was running around backstage. He was on the verge of hyperventilating, but when I showed him the money, he was real relieved. And happy. And he was lucky, too, because anybody else would have taken the money for themselves. But Mr. Brown never knew anything about the misadventure.

But Mr. Bobbit hadn't learned his lesson yet. When we were staying in a Dallas hotel, Mr. Bobbit came in tired one night after a concert. He had $50,000 in a shoebox, and as he passed the front desk, he must have had a lot of things in his hands and a lot on his mind because he got the shoebox and inadvertently stuffed it in the maid's supply room with some other office supplies.

When he woke up the next morning, he suddenly remembered where he had stashed the money, and when he ran downstairs, he found the shoebox, untouched right there on the shelf beside all the toilet paper, the detergents and maids' uniforms.

He said, "The good Lord must have been watching over me!" Maybe so, but there was so much money flowing around, and it was so mundane that you'd just forget that you had it. Money didn't have the same value anymore—it was just a responsibility.

* * *

Cash money wasn't the only problem—checks were, too, especially when you cash a check that's not payable to you! That can really cause some problems!

Brown owed $250,000 as the final payment on one of his radio stations, and we were already up to our ass in alligators with the FCC because we were already in default for another $500,000 on another note for another group.

To make things more interesting, Brown sent me to Texas to negotiate with Norman Fisher, one of the principles in the station. Rather than go to court, Fisher said he'd take less than the $250,000 … so after days of haggling and wrangling around with lawyers, he agreed to accept $125,000. Everybody was happy, and Brown made arrangements to draw the money from Polydor Records and charge it to one of his production accounts. So I went to New York to get the check, but the night before the meeting, Brown called me and said, "Tell Norman Fisher that we've changed our minds ... tell him I'll give him $90,000."

And man, that just deflated me! I had worked for two weeks thinking I was pulling a rabbit out of a hat by getting this man to accept $125,000—now I had to beat him down again. This is not how I would have handled it, but Brown was a wizard at pushing things to the brink and bluffing for some serious stuff ... and to add more pressure, the deadline for the payment was coming up fast—if we missed the deadline, we'd be in default.

When I broke the news to Norman Fisher, he went ballistic, "James Brown, that son-of-a-bitch! Does he think I'm gonna kiss his ass?" After that, I figured there was no more room to negotiate ... we had pushed it as far as it would go. But the next thing you know, I got Norman talking, and after two or three days of bluffing and threatening, I convinced him to take $90,000!

In the middle of all these negotiations, I still had to take care of the everyday business, and I was running all over the country on Delta, Eastern and United ... jumping on chartered planes, and even flying my personal plane for short hops between meetings. But somewhere along the line, I lost my airplane. Forgot where I left it. It was pitiful when I talked to people at airports, like I was a child... *I lost my plane,* but I finally found it in Oklahoma City or somewhere. Now I look back at this whole mess ... and shudder.

By this time, Brown goes to Australia to do some shows, so Al Garner and I finally headed off to New York to meet with Polydor and get the $90,000 check from the manager of business affairs, Dr. Ekke Schnabel. These German people were hardnosed.

We were getting down to the midnight hour, so to keep this deal together, Al and I had to deliver the $90,000 check to our FCC attorney, J. Ellis Parker III who lived in Upper Marlborough, Prince George County, Maryland. We were hanging from our fingernails on everything

… flying into New York and taking a helicopter to avoid the traffic, picking up the check, flying to Washington, D.C. and then driving to Prince George County-all before the clock strikes midnight!

First, I had to get the check, which sounds easy until we had to run up and down the floors in Polydor's 1700 Broadway office trying to get people to sign the check. The next hurdle came when we tried to get the check made out to Norman Fisher, but Polydor couldn't write it to a third party. The check had to be made out to James Brown, but I said, "No, you can't make the check out to James Brown … he can't endorse it because he's in Australia."

And Ekke Schnabel replied, "Well that's your problem, isn't it?" His attitude was like *I don't want to see you guys ever again! Get the hell out-and kiss my ass-and tell James Brown to kiss my ass, too.* And as Al and I turned and walked away, I could hear Dr. Schnabel yelling in his German accent. "James Brown—dat sonaffa bitch!"

Al and I looked at each other and said, "Shit man … what else is gonna get thrown in the mix? This is a damn nightmare." But it got worse and worse … as soon as you solve one problem another one comes along.

And now, it's about 5:30 in the afternoon, and everybody's leaving the Polydor offices. The only person left is a pretty little secretary who's running around getting the last of the paperwork done. Finally, she hands us the check, but it's made payable to James Brown, and not to his corporate name, JB Broadcasting of Baltimore Limited … and I'm thinking *Oh, shit! I'm not gonna forge his name … I'm not going to jail. And we've got to negotiate this check before midnight!*

Al and I were always pulling rabbits out of the hat, so we came up with another deal. While Al was starting to flirt with the secretary, I grabbed the check and stuck it into one of those old IBM typewriters with the letters on the ball. Al got the gal over by the coffee pot and was playing grab ass with her, and I got the check all straightened up, and where the check said, "Payable to James Brown," I simply provided an addendum with a few words … "Broadcasting of Baltimore Ltd." It looked perfect!

Then I walked over and I stuck the check in my briefcase and said, "Al, we need to get going." Then we skedaddled down to J. Ellis Parker

III's Maryland home by the midnight hour to meet with all the attorneys. As a corporate officer of James Brown Broadcasting of Baltimore Ltd., I endorsed the check and signed it over to Norman Fisher. Next thing I said was, "Damn. I need a drink."

A few weeks later after the check was processed, Dr. Ekke Schnabel got on the phone and was hollering and screaming that the check was forged. "James Brown-dat sonaffa bitch!" Apparently, Ekke was feeling heat from the auditors and the parent company in Germany.

I pretended like I didn't know what he was talking about and said, "That's y'all's problem … let your bookkeepers figure it out. If y'all can't clean this shit up, then you're all a bunch of sissies … let me and Al come over-we'll show you how to run your business."

It was just another day working for James Brown. Don't get me wrong … I had the sense not to forge Brown's name on the check. I was a credible and experienced banker … I knew better, but Brown always forced me to tiptoe on the brink of the law. Sometimes, I stubbed my toes, but I eventually learned to have a real respect for how fame, money and power can easily fog a man's principles.

At work in the Augusta office

Brown's Hawker Siddeley

We almost got thrown into a Baltimore jail.
(The Baltimore Sun)

This is when we met the Pope. According to Mr. Brown, this wasn't him meeting the Pope – it was the Pope meeting James Brown!

In my backyard in Riverdale, Georgia July, 1977—
several weeks before Elvis's death

Kelley and Pepper. Mr. Brown kept their school photos in his wallet.

March 10. 1979. Mr. Brown at the Grand Old Opry with Porter Wagoner. This is the only time James Brown got stage fright.

Pudjy suffered a tragic death from a swinging kitchen door accident. He received a Christian funeral and was buried in a $5700 coffin.
Photo Credit: Michael Ochs/Corbis

Brown's bulletproof Mafia limo. His chauffeur took my girls to school.

Mr. Brown listening to a track in his Augusta office

In the Augusta parking lot. This is where the police chase began. (Jet Magazine)

My daughter Kelley knew Mr. Brown since she was a toddler. He carried her school photo in his wallet.

Mr. Brown and I were best friends until his death.

Charles Bobbit, Jones DeVere and Fred Daviss at the 2014 Georgia Music Hall of Fame award ceremony

The James Brown Enterprises

1052 STEVENS CREEK ROAD
EXECUTIVE PARK SUITE 116
AUGUSTA, GEORGIA 30907

FRED DAVISS
EXECUTIVE VICE PRESIDENT
& COMPTROLLER

(404) 733-1052

CHAPTER 10

Lifestyles

To James Brown, money by itself, wasn't everything. He had so much of it stashed away … in shoeboxes, in trees, in grocery bags … and sometimes in banks … but what he really needed was a way to express his wealth through his possessions. He needed to turn cash into something tangible like cars, jets, homes and designer fashions for his wives … but he didn't really care about the possessions … he said that cars were "just pieces of tin." They were disposable, like a lotta things in his life. But his life was already sweet in so many ways because he was able to get whatever he wanted, which provided him with a pretty nice lifestyle.

James Brown was always buying cars. He'd drive them for a little while and get tired of them … and they'd end up in the backyard, rusting away. He was in a New York Cadillac dealership in the 70s when he discovered a custom-made limo ordered for a Mafia boss. It had bulletproof glass and was bomb proof on the underside and had a custom-made interior, but before the mob boss took delivery of it, somebody snuffed him out. James Brown just happened to be in the showroom when the salesman said, "Mr. Brown, I've got just the thing you need." Brown didn't necessarily need the bulletproof glass, but he bought it anyway.

The biggest enjoyment he got from this limo was during the days when he befriended Vince Dooley, the coach for the University of Georgia back during the Herschel Walker days. Brown had started going to some of the ballgames and even wrote a song called, "Dooley's Junkyard Dogs." It was never released, but became almost like a fight song for the Bulldogs.

A lot of times we would take the limo to the home games in Sanford Stadium in Athens, and all the Georgia fans got to where they recognized us ... I mean, how many bullet-proof Mafia limos are out there? And all these crazy, drunken Bulldog fans would honk their horns, and James Brown would crack the window and wave at them. It was almost like James Brown was an alumnus of the school ... and he would go right into the field house at halftime and even give the players some unsolicited advice right in the middle of Vince Dooley's serious ass-kicking pep talk.

There were times when Brown would fly to the ballgame and ask me to bring the limo from Atlanta, so June and I would have the limo to ourselves and keep it at the house. And sometimes the kids would have the chauffeur take them to school. Ya know, I got used to having my own limo and driver ... and I recommend it to everyone who might consider getting one.

Also at that time, James Brown met President Bongo of Libreville, Gabon, who invited him to play for his 19-year-old son's birthday party. Bongo sent his personal 747 jumbo jet to pick up James Brown and then chartered another 747 just to fly the band over. In other words, the President wouldn't stoop so low as to make Mr. Brown fly with the band. Then Bongo sweetened the deal by paying him about $250,000 for the gig.

Bongo and Brown developed a friendship over the years and out of the blue one day, Brown decided that he would give his limo to Mr. Bongo for a birthday present. Bongo had all the money in the world and could buy a fleet of limos, but James Brown decided to give him his personal limo because of all the history behind it. It was an ego thing so that Mr. Bongo could tell people that it was Mr. Brown's personal limo—and James Brown could say that it was an exclusive gift that nobody else could buy.

When we got it ready to ship, I had to get all the paperwork filled out and tidy it up a bit. Got new Double Eagle tires, washed and waxed it, and then I drove it to the dock in Norfolk. And I'm thinking *This is a helluva note. I'm losing my limo ... the car we used to go the football games in ... the car all the Bulldog fans crowded around in Athens ... the car that took my little girls to school ... and the car that I had so many happy memories with.* I really had a lot of nostalgic feelings about it, not like James Brown. He had no sentiment about anything ... a piece of tin. So the limo meant more to me than James Brown ... and probably more than President Bongo. As I stood on the docks, I got so sad ... I want my limo back!

* * *

During one of the seasons, the Georgia Bulldogs got invited to play the Cotton Bowl, and Mr. Brown invited me and June, plus Al Garner and his wife to fly with him and his wife, Deidre, on his jet. I don't think that all three couples had ever been together in a social setting. We all met in Atlanta for the flight, and it was amusing because all three wives had their mouths stuck out ... they didn't care anything about sitting on a flight to Dallas, Texas, much less having to put up with James Brown talking about himself all the way to the game ... and then back!

Brown also brought along his emcee, Danny Ray, and his hairdresser and bodyguard, and we had three stretch limos to take us to the stadium through this big crowd of drunken football fans. James Brown was in the first limo, and of course, he cracked the windows so that people could see who was in the limo. I heard 'em yelling out, "That's James Brown! James Brown's in the limo!"

Then the fans looked in the second limo and focused in on Danny Ray, who was sitting with June and me. Anybody familiar with the James Brown shows knows that Danny Ray is the spitting image of Sammy Davis, Jr., and one time on the Ed Sullivan Show, Ed turned around and did a double take at Danny Ray thinking that Sammy Davis, Jr. had sneaked up on the stage.

After seeing James Brown in one limo, the fans looked into the second limo and said, "Damn, that's Sammy Davis, Jr." But Danny Ray was sitting there with his mouth stuck out … he really didn't like to be confused with Sammy Davis, Jr.

The fans kept looking in the limo, and I was sitting there, waving and smiling, and this ol' drunk peeps in the window and yells out, "That's James Brown … and that's Sammy Davis, but who's *that guy?*" he said pointing to me.

His drunken buddy sputtered, "Hell, that's the Governor of Texas!"

I thought it was funny and got a big kick out of it. I was just some white guy sitting there minding my own business, but it only proves that just sitting in a limo makes you somebody famous.

* * *

Sittin' in a limo is one thing, but I knew my place because I was always being upstaged by Brown's dogs. We both flew in private jets, but they lived in a better neighborhood.

The dogs ruled because of Brown's second wife, Deidre Jenkins. He called her Deedee … I called her Mrs. Brown. Deedee had a thing about dogs, and when they moved from New York to Augusta, they bought this five acre home surrounded by a six-foot high, chain link fence. It was perfect because she would pick up stray dogs off the street, and the next thing I know, they had a small pack of dogs living at their Walton Way home.

She acquired a couple of those Afghan hounds, and she had a pair of sheep dogs … big, ol' fuzzy sheep dogs … you couldn't even see their damn eyes for all the hair hanging down. Then they got a nice pedigreed boxer named "J. B." Occasionally James Brown would get mad about something the dogs did and would yell at Deedee, "All the dogs have to go … except for J.B." Even though the boxer was a tough *man's dog* … Brown's favorite dog was a sissy little poodle.

The Browns had two little toy poodles, one black, and the white one was named Pudjy (pronounced Poo-gee). He was a lovable little dog, and he'd cock his head when you talked to him, and he'd priss around like he had the run of the house. Pudjy was such a spoiled dog. He flew on Brown's jet and got the whole VIP treatment from Brown's pilot, Doug Bell, a real meticulous guy who wore these nice blazers with the "JB" emblem on the breast pocket ... Doug also wore Gucci shoes and treated that plane like he owned it ... real particular, like, *Don't even breath on my airplane.*

I was a witness to the VIP treatment at the Los Angeles private fixed base operation. The crew would roll out the red carpet for the corporate jets, and they'd scurry around putting the chocks in the wheels and so forth, almost like the President was flying in. Then, they'd flip the door down and Mrs. Brown comes prissing down, making her grand entrance in her floor length, chinchilla coat—in 90° heat. Next, comes Pudjy, trotting down the steps running around under the plane looking for a tire to piss on. And while Mrs. Brown was standing there with her nose up, surveying the tarmac, Pudjy has gone and pissed on James Brown's plane. Next thing I know, Doug Bell is out there with these rags wiping off the tires. Doug didn't argue with Pudjy ... if Pudjy pissed on anything-it was perfectly alright.

Next thing I knew, it was dinnertime ... not for me, for Pudjy. They'd carry distilled water and some prime white chicken breast for him to eat ... that was because poor little Pudjy would get an upset stomach from flying through all those time zones, and he wouldn't eat right. So Doug Bell gets down on his knees and begins to talk to the dog. "Now Pudjy, it's din-din time."

Pudjy cocks his head and looks at Doug, who says, "Now, do you want your Mickey Mouse bowl today or do you want your Donald Duck bowl?"

Pudjy kinda cocks his head a little bit and Doug responds, "Oh, you want the Donald Duck bowl! Here, let me put some chicken in your Donald Duck bowl."

Then Doug serves some chicken and tops off the other bowl with distilled water. Pudjy sniffs at the chicken, eats a couple of bites and then goes off and pisses on the tire again. The whole time, James Brown is carrying on a business conversation with someone on the tarmac, and Deedee is posing in her fur coat for a non-existent audience while their highly trained and experienced pilot is on his hands and knees tending to the real boss … a toy poodle with a delicate stomach and a probable urinary tract infection. I was just glad I was James Brown's *Money Man* … and not his pilot.

* * *

It was evident that Deedee Brown had a thing about dogs. She showed her love for the dogs more than James Brown … but I knew he loved them, too, otherwise he wouldn't have let them take charge like he did.

The Browns had a big sectional sofa in their living room, and it had these little skirts around the bottom. And there were many times I'd be waiting on Brown in the living room when one of the dogs would walk into the room and look me in the eye like *Hey buddy, you'd better not say anything about this,* and then he'd hike his leg up and piss on the sofa.

Even when Wilford and I were waiting in the living room for Deanna to put on her tap shoes, a dog came in, sniffed around the skirt, and then pissed on the sofa. Brown was such a stickler for cleanliness, and if he had caught any dog doing that … he would probably have killed it … but the dogs got away with it every time.

I think the dogs knew they had a sweet deal. I was in the office one summer when I ran across a bill from a heating and air company for the Walton Way residence. I thought the $7,000 bill was kinda high, so I made some simple inquiries about what maintenance the Browns were doing and found out that they had installed some air-conditioning … in the dog houses! Now I was sure the dogs had a better lifestyle than I did!

* * *

Every morning, I would have a meeting with Brown, whether it was on his private jet, in his limo or in some concert location around the world. When he was in Augusta, we'd just hold court in his house. When I say "morning meeting", I mean 2 o'clock in the afternoon … that was his morning time. I always wore my usual business attire: a suit with a tie. Brown had his own business attire: pants, leather slippers and a bathrobe … always open, never tied, with no shirt underneath. Plus he always had his hair rolled up in big curlers.

As a matter of fact, Elvis dressed the same way … even the curlers. I don't know how they both ended up with the same fashion sense … it must have been bred into them somewhere along the way. But anyway, I had come up to Brown's house that *morning*—at 2 o'clock in the afternoon—and Brown was sitting at the kitchen table in his bathrobe and curlers. His wife, Deedee, was at the sink fooling around with some dishes, and Miss Ella Whitehead, Brown's maid for many years, had her little lace apron on and was doing her housekeeping thing. She was flitting around the house, humming, and going back and forth from the kitchen, in and out of the old-type swinging doors between the kitchen and dining room.

As I mentioned before, Pudjy, his spoiled-rotten poodle, was always with Brown, and that morning, he was trotting around the house and running up underneath the table and so forth. As Brown and I were at the table talking business, going over some contracts … Miss Ella had gone into the dining room. At the same time, Pudjy was trotting across the kitchen floor, when here comes Miss Ella in a big hurry. She swings this door open and … bam! She popped Pudjy in the head … and you could hear it crack out loud. Oh lawdy! And Brown was momentarily stunned as he watched Pudjy spinning around on this tile kitchen floor like a top. Just spinning. It knocked the hell out of him. And Miss Ella, she's jumping up and down in one spot fanning herself, "Lawdamercy! Lawdamercy!" She was all in a tizzy, and the dog was scrambling around, slipping on that waxed floor, and then Pudjy tears off down the hall, running cockeyed, yelping, and just raisin' hell.

And Miss Ella is still jumping up and down. "Lawdamercy! Lawdamercy!" And James Brown is in such a shock after seeing his dog get hit in the head. He finally jumps up out of his chair and yells, "Nigger, you done killed my dog!"

And Miss Ella's jumping up and down and says, "Lawd no, Mr. Brown! He wasn't dead when he come through here!" But Brown continued to raise hell about it, and Miss Ella kept apologizing.

As several days went by, the dog seemed to be walking around in a fog ... he wasn't as prissy as usual ... he didn't have as much spunk in him. Apparently he must have been really injured because about two weeks later, the dog died.

And so, Pudjy's death became the talk of the office and of the James Brown household. And it really affected Mr. Brown. He was sad, and he kinda got out of his normal routine of calling me on the phone all night long ... for that fact alone, I knew this must have been a period of deep mourning.

The next thing I know, his office called me with a bill for Pudjy's casket ... I think they spent $5700, give or take a $100, and I get word that they were having a funeral the next afternoon. They had already made a lot of preparations and apparently had enlisted the employees at his Augusta radio station, WRDW, to conduct the funeral ceremony. There was one guy, Bob, who was the engineer at the station. He was well educated ... very smart, but he was a big fat guy, about 375, and kind of rough-hewn. Another guy they got was Bill, the former policeman who helped out Pop when he shot the guy with the knife at the party. Bill was a typical old southern-talking boy ... his southern drawl was worse than mine—and he'd talk real slow. But they both kissed James Brown's ass, it was always "Mr. Brown this and Mr. Brown that." But basically, they were radio station engineers who kept the phasers in order and did all of Brown's go-fer work. But apparently, in this case, they had designated themselves as the funeral directors.

When I got to the house, part of Brown's family had already gathered there, including the in-laws. Miss Ella was crying as they ushered me in to the dining room where the funeral was set up. The mood was very somber. The drapes were closed, and I believe they had some flowers and some soft music playing. And in the middle of the room was Pudjy, who was lying in state, propped up in the white casket. He had his little paws drawn up under his chin, and his toenails were painted, and I swear, he had a little smile on his face.

I didn't see Mr. Brown yet. He was back in the bedroom getting ready. But that was normal, he was always late … even for his dog's funeral. So we waited, all standing around, lined up around the casket. That's when I noticed that Bob and Bill were wearing new, blue pinstripe suits. I didn't know they even owned ties! … but they took their jobs seriously and were playing the part of typical funeral home guys to the hilt.

And then here comes James Brown, and somebody had him by the arm, and he was slumped over, and oh man, he was crying and carrying on. And when he comes on in to the dining room, everything got real quiet. You could hear a pin drop, and Bill had Mr. Brown by the arm, and he's got his other arm around him, and he's hunched over as he whispered faintly into this ear, "Mr. Brown… Mr. Brown right this way." Typical funeral home conduct, like *What can we do for you, Mr. Brown?*

Oh man! It was so painful! It was all I could do to keep from laughing out loud. I was literally choking it back. There were people sniffling and such, but I had to bury my face in my hands to disguise the fact that I was on the verge of blurting something out. And I just kept thinking *Oh lawd knows! … what is the world comin' to?*

Somehow, I made it through the service, a Christian funeral (I never knew Pudjy was religious) and after the eulogy was read, I served as one of the pallbearers. We had a brief graveside service in the backyard, where the yardman had dug a little grave and put the little tombstone out there. Brown moved to another house a few years later, and I don't if the people who currently live there know about Pudjy … but that little dog flew in jets, lived like a rock star and was even buried in a $5700 casket … give or take a $100.

CHAPTER 11

Flying High

Mr. Brown loved expensive things … clothes, cars and jets. It was proof of his success. But it was kinda strange, his homes were rather modest, and since he was rarely home, he didn't need to invest a lot in making them showy. But he loved buying cars. He'd drive them around for a while and quickly lose interest and then park them in the yard. He loved jets, too, but he couldn't dispose of them so easily.

While I worked with him, Mr. Brown flew four jets: a Learjet 23 (their company's first model); a Jet Commander 1124B; a King Air 90; and a Hawker Siddeley DH125. He kept the Learjet for about five years and flew the hell out of it. Then I put together a deal for him to move up to a Jet Commander, a model which came out in 1970. It was a high wing jet versus the low wing, and being a pilot myself, I think the Jet Commander was probably the best all around executive jet that I could remember. It had an electrical system and an avionics package comparable to a 727 Whisper jet. It was a little bit larger inside than the Learjet, but still you couldn't stand up in it—you had to hunch your head down. It was fast, it was economical to fly, and it was a low maintenance plane. There were so many good things about the Jet Commander, but he only kept the plane for about three-and-a-half years.

Next, Mr. Brown wanted a plane that you could stand up in so I made a deal for him to trade in the Jet Commander for a King Air 90 turbo jet.

It gave him more headroom, but it didn't give him the speed he wanted, so he only kept it for about a year and a half. Then I went shopping for a big plane, the Hawker Siddeley DH125, which was one hog of a jet. Big ol' jet ... the size of a SabreLiner or the Lockheed Jetstar, which had four engines on it-very expensive to operate. But this Hawker Siddeley plane was still an expensive plane ... it was a gas-guzzler and had nice sofas ... Brown spent a ton of money customizing it. His planes were something he could show off to the world. When you've got a nice home, the public never sees it, but with a customized jet, you could show it off to people everywhere you went.

* * *

Mr. Brown was proud of his Learjet ... the only person who had more pride was the pilot, Doug Bell. At times, he believed it was his jet. A bit possessive. But he took pride in everything around him.

Doug was in his mid-50s and a real serious professional pilot ... a straight guy but so particular. He was a confirmed bachelor at the time, and a good-looking guy ... slim, tall with salt and pepper hair. He always had on these expensive sunglasses and a blazer with "James Brown Enterprises" embroidered on the pocket. He had several blazers including ones in yellow-gold and dark blue ... and his appearance and professionalism really added a little class to James Brown's business.

Doug treated this plane just like it was his own. He kept it spic and span, up to date on all the regulations, kept good logs and good expense records. As far as itemizing his bills, he would even record things down to five cents for a washer. It was like a brand new car to him, and he always carried a rag in his pocket to keep it dusted off, like *Don't nobody lean on the fender.*

It was a beautiful plane, and he had every right to be proud. The Lear had nice, black leather seats, and it had a little gold plaque on the bulkhead right next to James Brown's captain's chair that read, "Custom Interior for Mr. James Brown." We lost several of those plaques when people were servicing the plane—they made nice souvenirs.

Having the Lear at his disposal meant that he could unexpectedly pop into one of his radio stations to make sure everybody was doing their job and making sure that James Brown's hits were being played on his radio station. He had WRDW in Augusta, WJBE in Knoxville, WEBB in Baltimore and WNJR in Newark. However, there was an unknown individual in the James Brown radio organization who had obviously paid off somebody in the FAA to monitor James Brown's whereabouts and to let them know when he was about to pay an unannounced visit. They had even created a grapevine to alert the other stations because nobody wanted a surprise visit from James Brown.

One time, he was going to slip into Knoxville and land at the McGhee Tyson Airport on the Alcoa Highway. Somebody from the FAA called the radio station and somehow his arrival got back to the disk jockey, and he announced on-air that James Brown was going to be landing at the airport. Next thing we knew, half of eastern Tennessee showed up at the airport.

There must have been about 7,000 black people on the tarmac … there were even TV crews waiting for us to land. And since the airport security had gotten there too late to disperse the crowd, we had to make our way through this crowd of fans. We spewed kerosene fumes all over them as they rushed toward us and crawled under the moving plane. They didn't care … they were holding up signs up that read, "Soul Brother #1" and "We love you James."

As we taxied to a stop, the crowd began running their hands all over the fuselage and the wings. They were even lying on the wings and sitting on the gear under the plane and on the tires and trying to remove a piece off the plane for a souvenir.

By the time they got the plane's door open, Brown's security was looking for a way to get him outta the plane, but before that happened, Doug Bell was out there by himself with the co-pilot, and he's cussing and ranting and raving, "Get these damn people away from my aircraft!" I thought he was going to have a heart attack. He was just fit to be tied. And he was running around in his embroidered blazer and sunglasses and his Gucci loafers trying to push all these fans away from the plane. All of a sudden, he didn't seem to be very professional … he had lost control of his airplane.

And since he wasn't able to make the crowd back off, he took off one of his Gucci loafers, probably a $400 shoe, and he had it by the toe to get a little leverage, and he started swinging it around at the crowd yelling, "Get your damn hands off my airplane!" And to make it worse, they started laughing at him.

Even after the airport got a water hose to disperse the crowd, Doug was still running around like a wild man. And when he saw there were handprints all over the plane, he went into another hissy fit. I felt kinda sorry for Doug, but the co-pilot was just out there laughing away.

* * *

A jet was a serious status symbol, especially in the 1960s. Now, everybody has one. Having a jet back then, said you were *Number One* … but sometimes being first could make you a target.

Doug Bell was not the kind of guy who would clown around in a plane, but he is alleged to have done something that has made him some sort of legend. Apparently, he was deadheading somewhere with no passengers when several people reported to the FAA that a plane matching his description performed a barrel roll through the St. Louis arch. This was when the arch was new, and we all knew that some fool was going to do it, and it appeared that Doug Bell, in James Brown's plane, was the first guy to fly through the arch.

The FCC verified that the suspect plane was enroute to California, and coincidentally, Brown's Lear was in the same geographical area during that time of day. But when we asked Doug about it, he would just shake his head. He didn't know anything about it. Apparently, there were a lot of strange things that went on in Mr. Brown's planes.

* * *

It was pretty obvious that Doug *owned the plane* … Mr. Brown just paid the expenses. But Mr. Brown couldn't live without the Lear or Doug's services, like the time when Mr. Brown and I were shopping around, trying to purchase some FM radio stations. AM was on the way out, FM was the coming thing at the time. So we spent the day looking at some stations that were on the market.

Mr. Brown picked me up in Atlanta, and we flew to Columbus, Georgia, then we looked at a station near Chattanooga and another one near Mobile. We had started about 11 o'clock in the morning and by the time we flew back into Augusta, it was about midnight. The pilots were tired because they had been up the day before bringing Mr. Brown in from a concert. They hadn't had much sleep and so they were ready to go to bed in their hotel in Augusta.

When we landed at Bush Field by the Bobby Jones Expressway, Doug presumed he was through for the night, but suddenly it hit Mr. Brown, "Missa Daviss, you got your car here?"

And I said, "Naw, I don't have a car … can you drop me off at the hotel?"

Mr. Brown said, "Now wait a minute, you got business in Atlanta tomorrow … we picked you up in Atlanta, so you gotta get back there tonight." He turned around and made a little comment to Doug, "Missa Bell, you need to fly Missa Daviss back to Atlanta, and then y'all come on back … I'll meet y'all in the morning."

Doug didn't say a word, but I could really tell that he was pissed off. He didn't dare say anything to Mr. Brown, but I knew he was thinking that he *had to fly this son-of-a-bitch back to Atlanta before I even go to bed.* I could see the veins standing out on his neck, and he was slamming things around as he and the co-pilot climbed back into the cockpit and fired up the engines. I jumped back on the plane as Doug slams the door and locks it down.

As he wheels that plane around, I could see Mr. Brown's limo leaving the airport along the chain link fence. Doug taxies out to the runway real fast and did a quick run up, and then he wheels around to the end of the runway for takeoff. As he came down the runway, he pushed the throttle hard … all the way to the firewall. As the Lear came to the end of the runway like a slingshot, he pulls this damn plane straight up. I'm talking about pulling it straight up at full power!

It was no accident … but just as Brown's limo came around the perimeter fence, we hit the end of the runway, and Doug pulled the plane straight up at a 90 degree angle, and it's about to pull the skin off my face. But worse, the engines were pointed down at the limo, and from my window, I could see the kerosene exhaust spraying all over the damn limo. And I'm thinking *Brown is gonna raise hell tomorrow.*

But we leveled out and in no time we were on our way. The Learjet is much faster than the airline … it was actually based on a fighter plane design, so it was normally about a 20-minute flight from Augusta to Atlanta. I made a point of looking at my watch, and by the time we were getting ready to set down on the final in Atlanta; it had been something like 11 minutes. He was burning it up.

I tried to make a little chit chat with Doug, but he just stared out into space. And I'm thinking *What are you pissed off with me about, Mr. Brown's the one that made you fly me home.* But he didn't say a word all the way back.

When we touched down at the Atlanta airport, he was probably running 60 miles an hour on the taxi strip. Really hauling ass … it was almost 1 o'clock by then … and he's running across the airport, and he pulls up at Hangar One, where the corporate jets come in, and he pops the brakes down, and he rolls out of the seat, and he throws the door open. And he said, "Get your ass out! Get outta my plane!"

And I said, "Damn Doug, you don't have to be so crazy about this." Before I said another word, he slammed the door back up and twirled the airplane around to where it was spraying my ass with kerosene, and I'm thinking *When I see you tomorrow, first thing I'm gonna do is whup your ass! How dare you spray my damn $1500 suit with kerosene!*

* * *

Mr. Brown liked to customize his planes, but he didn't mess with the Learjet … it just had a black, silver and red stripe down the side. And he never changed the plane's number—it was always 123JB. The customization started out by painting the Jet Commander solid black. It made a dramatic statement. When he got the King Air, he decided to continue the black paint scheme, however, without my knowledge, he had upped the ante.

I hadn't seen the plane in about a week and didn't know what had happened to it, but he had mentioned on the phone that, "I added a few little odds and ends there to kinda put the finishing touches on it."

When I met him at the airport, Brown stood there like he was proudly presenting the airplane to me like *Look at this Missa Daviss!*

Well, my jaw dropped open when I saw the big black plane … that wasn't it, it was the gigantic red teardrops that dripped off the top of the wings. I was thinking, *Are we trying to compete with Jackie Wilson now with these 'lonely teardrops' on your wings? Mr. Brown! You have really fucked this plane up!* … (pardon my French) … *you have really messed the plane up!*

After a moment of me hyperventilating, Mr. Brown asked, "Whatta you think Missa Daviss?" I knew he kinda had his tongue in his cheek because I think Brown had realized that he had gone too far. He wouldn't admit he had made a mistake, and he was almost blaming it on Danny Ray or somebody else who had talked him into it. Then Brown added, "What do you think about those tires?"

And as I looked down at the landing gear, I'm thinking, "Gawdamighty! Gawdamighty! Look at those tires!"

And Brown added, "How do you like those whitewalls? They assured me that this is the only jet plane in the country that's got whitewall tires."

And while I'm standing there, I realize that James Brown was trying to be gangsta like the characters from the 1972 movie, *Super Fly.* Wide whitewalls were the big thing with pimp wannabes at that time. There was another song a couple of years later by William DeVaughn, *Be Thankful for What You Got.*

Though you may not drive a great big Cadillac
Diamond in the back, sunroof top,
diggin' the scene with a gangsta lean
Gangsta whitewalls, TV antennas in the back

Yeah, Mr. Brown <u>was</u> Super Fly … he not only had a Cadillac, he had a pimped out jet that could really fly … James Brown was *The Real Super Fly!*

When he asked me what I thought, I wasn't going to bring that up, I just stuttered around and said, "Mr. Brown I don't know. I'm gonna have to think about that."

Brown kept staring at me, not saying much. He just looked at me to get my reaction, wanting to pull it out of me, not suggesting anything … he wanted to see what I had to say about it.

I continued through the silence. "I don't know, Mr. Brown, I'll have to look at it a while. It's just such a shock. Most planes don't have whitewalls … and I'm gonna have to get over those teardrops first. It's just a little bit too much red against that black."

He could tell that I was shocked, and he knew what was in my mind because he knew that I was an ol' southern boy and that he couldn't suck any more out of me to force me to put my foot in my mouth.

He finally said, "Yeah, Missa Daviss. Those boys kinda niggered the plane up, didn't they?"

And that opened the gates for me. I laughed and said, "Well Mr. Brown, I guess the only thing they missed was the coon tail hanging on the tail of the plane."

That's when Brown broke up in laughter. "Aawawawaww!!!! Yeah Missa Daviss is gonna tell it like it is."

And while Robert Love, the pilot, was standing there rolling his eyes and drinking a Co-Cola, Brown said, "Missa Love, tell them to get them tires offa that plane right away."

As best I can recall, they left the teardrops on the wings until we traded in the plane to George Wallace, Governor of Alabama. He stripped the paint off and painted it red, white and blue … which only proves what Mr. Brown believed … just like with Paul Anka, *you can judge a man's place in this world by the quality of his jet.*

* * *

Most times, things can be explained reasonably. Other times Mr. Brown defied the supernatural, like the time he was in his solid black Jet Commander. His pilot, Bob Love, was bringing James Brown, Henry Stallings and Leon Austin back from a trip to the Bahamas, when all of a sudden, both engines flamed out. Bob was a flight instructor at

Ft. Benning in Columbus, Georgia … he was a good pilot. So was his co-pilot, Jim Wallace … they both were highly competent pilots.

I was not on the plane at the time, but I got James Brown's version of the story, Leon's version and the pilot's version. Of course, the pilot's version was most accurate. Bob Love said he went through all the emergency procedures, but they still couldn't light the engines. Then they went back through the emergency procedures and started pulling manuals out looking for something they had overlooked in the aircraft.

With every plane Brown had ever owned, he always sat on the right hand side of the fuselage where he could see the pilot. This way, he always could keep an eye on the pilot and be within voice range of the pilot. He always called them the "driver."

I asked Mr. Brown later if he was scared. He thought about it for a minute and said, "Well, let me put it this way, Missa Daviss, when I looked up in the cockpit, and I could see the driver's hand on the controls, and I could see the cat's hand kinda shaking … that's the time to get scared."

Bob Love thought that it was his last flight. But they kept on going through the emergency procedures, and he was figuring out how he was going to do a belly flop in the water, but at about 4,000 feet, he got the engines lit, and they flew out of it.

It must have been a helluva feeling to be gliding at such a steep rate of descent. All you could hear was the whisper of the wind. And everybody's looking at each other. I also asked one of the guys, and he said, "James Brown damn near turned white." Then I got the real story about how cool James Brown really was. Like when he was on his deathbed and told Mr. Bobbitt that he was soon to be leaving this world. Brown was cool—he had no fear. And that's what Bob Love said … he said James Brown sat there just as cool as a cucumber. He was the coolest person on the plane. He sat there and talked in a calm tone of voice and said, "Well fellas, y'all better pucker up. If it's time to go, we're all going. We've all had a good life. You guys better tighten your belt up because when we go, at least we know we're going. Can't be scared of it."

And he looked around the plane and asked, "Y'all aren't scared, are you? I ain't scared to die." He was just like that little boy in Augusta, "that little hard-headed piss ant" who poured the sack of feed in the levee.

When he referred to the episode later, he always swore, "You know Missa Daviss, we were in the Bermuda Triangle. There are strange things that happen there. But it wasn't my time to go. I still had things I needed to do. They still needed me, Missa Daviss."

Later, they took the plane into Hangar One in Atlanta and went over the plane with a fine tooth comb, but they could never find any type of problem. They had expert mechanics going over the plane because they were required to submit a report to consider the plane airworthy, but they never came up with an answer why it flamed out. The pilot couldn't figure it out either despite the many back up systems on the plane. But as usual, James Brown was right … it was the Bermuda Triangle that caused the flameout.

* * *

Mr. Brown was always right—even if he was wrong, even then, he knew he could turn anything around to his advantage. He was a master at manipulating people and in the art of intimidation, and he knew that even though he was wrong, he could still bluff his way out of most any situation … it was that Augusta street hustle thing from when he was a kid.

It didn't matter who he was hustling—even the President of the United States. One time when I couldn't get the President on the phone, it became my fault, like, *You mean we gotta make an appointment to talk to the President? I'm James Brown! You tell HIM that I've gotta talk to him NOW!* In other words, "I'm not going to kiss his ass—I don't care who he is."

In order to rule the world, James Brown always had to have the last word. He'd get you on the phone and force his conversation above yours. He'd talk faster and louder than you without letting you get a word in edgewise, then he'd hang up the phone. And if you dial him back, even five times, he wouldn't answer the phone. He knows it's you, and by not answering the phone, Brown would win.

On one occasion, I was having a very hard week. Brown had been riding my ass about putting a deal together, and I had just flown in … I was tired and dragging ass. Brown had been on the phone with me every waking minute of the day telling me, "I don't care how you get it done—just get it done."

I was pissed off. I was tired. I hadn't eaten and I had been up with two and three hours of sleep a night … I didn't know if I was coming or going. I had just walked into my house in Riverdale and dropped my leather bag and briefcase on the kitchen floor. It hadn't been there five minutes when the telephone rang. One of the girls answered and said, "Daddy, Mr. Brown … "

And I said, "Oh shit!" I had just gotten off the phone with him before I got on the plane, and now, we're having the same damn conversation that we had a couple of hours before! He's still spouting off all these orders and snapping his hands … "Do this–do this–and do this!" … and he's going on and on about all these things because he was going into a recording session later on, about 8:30 or 9:00, in New York, and he wanted to give me a few more orders before he got busy in the studio.

As I interrupted him, "Mr. Brown … "

And he yelled back, "Missa Daviss, I don't wanna hear that. I don't wanna hear it. Do you hear me? I don't wanna hear that!"

Then he went running off with diarrhea of the damn mouth, and I'm trying to get a word in edgewise but he just runs over my conversation. I have seen him doing the same thing with Congress people and Governors … he'd intimidate them into doing things for him that they wouldn't do for anybody else—and they'd be bustin' their ass to please him. People felt like they had to please James Brown. And he knew he had the power to make people follow his orders. It wasn't ass kissin', but close to it … but I was never an ass kisser.

So Brown was spouting all these orders, and before I could pop off at him, he hung the phone up. And I was standing there, my neck was red, and my hair was standing up on my neck, and I had steam coming out of my ears. If he had been standing there in front of me, I would have taken his damn head off! I was that angry. And I'm standing there beating the phone on the damn wall cussing out loud, "You muthafucka! … you hung up on me!" And I dialed the number back, and I'm grittin' my teeth, and he won't answer the damn telephone.

I was so angry—and I had to pop off at him to let him know that, *I'm not your boy—and you can also kiss my ass.* But I can't say it to him—he controls the situation—he's got me by the balls … he's even controlling what I'm doing right now. It's a little mind game he plays—he left me hanging where he wanted me, and usually he'd let me stew about it to the point to where he'd get me to do that extra 10%, to try a little harder, to force me to put a round peg in a square hole.

But I was bustin' a gut to the point where I wanted to cuss him out. I don't care if he fires me. He can kiss my ass. I'm gonna cuss him out. And back then, money didn't mean anything. Sleep didn't mean anything. I was steaming, and I'm telling my wife, "I'm gonna whup his ass! I'm gonna whup Mr. Brown's ass!"

And she says with real sarcasm, "Really? Are you really gonna whup Mr. Brown's ass?"

"That's right. 'Mr. Brown' is gonna get an ass whuppin'!"

And she kinda said, "Yeah … sure … "

I was serious. Brown had crossed the line. He knew that he had more power than I did, of course I was his employee, but I'd take a fall to bring him down. There was no need for him to insult me or belittle me—I'm a professional. *I'm the one that keeps your career going—you couldn't put these deals together without me. Mr. Brown, you can't do without me … but I can do without you! I've made enough money … I can always go back to the bank or I can go fly jetliners. I don't need this!*

So I picked up my bag from the kitchen floor—didn't call the airport—didn't make a reservation. This was in the 70s, and most of the time planes were never completely full except certain times of the day. I only lived 15 minutes from the Atlanta Airport, so I jumped in my car and pulled into the closest place I could get to the terminal … I didn't give a shit if it cost $100 an hour. I ran toward the terminal and the Eastern Air Lines gate because I knew a plane was leaving in 10 minutes. This was the old terminal where you could get to the gate in two and a half minutes and back then, you didn't have all the security you have now—you could even buy a ticket at the gate.

This whole story couldn't happen today at the Atlanta Airport, the world's busiest airport. I'd have to park the car in the deck—walk to the ticketing counter and stand in line—show my identification—wait in line while I took my shoes off and remove the metal stuff from my pockets while I went through security—walk to the underground shuttle train—ride the train to the concourse—take the escalator up-walk to the ticket counter ... and wait. All this taking the better part of an hour, much less the fact that today, when they discovered the pistol in my briefcase, I would have been arrested on the spot and made an appearance on the 11:00 evening TV news. Today, I would have time to cool off, but back then, plane travel was simple and immediate. Delta had a motto, "Delta is ready when you are," and I was ready to whup Brown's ass!

Within 30 to 35 minutes from the time I hung up the phone with Brown in my kitchen, they were backing the plane out of the gate with me on it. And I'm sitting there, so pissed off I was in knots. *Gawdamighty, I can't wait to hit the ground and grab a taxi—then I'm gonna whup his ass as soon as I see him. I'm going into the studio, and I'm fixin' to wreck the damn studio!*

When we landed in New York, I grabbed my bag off the luggage rack and jumped in the first taxicab I saw. I said, "Haul ass. I'll give you an extra $50 if you can get me there on time."

I actually wanted to beat James Brown to the studio and be waiting on his ass when he walked in the door. And light into him. Like, *Hey, you ain't hangin' the damn phone up on me now. You can't hide now! Don't you ever hide behind that telephone!*

It's just getting dark. It's around 8:30 or so, and I'm not sure Brown's there or not. Usually he'd be running late when he was going to the studio, but I jumped out of the cab. I'm paying the driver, and out of my peripheral vision, I catch Brown's limo pulling up to the curb as the chauffeur got out and opened his door.

And I started coming down the sidewalk, getting ready to whup James Brown right there on the street. Brown must have felt my presence … he didn't see me … *he felt me* coming because there was so much rage in me. But when Brown turned around and saw me, he smiles this *big James Brown smile* and calls out, "Missa Daviss!"

He had this look on his face where you could see the wheels clicking in his mind. Like, *Hell, I just got off the phone with you in Atlanta a few minutes ago! And I'm in New Yawk!"* That's the way he said it—"New Yawk."

He's thinking, *Missa Daviss is in Atlanta. How the hell is he here on the sidewalk? Somebody's done tricked me!*

It was no trick, actually it had been a little bit over two hours earlier, but he had no real concept of time … his strong point was manipulation … and he immediately changed into his hustle.

"Missa Daviss! Hey man, you wanna come to the studio?" He turned to his entourage and remarked, "Missa Daviss couldn't miss this … he loves to be in the studio. You need to hear the new tracks I got, don't you Missa Daviss?"

And I was trying to calm myself. "No, Mr. Brown. We got some business we ain't finished."

And he said, "Yeah? What business that be?"

I was on the verge of unloading on him when he slips his arm around me and says to the small group of people, "You know Missa Daviss-you know he's a genius. He don't miss nothing. Right now, he could be home with his ol' lady. He's been out there taking care of his business in Okalahoma City—he's doin' a helluva job. Missa Daviss, you're a helluva man. And you gotta know Missa Daviss … he could be with his ol' lady, but he loves me so much, here he is. By the way, Missa Daviss, how'd you get to New Yawk so fast? I just got offa the telephone with you. Wasn't it just a while ago we were talking?"

And I said, "Yeah, that's what I wanna talk to you about Mr. Brown."

He said, "That don't mean nothing—whatever we were talking about, Missa Daviss. The important thing is you're here—you brought me new energy. Let's go on in the studio, c'mon Missa Daviss—you're a helluva man."

He did it to me again! He knew I had every intention of taking a swing at him, and he knew exactly what to do-and it worked. He pushed me to the edge of the cliff, and I was willing to take us both over the edge, but he also knew the right words and gestures to shut me down. After that, I got what I wanted for the next two or three days ... but then, he started back on me again with a whole new cycle of bullshit.

CHAPTER 12

The Ladies

I've mentioned some of Mr. Brown's passions. He loved money and power—but the ladies were close, in third place. At times, Mr. Brown would get a bit too much impressed by the ladies to where nothing else mattered in the world, and occasionally he ended up making some unwise decisions.

James Brown was a "butt man." He loved a big ass on a woman. And since he was a celebrity and had guys who did his dirty work, if he saw a woman he liked, he wouldn't go over to meet her—he would send one of his bodyguards to fetch her over to him. Then, he'd get her telephone number and arrange a rendezvous in his hotel room.

It was business-as-usual one day outside the Polydor offices at 1700 Broadway as we all waited at the limo. Mr. Brown was sitting in the back of the limo and Henry Stallings, his bodyguard, was standing in the open door with his elbow propped on the roof. I'm standing on the other side of the door as Henry and I are chitchatting across the top of the car. James Brown was making remarks to us through the open door, and occasionally, people would walk by, and point, "There's James Brown!"

All of a sudden, this little black girl strutted down the street ... she was kinda skinny wearing a little ol' miniskirt with a big butt. It was just bouncing around like a pair of basketballs. As she's strutting down the street, she's giving James Brown the eye over her shoulder and kinda prissing around, knowing that all of us are looking at her. She was real flamboyant and had all this makeup on so I thought she was just a regular street whore, but all James Brown saw was that ass. When she had our total attention, she kinda slowed up and stood there on the sidewalk as she kinda twists around and adjusted her skirt, making a big thing about it and trying not to make it such an obvious tease.

James Brown said, "Man, look at the spank on that woman!" And he called Henry Stallings, "Du', go tell her to come here." And Brown kinda peeked out the door and gives her a little come on with his finger and says, "Come here, baby."

The gal comes prissing over to the limo, and she's just smiling, and we kinda stand back where she can lean over and talk to Brown through the open door. She says, "Hey baby, how's you doin'?

And James Brown said, "Hey baby, you be looking mighty good there."

And she said, "I know it. Don't I look good?"

And then she starts talking all this shit with Brown through the door. Then Brown slips over to the far side of the leather bench seat as he pats the seat and says, "Sit down, baby. Come here and talk to me." The girl carefully slips into the backseat as she tugs at her little ol' skirt, trying to keep it from riding up—it was already about halfway up her thighs. The two of them continued talking all this shit when Brown leaned back, and being cool he asked, "What's your telephone number, baby?"

And she hesitated in this little ol' squeaky girlish voice, "Well I don't know … "

Brown said, "You know baby, we need to get together at the hotel here. Where you headed? Where you going?"

Henry and I were standing in the open door, looking down at the couple in the seat. Then, Henry mumbled something to me across the roof of the car, "Missa Daviss, you know … she be a he."

I said, "What? What did you say?"

He repeated, "She be a he." And while I'm trying to decipher what he said, Henry looks off in the distance, real casual, like, *I ain't getting in Mr. Brown's business.*

All of a sudden I hear this squeaky, feminine voice drop several octaves, turning into a rough, raw voice—a manly voice. She says in a deep voice, "Mr. Brown, I just can't do this to you, brother."

Brown went into an instant shock, and as he leans back in his seat, this guy flips his little skirt up. Brown's eyes immediately felt to her lap as he discovers that this guy's got his privates taped to his thigh—with three strands of duct tape.

I have never seen Brown so shocked! I thought he was gonna turn white. He screamed out, "Good gawdamighty! Henry, Henry, get this nigger outta my car!"

As the he/she jumps up from her seat, pulling down her skirt, she returns to her squeaky voice and said, "I'm sorry Mr. Brown. I'm sorry brother. I want to go to the hotel with you but I can't … "

And then Brown cuts her off by shouting, "Get outta here! Get outta here!" and he stuttered and said, "Get away from me!"

The girl/boy made a quick exit from the limo as James Brown quietly sat alone in the back seat. He just stared into thin air, sorta trembling. His knees were drawn up, and he got his hands cupped in his lap, and he was thinking, *Damn, can you believe this?*

Henry said to me, "I told you, Missa Daviss."

And I said, "Man, I can't believe it." By this time I was looking at her and she was kinda half running and skipping away from the car. I whispered, "Damn, that's a man! I'm not used to seeing this kind of shit from where I'm from, and I wouldn't have believed it if I hadn't seen that thing taped to the leg! How did you know, Henry?"

Henry was from Harlem … he knew it right off the bat, but as streetwise as James Brown was, I can't believe that he was fooled. He was almost as innocent as I was, but Henry was laying back like, *Yeah. He played that brother.*

Brown was so embarrassed about the whole thing. He didn't say a word just, "You fellas get in the car … we finished our business here, we gotta go." And we all got in the car and there was no conversation all the way back to the hotel … Brown was just sitting there looking out the window—just had his mouth stuck out, pissed off and staring out in space. Had nothing to say. And we didn't dare say a word either. We had witnessed James Brown, a man of the world, being fooled. It was really funny to the guys who had been there, but to Brown, this was a humiliating attack on his sexuality.

If the same thing had happened to me, James Brown would be telling the story to everyone he met and be laughing in my face—but I think it's funnier since it happened to him ... he should have known better.

* * *

The thing was, James Brown demanded total control over his women. When his power was jeopardized, he had to take action.

When James Brown moved from St. Albans, in Queens, he lived at 3056 Walton Way Extension in Augusta, on about five acres. His entourage always congregated in the den which had a big picture window that faced the back yard. There was a living room and a dining room to the right and front of the house, but nobody ever seemed to go in there that much. As you were coming to the house, you'd come through the kitchen into the den where Brown had his hairdryer.

We were sitting in the den one day while Leon Austin was rolling Brown's hair. Henry Stalling was there, and Al Garner, the other white guy and myself were discussing various things during James Brown's little business session—a two-hour episode while he was getting his hair fixed. Leon rolled his hair into these great big round curlers, the kind the women used ... kinda pinkish purple, more of a lavender color. Then he'd sit under the clear bubble hair dryer, just like he was in a beauty shop. And while he's sitting there under the dryer, we'd have to talk a little louder for him to hear.

While he was sitting there in the chair, he had his terry cloth bathrobe on and had a towel around his neck. He wore leather slippers with socks, pants and no shirt. That's the way he dressed when he was getting his hair fixed, and that's what he wore after he'd get out of the shower at home when he first got up.

As we were all sitting around, talking loudly, Deedee was in the kitchen piddling around doing something in the kitchen sink. When the phone rang, she answered, and then she discreetly eased up to her husband over his shoulder and said, "Baby, Mister so-and-so called and wants to speak to you."

Brown turns around with this frown on his face and said, "Ask him what he wants. Tell him to tell you what he wants."

Then he continued to talk with us, and she goes back to the kitchen, and I could hear her talking on the phone and she said, "Yes, yes." And she put the phone back down and eases up to Brown and said, "Baby, he said it was personal, and he needs to talk directly to you."

By now, Brown was getting aggravated. He said he ain't got time to listen to this guy in Texas so he turns around and said it loud enough where the guy could hear it on the phone, "You tell that nigger to tell you what he wants or don't call my house no more."

Deedee goes back to the phone, and Al Garner and I look at each other. We could hear what she was saying while still paying attention to Mr. Brown talking business. We heard Deedee saying, "He what?! He what?!" And her eyes got real big and she says, "Really?!"

The next thing I know, Deedee slammed the phone down, and man, she blows a damn fuse! She stomps off across the hardwood floors in the den, and you could hear her heels clicking on the floor as she headed for the bedroom as she gathers up the children. Brown must have had a clue what was going on … his eyes were as big as saucers like, *Oh man, I have screwed up!*

I found out later that the guy on the phone worked for one of the radio stations in Texas, and James Brown had bought a new Pontiac for one of his girlfriends there and had left the paperwork up to this guy to take care of. There was some sort of snafu with the tags and the insurance so he needed to ask Mr. Brown about it. When he heard Mr. Brown's comments on the phone, he got mad and spilled the whole story to Mrs. Brown. That's what set Mrs. Brown off.

Knowing that a good offense is the best defense, Brown storms off into the bedroom with the curlers in his hair, and the next thing I hear is something slamming up against the wall in the bedroom. The force knocks a picture off the wall in the den and it falls off the wall with a "whump." We're all sitting in the den with our faces down acting like we weren't there.

Next thing I know, I hear these loud voices, and here comes Deedee stomping through the house dragging both young-uns with each hand and headed out to all these cars parked out in the driveway, which was a big car port and not a garage. Some of the cars were parked in the carport, and some of the cars were parked in a big concrete area.

Brown is right behind her, going out the back door and he's hollering and screaming at her, "You better not leave this damn house!" Before she gets her keys off the wall in the kitchen to get her Mercedes coupe and leave the house, he goes back into the bedroom and comes back through there dragging an armload of clothes draped over his arms. Suddenly he stops at Henry's side, sitting there with his head down, trying to look invisible. Brown said, "Du', you gotta match?" And I'm wondering why James Brown wants a match—I know he ain't gonna light a cigarette … he doesn't smoke. But he snatched some matches out of Henry's hands and continued to stomp outside. By then, we were all peeping through the windows trying to figure out what was going on.

Next, Brown throws half the clothes in a pile in the middle of the driveway. Then he grabs a can of gasoline near the riding lawn mower, and he douses this pile of clothes with gas and throws a match on it. He lit it up. *Whomp!* And while he was standing there arguing with her, he still has some clothes draped over his arm and he said, "And I'll tell you one more thing … "

But she wasn't listening—she was dancing around the fire jumping up and down saying, "Baby, baby don't throw that … not that one! … please don't burn that baby!" But he throws another designer dress on the burning pile, and he kept throwing three and four more outfits on the fire, just chewing her ass out about this and that while he dances around the fire, just laughing. Finally, he's got her floor length chinchilla coat which he dangles over the flames. I was with him when he bought it—he paid over $12,000 for it. Then he throws this chinchilla coat in the fire. I guess being his *Money Man*, I kinda mentally added up what he threw in the fire … it had to be in excess of $20,000 worth of clothes.

The chinchilla really broke Deedee down. She was crying to the point where she slumped down and goes back in the house holding the young-uns' hands. They go in and she quietly goes through the den with her head down crying—dragging the kids across the floor and goes back to the bedroom. Brown's about six feet behind her and walking with a purpose as he follows her to the bedroom. We're all keeping our heads down—nobody said a word—but we were looking out the picture window at the yard man who was raking leaves. He was constantly working in the yard, but now he's over there tending the fire with his little rake. Just like it's a burning pile of leaves, he's just kinda keeping the fire in order as the pile of clothes continued smoldering and burning.

Henry said, "Missa Daviss, I see some bucks sticking out of the pocket." And sure enough, I could see some $100 bills smoldering in the middle of all that chinchilla fluff. So Henry eases out the door and into the driveway and pulls a couple of wads of half burned money from the pile. Then he took a stick and was digging around in the fire and pulls out this molten jewelry, now just a chunk of gold the size of a lemon. Henry rolls it out and kicks it around on the ground before picking it up. Then he blows on it and pitches it back and forth like a hot potato in his hands trying to cool it off. He said, "Damn. I can go pawn this!"

* * *

James Brown had a reputation for cheating on his wives. I suppose it was his conservative nature that forced him to try to hide it … remember, this is the same guy who looked down on people smoking cigarettes and drinking alcohol. He was a puritan at heart, and musta had a conscience somewhere deep, deep down inside.

When he was married to Deedee, there was a woman he wanted to see, and he needed me to back up his alibi. He explained the scenario to me … when we left the office, he wanted me to ride home with him and tell Deedee that he and I needed to take care of some business and he was going to be late coming in that night.

Deedee instantly saw through it, but Brown had a back up plan. He told me before we got to the house, "I'm gonna start an argument with her, and that way I'll have an excuse to leave." And he did. We went in the house, and we weren't there five minutes when he started picking at her in the kitchen. Of course, she turned around and snapped back at him … next thing you know, she gave him an excuse to storm outta the house.

Brown's parting words to Deedee were, "I'll see you when I see ya." It was like, *You pissed me off, I'm leaving,* and apparently Brown thought he was slick. I'm sorry, but I could think of a dozen other ways to get outta pocket … something a little more sophisticated … but that was the way James Brown did it.

* * *

James Brown and his family lived on another planet, I mean, with their money, they were able to buy things and afford a lifestyle that only the very wealthy could enjoy. Even with all that money, Brown's relationship with his wife never got better. Money can't make you happy … happiness is something you can't buy—it's something you can only rent.

After moving out of his Walton Way home, Brown bought a nice 60-acre estate on Douglas Drive in Beech Island, South Carolina. It was just over the Savannah River into South Carolina in a very rural and sparsely populated country area. He had a great big gate at the entrance, and his driveway had a curved gutter, nice manicured driveway. You couldn't see his house from the road, but as you approached it, there was a manmade small pond and a nice barn with stalls for horses. Between the house and the barn, there was a long shed area where he parked a lot of his cars, and if you weren't parking your car there, you could follow the driveway as it curved around to create a cul-de-sac, landscaped island in front of his house.

The house was a real contemporary wood and glass-type structure that was about nine months old when Brown bought it. The owner had built about 38 sliding glass doors in the house because he had been in a house fire once and never wanted to be trapped in a house again, so there was a door on every corner of the house and in every little nook and cranny. To walk out of this house, you'd just slide a wall back and walk out.

To the left of the house was a pool and a long contemporary-style pool house about the size of most peoples' homes. James Brown used his pool house to store a lot of his wardrobe, and he had long racks of outfits and clothes and leather coats and various costumes he wore on stage. And he also liked to watch movies and TV shows on one of these gigantic television screens that hung down from the ceiling—must have been about a 100-inch screen.

With all this luxury, Brown still couldn't find happiness with his marriage. One day, he and Deedee had a fight, and she stormed out of the house and jumped into this little blue Mercedes 500 Coupe. It was a convertible that came with the little hardtop that you could snap loose. That day she had the hardtop on, and she had pulled up in front of the house to pop off a few more comments to Brown before taking off down the driveway … like, *Screw you, I'm leaving you!*

She had the window down, and Brown was bent over and was just giving her hell when he reaches in the car and grabs a wad of hair with his right hand. He snaps her head back and got her head pinned back to the headrest where she can't move her head.

She had to cut her eyes over to look at him while he continued to give her hell. I was standing about six feet away, so I could see her eyes glancing down at the armrest on the door. That's when she reaches over with her left hand and hits the electric window button, and before he realizes it, she had let the window up on his right arm … completely pinning it between the glass window and the roof—I'm talking about being pinned tight! At the same instant, she reaches over in the console and snatched this son-of-a-bitch in low gear, and she floorboards the Mercedes. The tires were squalling, and she tears off, hauling ass down this asphalt driveway!

As the car lurched forward, so did Brown, and he's bouncing on the asphalt like a rag doll on his knees. I'm talking about his damn knees are bouncing up and down on this pavement. My first thought is that she is going to kill him, if not, she was surely going to pull his arm out of his socket.

First, he tried to run along the car, but hell, in less than a half a dozen steps as she picked up speed, his knees were bouncing up and down on the pavement while swinging by his right arm. About 50 yards down the driveway, Deedee hits the brakes and Brown pivots from his arm like a door hinge as his whole left side of his body slams up against the front fender ... but he's still got his arm hanging in the window.

He was screaming, "Deedee, let the window down! Let this window down woman!" As soon as she lets the windows down, he collapses on the driveway, and he's laying there holding his arm. As she stomps down on the gas, she spins off and damn near slams him in the head with the back end of the car ... then I could hear her hauling ass down the driveway hoping that the guard would open the gates up before she reached Douglas Drive.

Brown rolled over on the driveway, but I'm thinking that she had probably broke his legs all to pieces. We started picking him up, and man, he's hobbling and groaning and pissing and moaning. It didn't just skin his knees ... it damn near decapitated his kneecaps! They looked like somebody had sliced the top of them off—they were raw and looked like a piece of ground up hamburger.

Miss Ella got him in a sitting position, and we hauled his ass back to the house, but she kept her cool, not like when she was running around the time when Pudjy got bonked in the head ... but we got some antiseptic to clean up his knees, but Brown kept telling us, "Oh, it's not a big deal." He was acting like there was nothing to it. We tried to get him to go to the doctor, but he was too embarrassed to go to the doctor. He didn't want to tell anybody that his wife had drug his ass up the driveway, and that he had put himself in that position and let a woman do this to him.

James Brown always had the upper hand, and I was surprised that Deedee had the guts to do it, because most of the time a woman will back down from Brown. Just as soon as he raised his voice, the women were so intimidated that he could back them down without any physical violence. That day, she meant business, and as Brown sat there in pain, he got to joking about it and said, "Man, I think I must have pissed Deedee off worse than I've ever seen her. She better not be gone overnight. She better have her ass back to the house before sundown." And I think she did come back later on that day because she was there the next day.

We doctored on his knees and put some Methialate on, and over the next several days he developed a huge, crusty scab, a half-inch thick. Then it cracked when he walked, and it never ceased to amaze me that within three days, he was performing on stage. It took several weeks to heal, but the first few shows, he'd put some gauze over his knees to stop the bleeding. It was bleeding so bad that you could see the blood coming through his pants when he was on stage, and he would have to come off stage and change outfits two or three times.

People say, "He's the hardest working man in show business." I guarandamntee you, that convinced me! Anybody who would break those scabs in a performance had to be tough, and by the time they hardened up the next day, he'd crack them again. I don't know how they ever healed. Maybe it was because of him dropping to his knees so many times on stage, year after year. I've seen his knees, and they always looked like they're had big old calluses on them, a permanent scab. He was an amazing man, and despite the fact that Deedee tried to bring James Brown to his knees—he just wouldn't let it happen.

* * *

James Brown and Deedee eventually got a divorce—then Brown married Adrienne Rodriguez, Wife #3, in September 1984. He had met her when he was a guest on the TV show, *Solid Gold*. I was there at their first encounter … she was outside his dressing room as we both watched her swing her ample rear end down the hall … James Brown instantly fell in love!

"Alfie," as Brown called her, had gone after James Brown from Day One. She knew exactly what to do in order to manipulate him. In that way, she was different from Deedee, who was more refined and raised in an upper middle class family from Baltimore. Alfie was more the star-struck, Hollywood type—she even claimed that she once dated Elvis Presley, something that was never confirmed. As a matter of fact, James Brown mentioned in a book that the only other man she had dated was Elvis. But since Alfie was divorced, the truth is neither here nor there.

Alfie played the part of Mrs. Brown, and the newlyweds would get silly at times. During their good times, Alfie and Brown would fantasize that they were the inspiration for the TV show, *Hart to Hart,* which aired from 1979 to 1984. The series starred Robert Wagner and Stefanie Powers, a jet-set couple constantly involved in one adventure after another. Brown got so infatuated with his fantasy relationship with Alfie that he started coming up with some weird comments to me, like, *Alfie and I were laying up in bed looking at Hart to Hart ... and we're exactly like that couple. Ya know, we can hop on our private jet and go here and go there. You know, we're living just like them. Missa Daviss ... you know they probably made the show about us. We're just like them.*

They started living in a make-believe world, and she had got him believing his own bullshit ... you know, laying up in bed blowing smoke up his ass ... telling him what he wanted to hear. But then it finally came down to the inevitable ... there was gonna come the day when you had the first fight—and there's gonna be an ass whuppin'.

It started out with a little shoving and a little slapping, but Brown got to his old ways—just like an ol' dog running in the middle of the night. And he'd be telling her he was going down to the studio or he had to go down and take care of some business, and he'd go out and he'd be with some lady friend ... then, come in at four or five in the morning.

Alfie was the jealous type ... real possessive, and when I was living in Augusta, she would call me at 2 and 3 o'clock in the morning and go on and on and crying, "I know you know Mr. Daviss ... who is he out with? Is he out with that damn Estella Johnson tonight?" It was like Alfie had latched on to me because she had nobody else she could talk to, and she knew I wouldn't run my mouth.

And I'd say, "Alfie, if James Brown finds out about all these telephone calls, he's gonna fire me and shoot you! You know James Brown is out screwing around—you knew that when you met him—so what do you want me to do? Confirm it? And as a matter of fact, I don't know who in the hell he's with tonight, but you're right, he's out with somebody."

"Have you heard from him?"

"Naw, I won't hear from him until he comes home—then he's gonna get it on with you, and after he gets tired, and he's tired of you, then he's gonna call me and keep me up the rest of the night."

I knew his routine. And then I gotta get up and take care of the legitimate business the next day while Brown is laying up there in the bed sleeping. So I not only had to stay up all night talking to James Brown, hell, I'm having to stay up and talk with somebody's wife because he ain't home.

Everything changed one night. It would eventually lead to her death and his arrest and incarceration. It's funny how your world can change so quickly, but Alfie called about 1 o'clock in the morning, maybe even 12:30. It wasn't all that late. But she called, and she's crying, "Lawd knows, this man is trying to kill me … he's beat me up so bad."

I said, "Where are you at?"

She said, "Well, I just took off running from the house—I escaped." Apparently, all she had on was her bedroom shoes and her housecoat, and she had run up the road from their Beech Island house, which was way off of the main highway. She had wandered up into some subdivision and banged on somebody's door and asked to use their phone. She gave me their address and pleaded, "Please save my life, Mr. Daviss."

I didn't think twice about it. "Sure, I'll be able to pick you up." And so I get into my car, a custom, limited edition Cadillac Elegante, which everybody in Augusta recognized.

I didn't realize it until the next day, but Brown had various employees and members of his entourage riding up and down the road looking for Alfie, and to this day, I can't believe that nobody recognized my car. James Brown would certainly hit the ceiling if he knew that I was in his business and that I had even considered coming to pick her up without him knowing it.

But I went over to the house and picked her up. I noticed she had a black eye, with a little cut on her lips and a couple of skinned places on her face where he had slapped her. I know all this wife beating that everybody heard about with James Brown was mostly shoving and slapping around, not really all out ass whuppin' … just a lot of slapping and shoving which resulted in him storming out of the house.

And I got to thinking, what if James Brown somehow found out that she had gone to my house, there's no telling what he would have conjured up in his mind. So I took her to a motel no more than about three blocks from his office, right up on Washington Road. I put her up in a room, paid her hotel bill and gave her some cash for some food. The next day, I borrowed some clothes for her, and so she stayed holed up in this motel for about three or four days … just kinda hiding out. I'd go over and check on her every day.

The next day at the office, James Brown told me that he had a fight with his old lady. He said, "She done screwed up now, Missa Daviss. Any woman that stays out all night and never comes back to my house … ain't no telling where she's been." He had a real thing about that … he kept asking me if I had heard from her, and it wasn't that I often lied to James Brown, but I certainly couldn't tell him any part of the story.

I was thinking to myself, *What kind of mess have I gotten myself into?* What if they get lovey-dovey again, and she slips up and tells James Brown that I'm the one who came and picked her up … he's certainly gonna be questioning where she was at and how she got there. And I'm thinking, *Lawd knows, how did I get in the middle of all this damn crazy mess?*

And he's talking to me for the next two or three days asking me if I'd heard from her. I played dumb but the whole time I'm going over to the hotel checking on her every day. She's trying to figure out what she's going to say to him and how she's going to go about it. I didn't think she was going to be able to smooth things out, but all she was interested in was being "Mrs. Brown." It made her a star. She was so hell bent on getting hooked up with James Brown, she'd do anything necessary to stay married to him. And she had woven this web around him and did everything she could to make him think she was the greatest thing that ever was … even playing this little *Hart to Hart* stuff like they were something special. But I didn't think that she could ever make up to him.

But she told me, "No, I know James. I know him better than any woman has ever known him, and if I can ever get him to give me enough conversation I will convince him to take me back."

I didn't believe her but then she looked at me, and I could see her just kinda staring out into space-dreaming and scheming. She said, "Yeah, I'm going to tell you one thing … I'm gonna get back into that house and when I do and when everything gets back on track." She took a breath and began to grit her teeth, "I'm gonna bring this nigger to his knees!"

Somehow or another, she called him and told him something to baby him up. The next thing you know they were hugging and kissing so she never said anything to him that I was the one who had carried her over there. 'Cause if she did, she might have gotten a bigger ass whuppin' from me! *Not really.*

At the time, I didn't think much about the comment, "I'm gonna bring this nigger to his knees!" but about that time, James Brown started drifting into the drugs and none of us knew that it was the beginning of his problems, starting with his arrest for the car chase and his subsequent jail sentence. I didn't see the connection but Miss Ella, the maid, swore up and down that in addition to them doing the drugs together, Alfie, (or "Mrs. Brown" as Ella said), was actually slipping PCP into his creamed corn and in his strawberry ice cream, his favorite foods. Several times, Miss Ella would say, "Lawd, Missa Fred, I think the woman is feeding him that shit." After Miss Ella said that, I began to focus on it how Alfie babied over him and noticing that Alfie was always around to put food in front of him.

James Brown was getting into more bizarre and risky behavior … and I think it was due to drugs. One day, Alfie showed me some dental work she had done … she had beautiful teeth, but she had her front teeth replaced with a bridge. And she told me in these exact words, "The son-of-a-bitch jammed a double barreled shot gun in my mouth and knocked my two front teeth out." And the pushing and shoving that had gone on before had escalated into more than just a little slapping around. It was the drugs, not the James Brown I knew.

The more I thought about it and the more I saw him drift off into the drugs, I believe that Miss Ella was right. I remember how Mrs. Brown told me that she was going to "bring that nigger to his knees." But she didn't realize the other consequences that would come with it … that James Brown would become so deeply involved in drugs that he would go to jail. But worse for her … Alfie died.

* * *

James Brown was proud of his women and how they looked. After all, he got Alfie some new front teeth, then he decided that she could use a butt tuck, a breast lift and some liposuction in this posh Beverly Hills clinic. The surgery went well but, according to a lady I knew in California, the first thing Alfie did when she came out from under the anesthesia was to call her girlfriend and order a double cheeseburger and two Twinkies … and some PCP. In reality, her body just couldn't cope with the PCP on top of the painkillers and anesthesia already in her system.

At the time when Alfie died, I was no longer working for James Brown, but I continued to talk to him about every other day. When I heard the news that Alfie had died, I immediately called Mr. Brown at his home. He was eating while I was talking to him, and he seemed a little melancholy and kinda nonchalant. I told him I was sorry to hear about Mrs. Brown, but I didn't reference anything to her drug use, but I did ask what happened to her.

He said, "Well, Missa Daviss," and even though he was on the phone I could imagine him staring up at the ceiling in deep thought. He said, "You know Alfie was killed."

I was thinking that he was gonna come up with this big conspiracy theory … like it was one of his favorite villains … the phone company.

"She was killed? I didn't read that in the paper, Mr. Brown. Who killed her?"

"Missa Daviss, God killed Alfie … "

"God killed her? Why did he do that?"

"God killed her. You know I'm a spiritual man—you know how spiritual I am. I'm so spiritual, I can pray to God, and he'd give me anything I want. Yeah! You believe that, Missa Daviss? If I need a million dollars, I pray to God that I need a million dollars, and God will give me that million dollars in less than 24 hours. If I pray to God right now … if I need a million dollars … he'll give it to me in less than 24 hours."

"That's really something, Mr. Brown. I wish I could get something that fast. That's the power of prayer."

"Yeah, Missa Daviss, what happened was, I prayed to God. Alfie and I had a little spat before she went out there, and I prayed to God to 'get rid of Alfie'."

"You prayed to God to get rid of her?"

I could hear him smacking his lips, chewing his food, slopping his creamed corn as he continued. "Yep, I prayed to God to get rid of Alfie, and you know Missa Daviss … ", I knew a real deep thought was about to emerge." … you know Missa Daviss, God misunderstood me. When I told him *to get rid of her*, he killed her. What I meant was *I just didn't want to be around her no mo'*. And he misunderstood me and killed her. But it was too late then. I just asked him in the wrong way, but he took care of her for me. God killed her."

I really didn't know what to say, and I'm thinking, *You're smokin' that shit again*. But he was real philosophical about this. We continued talking and within 20 minutes, he was convinced that the Mafia had something to do with Alfie's death … "the Mafia done killed her." He forgot that he had just told me 20 minutes before that "God had killed her", but now it was the Mafia … "

Her funeral was a big deal. My dad, my wife and I went down to this old theater on Broad Street in Augusta where there must have been 10,000 people milling around. They put my dad and wife in the family section, but I went out to smoke a cigarette, and the next thing I know, a State Patrolman walked up to me and said, "You've got to move back behind the rope."

Then Danny Ray came out and told the trooper, "Get away, this is Missa Daviss, he be the man. Missa Daviss is family."

And as so I stood there smoking my cigarette with all these TV cameras, a bunch of celebrities started getting out of their limos ... Alfie's friend, Nancy, wife of Senator Strom Thurmond and Reverend Al Sharpton with his wife, Kathy. I hadn't seen Rev in a couple of years, and Rev comes running over and hugs me around the neck, and then he picks me up off the ground in front of 10,000 people and the TV cameras, and I'm saying, "Rev, Rev, put my ass down! These white people are gonna burn my damn house down!"

But that caused Rev to start laughing, and of course we made a big joke out of it. Then he bends down and looks right into this TV camera and points at me and repeated, "I love Fred. I love Fred."

And I said, "Rev, you're going to get my ass killed." So we made a big joke about that later ... we still joke about it.

After the long funeral service, we drove out to the cemetery, and I stood there next to Bob Patton, but as soon as they got through with the graveside services everybody drifted away, leaving the casket unattended. As we were standing next to the limo, talking with James Brown, we were about 25 yards from the grave when I became conscious of a noise ... some machinery running. As I turned around from the conversation and glanced over my shoulder, there's a damn backhoe dumping dirt on her grave, covering her up ... and we were still standing out there by the limo!

Brown had his back turned to the grave, and I didn't say a word, but I know he was aware of what was going on. He just never liked to see people put in the ground. He hated funerals.

* * *

I wonder why he hated funerals so much ... maybe because he had no control over death. James Brown needed to have control over his world—including his women. I never knew how possessive he was until we were on a European tour.

Everything was on schedule. The whole entourage, the promoters, everything was working like clockwork as we traveled all over Europe … France, Switzerland, Italy and Germany. I had been on the tour for about two-and-a-half weeks handling the money and working with some of the promoters and was not used to spending every day with James Brown. I had my gut full of Brown, and things were getting to the point where they were about to boil over. Going to bed at 3 AM, and sometimes, no sleep at all. I was ready to get away and looking forward to get back home and taking care of some of the business.

But the tour wasn't bad … we stayed at the very best hotels, and pretty much lived and ate well. When we were on the French Riviera, we stayed at the Negresco Hotel, which was a really fancy place. The bellmen wore tuxedos.

Brown had a woman with him named Gloria. I had never realized how jealous James Brown was. A few days before, in Belgium, Gloria had gotten sick and was running a fever so the hotel got a doctor to come to her room. Through a translator, Brown was told that Gloria needed a shot, and the doctor needed to give it to her in her ass—her hip. But Brown got so jealous at this young doctor that he was ready to walk out of the room. He told me, "Missa Daviss, he just wants to see her spank. He wants to see her butt. I know what this man's after. A woman with a spank on her like that … does the man think I'm crazy? I told him he could give it to her in the arm. But he said he needed to give it to her in the buttocks."

So Brown made Gloria put on a pair of leotards and made the doctor give her the shot through the material. I thought that was the most ridiculous thing I've ever seen. And the doctor didn't know what the hell was going with this crazy bunch. But Brown was really getting hot under the collar about it … he just didn't want this doctor to see her bare ass.

A few days later in Nice, Brown had to drive to Monte Carlo for a radio interview. I had to stay at the hotel to receive a fax and really wanted to relax and walk on the beach to look at the nekked women. Henry Stallings, his bodyguard, stayed back at the hotel as did Gloria. We all had a few hours of peace without James Brown. I ran into Henry on the sidewalk, and we spent some time together, and as we were coming back to the hotel, Gloria waved to us from her second story suite.

When Brown got back, he called me and started questioned me about some things that were going on while he was in Monte Carlo. He was asking questions about Henry and Gloria … I didn't know what he was getting at, and I knew he was real strict about socializing … he didn't want the employees to get too tight with each other.

He called a couple of more times questioning me … "How much did you see Mr. Stallings today? Where was he at?"—all these questions 'bout Mr. Stallings. Well it all made sense later on when I come to find out that he was jealous, thinking that Henry might have been screwing around with Gloria while he was in Monte Carlo.

The next morning, Brown called to question me again about Henry, and after I got through with the interrogation, Henry shows up at my door. He told me that Brown had accused him of screwing around with Gloria. As close as I was to James Brown, I figured I could talk to him and ease his feelings. So I called him back and could tell I got in the middle of a hollering and screaming session with Gloria. I was being the good guy!

"Mister Brown, I see what you were talking about. You don't have to worry about Mr. Stallings and Miss Gloria. Mr. Stallings was with me down in the lobby most of the day, and I could see him down on the streets shopping. (I didn't tell him I was with him.) And as a matter of fact, I was on the street looking in the windows and passed Henry several times. He was outside sightseeing, and I saw Miss Gloria sitting up on the balcony, and I talked to her and she was in a suite by herself all day. You've got nothing to be jealous about." But this really hurt his ego because it only acknowledged his petty jealousy.

The next thing I know, he blew up and got mad at me, accusing me of sticking my nose in his business. He flew into a rage on the phone, and his last word was, "You keep your nose outta my business … you sorry-ass nigger!"

And he hung up. And I was standing there holding the phone like, *My gawd, I can't believe it. Man! That pisses me off. I fixin' to call him back, and I'm gonna damn light into his ass! I ain't listening to this bullshit.* And I called him back, but one of the guys answered the phone and relayed my message to Brown. In 10 minutes, I had simmered down and I was sitting there in my suite enjoying my breakfast with the shutters open, looking at the Mediterranean from my balcony. It was so nice.

All of a sudden, I heard this hollering and screaming, "Missa Daviss! Missa Daviss! He's done carrying on … he's gonna kill me!" And I got up and opened the door as Gloria, in her housecoat with her hair in curlers, comes running by me and into my room, "Lawd, he's gonna kill me. He's gonna kill me, Missa Daviss!"

Right behind her, here comes James Brown down the hall with his hair in curlers, wearing nothing but his pants, his bathrobe and his sock feet, and I'm standing there holding the door open, and he runs by me like he doesn't even see me. And as he goes past, he grabs a wine bottle off a table and chases her into the bathroom.

And I'm still standing in the door with my hand on the doorknob with my mouth open, like, *What in the hell is going on?*

As many years as I was around James Brown, I never saw any abuse firsthand, but this time he proceeded to beat the hell outta her in the bathroom. Next thing I know, he chases her out of the bathroom and into the hall. Gloria runs up and stops on the staircase and Brown stops in my doorway holding the wine bottle as he glares at Gloria, telling her, "I'm gonna beat your ass."

Gloria looks like she is going to run again, but Brown throws the wine bottle down and stalks off down the hall to his suite. Gloria disappeared somewhere in search of the hotel security, and I went back in my bathroom to find great big chunks of her hair lying on the floor.

Within 15 minutes I started getting telephone calls from hotel security in the hotel wanting to know what's going on. Then Gloria called, and she was crying. I was so pissed off, I told her, "Mr. Brown is not coming in my suite, acting like a fool. I've had it. Screw this. I'm ready to go home."

Gloria told me that she couldn't go back to his suite … she had no clothes, but I said, "Gloria, I've got everybody's airline ticket. I've got your ticket to go home with, and I've got plenty of money. We can buy some clothes. Don't worry about it. Screw it."

She said, "Thank you Missa Daviss. You're a good man."

Then I got a call from one of Mr. Brown's guys, and I told him that I didn't want to talk to Mr. Brown until he apologizes to me. When I heard them telling Mr. Brown that he was supposed to apologize to me, I heard his reaction over the phone.

"What!!! What!!! Apologize for what? You tell Fred Daviss to come down to my room and I'll apologize to him alright."

And I said, "You tell Mr. Brown to fuck off. I ain't coming to his room." I hung up the phone. A few minutes later, two or three of his guys came down to the room wanting to know what my problem was.

I said, "Tell Mr. Brown that my problem is ... I don't know how all this came about for me to get involved in the middle of his damn crazy shit goin' on. Mr. Brown called me a nigger, and he's gonna apologize before it goes any further. I don't care about talking to him. He's gonna apologize to me. You go tell Mr. Brown that I've had enough of this, that I need a vacation anyway, and tell him I'm fixin' to buy myself a bathing suit and go down on the beach with all these pretty people. I've got everybody's ticket, and he can meet me in the lobby in front of everybody, because I'm not going to meet him anywhere by myself-not in his rage, because I'll end up killing him before it's over. As much as I love Mr. Brown—this is damn crazy! I'm just a bystander in the middle of all this shit ... and I'm the bad guy? I'll meet him in the lobby. I've got roughly half a million dollars in my bags, and I need a receipt for it. I've got everybody's airline ticket. I need a receipt for that, too. We need to clear up all this business. I'm gonna stay here on the French Riviera and enjoy myself and let Mr. Brown do his thing. I'm tired. I've had enough of this shit. You tell him just like I said it."

So apparently they told him. One of them called back, and we made an appointment to meet in the lobby. Of course, the whole James Brown organization is on a schedule to get on the train and go to Montpelier for the next gig ... but I'm not going anywhere.

When it came time to meet Brown in the lobby, all the promoters, all the people, all the buses were sitting out there … the band was all packed and ready to go. The entourage, the limousines, all this stuff. Everybody is walking around looking like the world is falling in on them … right in the middle of this expensive tour.

I'm sitting there in the lobby, under this big Victorian rotunda … a beautiful rotunda in this big gigantic room, and here comes Brown exiting the elevator off of the mezzanine level. The elevator only comes down to a certain level, then you come down this wide staircase into the lobby. So here comes Brown with his entourage, all coming down the staircase … and guess who's on his arm—Gloria! And she's all decked out, and she's locked on his arm looking at me like, *We made up in the last couple of hours.*

Brown asked, "Missa Daviss, you got a problem?"

"Hell yeah, I got a problem," I barked as I gestured to my briefcase, "you need to sign a receipt for this stuff."

As we sit down on this sofa, I could hear all the people in the hotel hunched over whispering about us. The entourage is lined up on the street outside. Everybody is looking at their watches. Everything is so quiet you can hear a pin drop. And I flipped my briefcase open, I've got the tickets bundled up … I've got another bag with approximately half a million dollars in it. I got my receipts made out and Brown comes up to me real sad … and he sits down beside me, and we both are looking at each other like, *Where do we start this conversation?*

Missa Daviss, you gotta problem?"

And I'm grittin' my teeth. I said, "You damn right, I gotta problem."

"But Missa Daviss, we're family."

Brown was about to explode, so he got Gloria and they simply walked out of the Negresco and down the sidewalk. I tore out a piece of paper from my notebook, and I wrote him a little note that said, "Mr. Brown, I don't know why it came to this, but you need to stand up and be a man. You're right. We're like family, and I do love you Mr. Brown, and I hate for it to end this way, but I'm not going to kiss your ass." And I folded my little note and even addressed the note to "James." And I signed it, "I still love you, Fred."

Then I ran outside and walked right up in his face and he says, "What do you want, Missa Daviss?"

I said, "Before we part company I want to leave you this little note." And I gave it to him and he starts reading it and I said, "I'll meet you in the hotel, and you sign these receipts for me."

I headed back to the hotel, and soon he walks over to me with the note in his hand, and he started crying. And Brown looks at me with his sad eyes, and he pats me on the knee and he leans up real close and said, "Missa Daviss. Call me *James.*"

"Okay *James*, let's get this over with."

"Get what over with?"

"Mr. Brown, I'm leaving you. I want you to sign these receipts for this money and for the airline tickets. I'm giving you the whole stuff. I'm tired and ready to take a vacation."

"Missa Daviss, this can't end this way. You know I love ya." And a tear rolls down his cheek. "I love you Missa Daviss. We're like family."

"I love you too Mr. Brown. We're like family. We'll still be like family. But I'm not your boy. I ain't gonna be your whippin' horse. Here I am, standing up for you. I'm trying to ease your mind or whatever the hell is going on with you and Gloria—and nothing was going on—and you get me in the middle of all this bullshit!"

"Well what's your problem?"

"My problem is that you're gonna apologize to me."

"Missa Daviss, we're like family." And then he starts crying and he puts his head on my shoulder … he's crying like a little baby, and I get to feeling sorry for him. And I put my arm around him, and we're hugging each other, and I get to crying a little bit. We're both hanging on each other just kinda crying. And all of a sudden we ease up, and he smiles, and I smile a bit … and we talk and he gets up and all of a sudden, he thinks everything is alright.

"Well, good Missa Daviss, I'm glad all this is behind us. Do you have your bags packed? Are you ready to go?"

And I looked at him and said, "*Ready to go?* I ain't going nowhere."

"What? What's your problem? Are you getting *an attitude* with me Missa Daviss?" All of a sudden, he bucks up.

"Mr. Brown, you're the one who got *an attitude*."

"But what is your problem? You've got *a problem*?"

"Yeah, I've got *a problem*. You haven't apologized to me."

He said, "*Apologize for what?* I thought all that was behind us."

"You haven't apologized", and by this time he was gritting his teeth. I said, "Mr. Brown, you called me a nigger. I've never called you a nigger, and I won't put up with this kinda mess. I ain't your boy."

He looked at me real hard, and I'm standing there looking at him like, *I'm waiting for your apology.* And he looks out at everybody in the lobby, and they're trying to look nonchalant, and he looks back at me staring at the ceiling ... he clenches his teeth together for a few seconds ... then he looks back at me, and I could see the hairs standing up on his neck.

As he leans over, he utters something through gritted teeth, "Uhhh, uhhhh, uhhhh, I'm sorry."

"What you say, Mr. Brown? I didn't understand what you said." And he looked at me like he could have swung on me. And then he made it real plain.

"I'm sorry ... "

"You're sorry for calling me a nigger?"

"Yes, I'm sorry," like, *I'm not sure I actually called you a nigger.*

But from that point, I started barking out orders and got the whole show on the road. Everybody was hopping ... all the gears were meshing together now. And everybody starts moving. Brown's standing there smiling, *Get 'em Missa Daviss.* And he puts his arm around me and says, "Missa Daviss is a genius. Yeah, I love Missa Daviss. You know, Missa Daviss, we're family."

Right after than, the tour cranked up and the promoters were wiping the sweat off of their face. We get in the limos, the bus takes off up the road toward Montpelier and we head to the train station. I knew somehow that Brown and I were never splitting up.

* * *

James Brown was a very insecure man when it came to his girlfriends and wives—he was very jealous. I guess it's because he had done so much behind his wives' back so he figured that if his girlfriend or wife got a chance to screw somebody behind his back, they'd do it … just like he would. He could never believe that anyone was 100% loyal to him. For a long time I never realized how jealous he was until the maid, Miss Ella, clued me in.

When James Brown went out of town and left his wife at home, he had a lot of his staff to keep an eye on her. There was a guard at the gate who could keep tabs on his wife's comings and goings, and if she went to the store, she had to take the maid or the guard with her. She was constantly chaperoned and watched … not only outside the gate, but also in the home.

James Brown made a remark to me one time when we were talking about soap operas. He said, "Missa Daviss, don't let your old lady look at them soap operas. It'll ruin 'em."

"What are you talkin' about? I don't care what she looks at on TV."

"Naw, don't ever let her look at those soap operas … those cats come up with stuff on there … they slip in some real subtle stuff … and if you don't watch it, it'll turn the women around."

"What do you mean, *turn them around*?" He was always talking left handed. "Turn them around for what?"

"It'll make a lesbian out of them, Missa Daviss."

"How do you make a lesbian out of somebody? You know, it's like being a little bit pregnant." He had an idea that with all the back stabbing and affairs going on that if the women looked at them long enough they would get tuned into on what was going on. And he thought that they wouldn't just be screwing around with a guy behind their husband's back … they'd be screwing around with their best friend … which was another woman!

He was so jealous that he'd given everybody in his household strict orders about watching the soaps. He even turned Miss Ella into a spy and used her as an informant. He threatened his wife by saying, "Miss Ella is gonna tell me if you're watching them soap operas, and if I catch you watching one, I'm gonna beat the hell out of you!

And she said, "Yeah, baby, I won't watch 'em if you don't want me to."

And Brown extended the TV ban to everyone by adding, "And I don't want you to watch them either, Miss Ella, even if my old lady ain't there, 'cause it'll turn you around ... next thing I know, you'll be on my old lady."

I mean, he had all these crazy ideas about this, and he didn't want his wife or anybody in his house who was female exposed to the soap operas. To get double insurance on the whole thing, he'd get Miss Suzie to catch the Greyhound bus up from Bamberg, South Carolina to stay for a week. And he'd say, "Now mama, don't you let Miss Ella and my old lady look at soap operas."

And she said, "James, I'm gonna do just like you told me to, Baby. I won't let 'em look at it." And what was so funny was, they all convinced him that they were watching each other ... and he was convinced that one of them was going to tell on the other. He had all the bases covered.

But it was just as I expected. I had to go to his house in the middle of the day to pick up some paperwork and there it was ... Miss Suzie, Miss Ella and Mrs. Brown would all be huddled up around the TV watching their soap operas ... James Brown's biggest fear-all the women in his life were becoming soap opera lesbians!

* * *

While I was still working at the bank, Mr. Brown had his Learjet, but he wanted a bigger plane-the Grumman Gulfstream II ... the finest corporate jet made. There was a two year waiting list, because there were only about six of them in the country, and they cost about $6 or $7 million dollars. I think Co-Cola owned one ... Colgate Palmolive owned one or two—they were very hard to get.

There was a guy named Tom Fowler who was trying to work out a deal with Brown to buy one, so Tom ended up going to a gig in Columbus,

Ohio, at the Ohio State Fair. There was no time to drive a bus to the venue so Brown got me to charter a DC9 from Delta to carry the band. I also went along on the DC9 to babysit Tom Fowler.

Once we got to the concert, we were all assigned some front row seats. It was Tom and me, the stewardess, the pilot—who was a pretty straight guy in his late 50s … and the co-pilot, who was probably in his 30s. We also sat next to the Ohio Governor and a bunch of dignitaries. I was really impressed! … this was the most people I had ever seen at a concert—about 85,000 people! The only thing that separated us from a solid mass of black people was a little old chain link fence about 10 feet tall to hold them back from the stage. The old pilot was so uneasy. He wasn't used to being around so many black people.

As the concert started, the young co-pilot was sitting there in awe as this light-skinned black girl was dancing on the stage right in front of him. His mouth was hanging open as he mumbled, "Oh man, that's the best looking woman I've ever seen." She had zeroed in on this white boy, too—and she was bumping and a grinding just for him! He wouldn't even take his eyes off her, and outta the corner of his mouth he says, "Tom, look at the ass on that gal!"

The co-pilot still hasn't taken his eyes off the dancer … his mouth is hanging wide open, but Tom replies, like he's disgusted, "Man, that's a nagger!"

Without taking his eyes off her, the co-pilot replies, "Naw man, she's Polynesian."

Later, when I told the story to Brown, I thought he was gonna fall outta his seat laughing and it immediately became a private, inside joke between Mr. Brown and me. He knew the type of women I liked, and he was always kidding me, "Missa Daviss, you need to have a sister at least one time."

"Naw, Mr. Brown, I'll stay with the white girls."

"Naw, you need to have a sister one time. You need to sample one." He was always joking about it, but after I told him the story about the Polynesian, we would be somewhere, maybe at a concourse of an airport or at a restaurant, and there would be a good-looking, light-skinned black girl, and he would always say tongue-in-cheek, and would elbow me and say, "Missa Daviss, she'd be Polynesian."

People would always want to know what we were talking about. But what would get me in trouble is when I'd have my wife around us, and Brown would say, "Missa Daviss … she's Polynesian."

June would always say, "What the hell is he talking about?" I tried to act innocent … I simply told her that Mr. Brown thought the girl looked Polynesian and hoped that would satisfy her curiosity.

* * *

It may not come as a surprise, but eventually June and I got divorced. Now I'm married to the coolest wife you'll ever meet. She's heard all my James Brown stories, and she puts up with all my mess … but she knows how to treat me, and she's just a sweet woman all the way around. And even though she was born the year I graduated from high school, we seem to get along very well despite the age difference.

After going together for a few years, and after having a few drinks at dinner, I said, "You know, why don't we take the whole family on a trip and treat them to a trip to Las Vegas … and we can even get married out there."

I didn't think she'd go for it, but she said, "Oh yeah, that'd be fun." So we got talkin' about it, and we planned the trip … we took my dad, my two daughters, one of my daughter's friends, and my other daughter's spouse, and we all stayed at the Luxor Hotel … which was fairly new in 1995.

Mr. Bobbit arranged for some limos to pick us up at the airport, and once we checked into the hotel, I learned that Mr. Bobbit had told Wayne Newton that I was there to get married. I met him years before during the time I worked for James Brown, and we knew each other from that relationship … but I was really surprised when he upgraded our suites and sent up a magnum of champagne and invited us all to his show.

Best of all, the seats were right next to the stage. Then about 10 minutes into the show, Wayne Newton stopped everything and mentioned that his friend, Fred Daviss, who had worked for James Brown, was getting married. Wayne put the spotlight on Cynthia and me, and as Wayne leans over, he says in his deep, serious voice, "Cynthia, Fred is a dog."

Cynthia locked her jaws in a big ol' smile while she's bobbing her head up and down, like, *Yes… yes…*

He continued, "Cynthia, you're not going to marry this guy! He is a dog!" Cynthia continues nodding and one of my girls put her hands up over her face like, *Oh my gawd, what is this?* My dad was even rolling his eyes in embarrassment.

But Wayne wouldn't stop, and said, "Cynthia, you just don't know about this guy. We used to run the same women … kinda swapping them back and forth … "

Without stopping, Cynthia kept on like, *I know, I know.* But he carries on with her, and the next thing you know, they bring her out several dozen roses and set them on our table. It was pretty neat, and he had us all going with his practical joke … but I was still red in the face.

Wayne continued, "Fred… you dog! You're nothing but a dog! But I want the audience to know that Fred was good friends with Elvis … he was at his house the night after he died. So I want to sing Cynthia a song … I want to sing her an Elvis song." And then as the lights dimmed, he sang *Love Me Tender* to Cynthia. It was a pretty neat evening.

The following night, we got married, and as we were eating dinner, my Daddy was choking to death on a piece of roast beef. I jumped up and performed the Heimlich Maneuver in front of 500 people, who began to applaud. My daughter's friend was amazed, and said, "Mr. Fred, that was about the coolest thing I have ever seen!"

And Cynthia added, "Yeah, Fred's the guy you want to be with if you've got an emergency."

In the end, the Vegas trip turned out to be a good time. I won a bunch of money, got married, and saved my Daddy's life … maybe we can go back and do it again sometime—but now, thanks to Wayne Newton … the whole world knows I'm a dog!

CHAPTER 13

TMI—Too Much Information

People might think I'm saying too much personal stuff about James Brown. In many cases, I'm the only person who could tell these stories … I'm probably the only one who he really opened up to … he could trust me, and I don't feel like I'm betraying his trust. He was a person, like everybody else, but by revealing the truth about him, I believe I'm proving that *he was more of a person than most everybody else* … he was a great performer and a great man, even though he sometimes stumbled made some bad decisions—but he always got up and carried on. I suppose it's a matter of debate if I'm revealing *Too Much Information.*

A lot of things went on while Brown was on stage—I mean, besides the concert. Everybody talks about his performance … his dancing, his style, the band, the dancers and so forth, but the real show was going on between Brown and his entourage. It was a drama that could have been on Broadway!

Brown was a perfectionist, and he'd fine people for a number of reasons … if they were hitting the wrong notes or if one of them had a button missing on his uniform. Something like $50 or $100 bucks, and he'd dance across the stage and get up in their face and start counting out the fine by opening and closing his hands to the beat of the music-$10, $20, $30, $40—he just kept adding it up, and you could see the panic in their eyes, not knowing when James Brown was going to quit.

When I was at the Howard Theater in Washington, D.C., I was watching the show and he was fining the hell out of three or four people up there. I kept track of the fines by taking notes in my little pad 'cause I was doing the payroll that night. When we got backstage after the show, Brown was fixin' to tell me how much to take out of people's paychecks when I said, "I already got it, Mr. Brown."

He said, "Whatta you talkin' about?"

"I saw you fine them."

And he said, "Missa Daviss, don't be getting so far ahead of me." He really got his mouth stuck out because I had caught on to something private that was between him and the band. He wanted to maintain control over me, and said, "Yeah Missa Daviss, you think you've got all my moves, dontcha?" And as he turned to his entourage, he was kinda bitter about it. "Yeah, next time, Missa Daviss will be out there trying to do the show." And even though he was pissed off at the time, we'd laugh about it later when he was in one of his mellow moods.

Other stuff happened on stage, too. There were times when I saw him split his pants, and he'd dance off the stage and change into something while one of the guitar players or horn players did a solo. He had the coolest horn players that ever were … Holley Farris, the whiteboy horn player, and of course, Maceo … and St. Clair Pinckney and Pee Wee Ellis. The audience saw the performance but was not aware of all the other things that would happen on stage.

In later years, James Brown was having trouble with his teeth and had his teeth pulled. Then he had these implants put in his mouth with these little pegs that they implanted into his jawbone. The whole plate was then clipped on and hooked into these two little pegs.

As a matter of fact, the dentist he went to for years was up on West Peachtree in Atlanta across the street from Crawford Long Hospital. Brown went to see him right before he died, and strangely enough, Elvis also went to see his dentist right before he died, too.

Anyway, Brown was trying to get used to his teeth during the first couple of weeks he had them. I was at the show, and he was all over the stage dancing and twirling around … he did a split and came up off the stage and whirled around—very athletic. I was standing at the corner of the stage, and the next thing I knew, his teeth came flying outta his mouth … his plate bounces across the stage, and of course nobody in the audience saw it, (I don't think) and Danny Ray was scrambling around on his knees trying to grab a towel and brush them off.

Then Mr. Brown dances over to Danny and twirls around so his back is to the audience. Then, Danny passes the plate to him as he slaps them back in his mouth, twirls around and continues dancing with this big ol' smile—he called it his "alligator grin." I was just amazed and said to myself, "Man, that's showmanship! He never missed a beat!"

* * *

James Brown always tried to be the leader of the pack … the pack meaning his entourage, band, wives, children and the rest of humanity. He had the answer to every one of life's problems … including health problems. This was his little game to keep us down so that we had to rely on him for everything. One day in the office, outta the blue, he called a little meeting, and he got to talking about how pretty his teeth were—and they were! But they weren't really his teeth—he had gone out and bought them at the dentist. He told us that everybody in the office needed new teeth, and he was going to do us a big favor by making us all an appointment with his dentist. Everybody was gonna be looking good!

Of course, most of the guys at work were intimidated by James Brown more than I was, in fact, I said, "Mr. Brown, I don't have any problem with my teeth—also I've got to be in New York tomorrow, so I can't go to the dentist." I walked out of the meeting and left the guys all excited about getting their new teeth. I went to New York and was gone for a few days and kinda forgot about the whole thing.

When I came back I noticed that several of the guys in the office were toothless. Every tooth gone. And I felt like something was going on that I didn't quite understand.

I grabbed hold of Willie Glenn and asked him about his teeth. When I was looking at him, I notice how sunk in his face was—then he got this real concentrated look on his face and mumbled worse than ever, "Mitha Daviss, we been in a helluva mess ... well, er uh ... you know, Mitha Brown thent uth all to the denith offith, and he pulled out all our teef ... now, it makth it real hard to talk."

And I asked him about when he was gonna get the new dentures. But apparently when Brown got wind of how much the teeth would cost, he got amnesia—couldn't remember anything about "buying" new teeth, he just said he would pay to get their teeth pulled. That was a helluva mess! I couldn't help but see the humor in it, but it was horrible at the same time. A lot of times, the line between laughter and pain is very thin.

* * *

Bob Love, the pilot, was like everybody else ... always trying to keep Mr. Brown happy-whether you were the pilot, whether you were his hairdresser, his bodyguard or somebody in the band ... whatever it took to make Mr. Brown happy—because Mr. Brown was "The Man"—he was the boss.

Robert's job was not only to make sure the plane was well maintained, more importantly, he always had to be ready to fly. When Mr. Brown's limo rolled up, the jet would have to be running when he hit the steps. When Mr. Brown was ready to go, he didn't want to wait in the limousine.

Mr. Brown had all his pilots dress in uniforms. He believed in uniforms—said uniforms made you look important. And Brown always sat in his favorite chair, so he could watch the pilot, and nobody dare sat there. Bob always made sure Brown had his Kleenex where he wanted ... and his cup holders and all these little personal items like his telephones and his TV controls had to be in their place. And after a concert, at 2 or 3 o'clock in the morning, Bob always made sure they had plenty of sodas on the plane. Brown was not a drinker, not a liquor drinker, but he did have liquor on the plane for any guest who wanted a highball or something.

Brown might have a cold beer occasionally, so Bob always kept a few cans of beer on the plane, but plenty of soda pop and mostly orange and grape. He loved the orange Nehi, and years later, he liked the Suncrest soda. We'd drink tea or coffee, and Brown would drink coffee occasionally, but he would always drink sodas with his meal. He was a steak and potatoes man—loved creamed corn and strawberry ice cream if he could get it. Wasn't much of a bread eater. He liked the potatoes, the corn and the steak. And he would eat chicken. He liked chicken wings and fried chicken.

Usually Bob got a charbroiled steak from a restaurant. The plane had ovens, just like an airliner, where you could heat up the food. One time, Bob thought he was going to get a feather in his cap by getting some baby back ribs from some famous rib place in town … the meat would just fall off the bone. When we got up in the air and one of Brown's assistants started to get the food out, Brown asked, "What did Mr. Love get me to eat tonight?"

The assistant said, "Mr. Brown, we got some ribs."

He said, "We got what?!"

"We got ribs, Mr. Brown, these are baby back ribs."

Bob looked back from the cockpit with this big smile and said, "Yeah, Mr. Brown. We got you the best ribs in town!"

Mr. Brown looked at me, kinda distressed, and said, "Missa Daviss, you gotta talk to these boys." Then he turned his direction to the pilot and said, "Missa Love!"—and you could tell from the tone of his voice and the look on his face that something had gone wrong … we had just leveled out at cruising altitude, and as Bob Love looked over his shoulder, he knew something was wrong. Brown said in a serious tone, "Missa Love, are y'all trying to kill me?"

Bob said, "I don't know what you're talking about Mr. Brown."

Brown said to me, "Tell him, Missa Daviss."

But I didn't know what the hell he was talkin' about. And I said, "Whatcha talkin' about Mr. Brown? You want me to check these ribs out?"

But Mr. Brown was not happy as he said, "Naw, y'all know better than to feed me pork! It'll run my blood pressure up … I bet I'll be having a stroke. No pork!"

And I think Pop was with us that night, and he said, "I'll eat it Ju-Ju-Ju-Junior. Pa-pa-pa-pass the ribs over here" as everybody on the plane devoured the ribs—just tore them damn ribs up!

I wanted me some of them, but Brown said, "Naw, Missa Daviss. Let the rest of them eat them if they want to die, but I've got to watch out for you. You need some chicken, Missa Daviss."

But I said, "Mr. Brown, I don't like chicken—I like pork."

Mr. Brown really got pissed off at Bob Love that night, and after that, he never mentioned pork again—that is, until one Saturday I met Mr. Brown and Alfie at a little delicatessen near his corporate offices in Augusta. I was going to drive them to a football game in Athens in my Cadillac Seville. He said that we were going to need something to eat, because we hadn't had any breakfast … so I got me two hot dogs and a Co-Cola and was standing there, biting into one of the hotdogs when Brown snatched that hotdog outta my hand and throwed it into the trash can.

"Hey, hey, hey, what you doing with my hot dog?"

"Missa Daviss, it's gonna kill ya. That stuff'll kill ya."

"Mr. Brown, that was a good hot dog!"

"You know what's in them things?"

"Yessir, but I love 'em anyway … "

"Oh, Missa Daviss, you can't have no hotdog!" Then he took it on his own to order me some sorta damn sandwich that I didn't care nothing about.

So rather than eat it there, I compromised and said, "Well, I'll take it with me to eat."

It's kinda ironic, but pork is the essence of soul food. Think about it … chitlins, pig feet, pig ears, hog jowls, pigtails, fried pork rinds and ham hocks. I knew he had been brought up eating all that stuff, but in reality, the *Godfather of Soul* rejected traditional southern fare and was some sort of damn health nut.

* * *

During the Vince Dooley era, when the University of Georgia won the national championship with Herschel Walker, their famous running back, James Brown had become synonymous with the Georgia Bulldogs through his recording, *"Dooley's Junkyard Dogs."* The school had gone crazy over it, and all these Bulldog fans naturally related James Brown to their football team.

As a tribute to James Brown and his music, the school's musical director, Roger Dancz, dedicated a halftime show in his honor. I didn't realize what a complicated thing it was to do a halftime show with a marching band ... hell, we did 300 concerts a year!—what's the big deal? But they started doing the arrangements several months before the show, and I'm sure it was a big deal to get two or three hundred musicians out there on the field playing *I Feel Good* and *Dooley's Junkyard Dogs.*

Everybody knew that James Brown was gonna be on the halftime show—they had advertised it on TV for weeks—and they were building up all this hullabaloo and the fact that it was going to be on national television with an estimated audience of about 40 million people. Now, some people naturally get star struck when they see their favorite movie stars, or musical legends. It's just natural ... what's unnatural is how the fans perceive their idols to be almost un-human in the way they live.

It reminds me of an ol' boy at the bank ... one time we were talking about crazy things, and this ol' boy mentioned Elizabeth Taylor and said, "Fred, can you imagine Elizabeth Taylor sitting on the toilet taking a dump?"

And I thought about it, and said, "No, I can't. She's a superstar ... I can't even imagine it." I couldn't ... you just can't imagine it because of all the glamour and hoopla surrounding famous people—but it was something I came face to face with at the University of Georgia. Shortly before halftime, that day in Athens, we arrived in James Brown's bulletproof limo ... and of course, all the Georgia Bulldog fans recognized James Brown's limo as we entered the bowels of Sanford Stadium—this big ol' concrete structure wedged between a bridge and a railroad track.

Everybody knew what to expect from James Brown. They were all familiar with the red jumpsuit he used to wear—it had this zipper all the way down the front, and he had his real fancy, thin sole boots with the slick leather soles where he could slide around the stage and dance. But this day, James Brown wore this long raincoat over his jumpsuit, trying to be incognito. And since he didn't have an entourage around him, he was able to slip into the stadium unnoticed. We hid under the grandstands, kinda huddled over in a corner.

As we're waiting around for halftime, and I'm smoking my cigarette, and Brown is hunched up with his collar pulled up as high as he could around his teased up hairdo, trying to disappear from recognition ... but inevitably, people come up and yelled out, "Hey, James Brown! Hey, James!"

Normally, we'd get our field passes, and we'd walk up and down the sidelines, and James Brown would talk to the ball players and Vince Dooley (giving them helpful advice) and the people in the stands would yell, "Hey, James Brown!" And they would all be hanging on the fence before the ballgame wanting autographs and such, but this time, James Brown had to stay out of sight until halftime. There was nowhere to hide, but fortunately, it was only minutes until halftime. And so we're hanging out with all these thousands of people ... all these drunk, redneck Bulldogs fans under the stands who've been drinking beer for hours and now were pushing their way to these toilets under the stands. We're seeing all this going on because we're standing right outside the bathroom entrance.

James Brown said to us as he walked into the bathroom, "Hey fellas, let me stop." Apparently, he wanted to take a leak before the halftime show—this was his last chance. So Henry Stallings, his bodyguard, and I were right there by the entrance watching all these guys going in and out of the toilets. The toilets were actually these long troughs with this pipe dribbling water down the wall. It's like a pig trough, and all these guys are standing there urinating into this long trough like a bunch of cattle lined up in there. There must be 200 drunks in the bathroom, and I figure with so much pushing and shoving, someone was bound to get their shoes wet. It was not a pleasant atmosphere, and they also had these stalls with toilets, but they've got no doors on them. They're just stalls—no doors.

So Brown goes in there, and he's covered up with this trench coat, and we're standing there smoking, and we thought he'd be three or four minutes. After seven or eight minutes, we realized that Brown's not back yet.

I said, "Henry, Brown's not back. What's going on?"

He said, "I don't know, Mr. Fred." So we peeped in and saw people going in and out, and I looked down the bathroom, and I don't see him. I don't see the red jumpsuit or the trench coat. I knew he had plenty of time to go to the bathroom, but then we got concerned. *Hell, maybe somebody's kidnapped him!* So we decided we'd look for him, and as we push through the crowd, Henry was on one side of the bathroom, and I'm on the other side. We finally got down to the stalls with no doors … and we had to be kinda discreet about it-you know, you don't want to be snooping around there with all these guys sitting on the toilets, but we kinda walked down through there peeping into each stall.

At face value, this story isn't all that significant, but when you add the celebrity factor to it—it becomes real strange. Here we are, looking for the star attraction of a halftime show that's fixin' to perform live in front of 40 million people on television plus 80,000 people in the stands! The whole show is built around this one individual, who has disappeared in a crowd of drunks in a public toilet.

But all of a sudden I go past a stall, and I do a double take, and I back up, and that's when I found James Brown. He had his trench coat laying on the wet, sticky concrete floor, and he's got his jumpsuit unzipped. It's not just like you're pulling your pants down … I mean, it's like some gal in her jumpsuit. He's got it unzipped, and he had to pull his jumpsuit all the way down to his ankles and over his boots, and he's sitting there on the toilet, naked as a jaybird. Brown is up on his elbows, and his hands cupped over his face, and he's staring between his legs and the floor and apparently was constipated.

And I'm standing there as this human herd of fans keep pushing past me, and it comes to my mind that here's this superstar, James Brown, who's fixin' to be on national television five minutes from now, and he's sitting there for all to see, like, *Hey folks, the show's not out on the field, it's right here under the west stands!*

And I'm thinking he's got to pull this red jumpsuit up right quick—it's almost halftime! I said, "Mr. Brown are you alright?"

And he said, "Missa Daviss, I'm kinda stove up a little bit. I told Alfie we shouldn't have eaten them damn hamburgers last night." But he finally gets through, and he gets that jumpsuit back on and has a minute or two to tease his hair a little bit, and then after that, here he comes out on the field and everybody is whooping and hollering, "James Brown! James Brown!"

The halftime show was a big success, and I think about that day many times. Mr. Brown was just one of the guys … one of many in the stalls, but even then, he was the center of attention, especially with all these drunk guys whooping and hollering and the ones that would pass him and say, "Hey James! Hey!" And he's trying to sit there and shit, but he's still the center of attention, even in the bathroom, and everybody is talking, "Hey, James Brown is taking a shit over there."

I'm sure I'm not the first person to tell this story. There were so many other people who happened to be in the bathroom that day. I'm not teasing or making fun of James Brown because he was constipated. I just want people to see the human side of James Brown and all the everyday things he went through … 'cause no matter how much fame—and no matter how much money you have—and all the notoriety—you still get constipated from time to time, and you still gotta go through the same thing with a bellyache. But for James Brown, it was twice as hard for him, because when he had to go, everybody who passed the toilet was pointing at him. Nobody likes when people point … especially then … so even the most routine things in his life ended up being twice as hard.

* * *

James Brown was just like every other guy … he put on his jumpsuit one leg at a time. I was fortunate enough to get to know him very well … I'd even say intimately—I'd say "intimately" in the academic sense of the word. But sometimes our close relationship may have been too close for comfort, but one thing it did … it made me see him as a real person, just like everyone else.

Miss Ella had her own close relationship with James Brown—working in a domestic situation for someone doesn't allow much room for hero worship—you get to see the real dirt that nobody else ever will.

One time Brown was out of town and I had to go over to his house in Beech Island to pick up some papers or something. It was in the middle of the day, and Miss Ella was there at the house—nobody there except the yardman and the guy on the gate.

Miss Ella was doing her typical housework. She always had this lacey little short apron on and her matronly shoes. And her hair was always fixed up, and she'd priss around in the house—I mean, *that was her house!* And she would cook anything Mr. Brown wanted ... she was totally at his beck and call.

But like all the rest of the employees, when Brown was not there, they could all talk freely among themselves and knew that it wouldn't get back to James Brown. They loved to talk and gossip about him. Even his children. Even Teddy, the oldest son who got killed, he'd talk about his Daddy in a bull session just like we would.

So I had the same sorta trust and relationship with Miss Ella, and when I dropped by the house, I found her doing laundry ... and she wasn't happy about it. Although most of Brown's clothes were dry cleaned, his personal laundry had to be done at home ... stuff like his socks and underwear. He had all these bikini-looking underwear drawers—not your typical boxers or briefs—they were the sexy, red bikini drawers.

And he had all this laundry that went in this big drawstring-type laundry bag, and from time to time, the people who handled his clothes and luggage had to wash all this stuff. And there were people who had to deal with his shoes and luggage and all his personal items ... his toiletries and things. He had his personal tastes about things ... he still shaved with an old double edge Gillette where you put in the blade and screwed it up tight and put the lather on. I've seen him many times in a hotel suite, and we'd be talking, and I'd be standing in the bathroom door, and he'd be shaving with that old style razor ... the kind my Daddy and Granddaddy shaved with. One time I forgot my razor and Mr. Brown loaned me his personal razor ... that's pretty intimate, isn't it?

Usually, Miss Ella was humming and carrying on and prissing around in the house … just always stayed busy. A little dynamo. But on this day, Miss Ella was grumbling … she was there by herself and could say anything she wanted. But she was really pissed off about the laundry, and she was in the laundry room sorting the socks and the underwear and was saying, "Lawd kno', Mr. Fred! I just can't believe it! They bring all these damn drawls in here! You know, the nigger's got skeet marks all in his drawls! Yeah, he skeeted in his drawls!"

And I kinda laughed, and she's down on her knees throwing these drawers in the washer. I said, "Miss Ella you know that's a man thing. You know he probably gets these skid marks from doing those splits."

She says, "Yeah, James comes in with these damn dirty drawls—I've got to wash all the shit out of his drawls. He comes home, and the nigger done shit in his drawls … every time he put 'em on!"

And sure enough, every one of them had skid marks in them—every pair of *drawls.* Or is that *too much information?*

CHAPTER 14

Thin Ice

It seems like I was always ending up in strange situations—not your regular ol' strange situations, but situations of life or death—or worse! They usually involved firearms or armed revolutions in Third World countries, or the FBI, or going to jail … and sometimes, I simply made a bad decision and had to face the consequences. But usually I just happened to be in the wrong place at the wrong time. In any case, every day with James Brown was like a slippery stroll on thin ice.

I spent a lot of time in Brown's jets, and many times we'd drop Brown off in Augusta and fly back to our base in Atlanta. It was a short trip, and I would move up into the cockpit while Jim Wallace, the co-pilot, would relax and go back and sit in Brown's favorite chair. Jim would take his shoes off, prop up his feet, make him a drink and turn the stereo up-chillin' out. Never even put his seat belt on.

On this night, about one o'clock in the morning, I was in the co-pilot's seat and had folded up my left armrest so I could lean over and talk to Bob Love, the pilot. We had had the Jet Commander about six months, and Bob was very proud of it, but as we left Augusta, I thought it was strange that he quickly got up to about 24,000 feet … we usually went only up to 12 to 15,000 feet, because once we got up, it was time to come down. Bob was trying to tell me something about the plane, and I was having trouble understanding what he was saying. As I leaned over, he started slowly rolling the plane to the left, and I was thinking, *What the hell is he doing?*

The next thing I know, Bob had rolled us upside down—more than 180 degrees! There's nothing dangerous about rolling a plane, but you need a horizon to tell where you're at … and when you're flying from Augusta to Atlanta at night—it's sparsely populated with a lotta dark—there is no up or down, just black. Plus, at that speed, if you let one thing get away, it multiplies on you 10 times as fast. It's not a forgiving situation.

As I suspected, Bob lost the horizon. And as I looked at the instruments, all the dials were rapidly tumbling as the plane rolled—Bob had lost control. As you go in a roll, your nose is high with the yoke pulled back toward you—you're pulling back on the yoke … but as you roll over 180 degrees with the yoke still pulled back, that means that the nose is now pointing toward the ground! And because the nose is pointed at the ground, you start to build up airspeed. Before we know it, the damn airspeed had jumped to 700 knots, and we're going faster and faster! Immediately, the g-force became overpowering. Bob had his right hand on the console near the throttles, but my left hand was being forced down by my side.

The g-force is pulling the damn skin off of my face, and the plane is violently shuddering and making a racket—just raising hell. I'm looking at the altimeter, and it's spinning like a bat outta hell-falling fast … and the roar of the air, and the engines are revved up to cruise speed! Bob's hand is pinned to the console—he can't move it!

We've got one minute to live—then, we're simply going to plow nose first into the ground at full throttle. Whatta bitch! Then, all of this shit started running through my head … all these things that I haven't finished … we're in the middle of this shit with the Internal Revenue, and I gotta meet with the lawyers tomorrow … the radio station needs attention in Baltimore and Brown is involved in a damn paternity suit. All this business stuff is bouncing around in my head—stuff that hadn't been completed. My whole mind is like a fast forward video.

And I'm thinking, *What is this son-of-a-bitch doing, rolling the plane and didn't even tell me? Bob Love is going to kill me right here, right now!*

I'm getting so pissed off. In that short period of time, it's surprising how fast your mind works. It's true, I saw my whole life flash before my eyes. They say, you should always *live in the moment*, so I relaxed, calmed down a little and tried to enjoy the ride. I looked up at the two elongated panels in the roof of the cockpit—almost like a sunroof in a car. I could look outta the top of the cockpit and see the bright stars winking in the dark sky. It was a pretty sight, but then I started to comprehend all this and thought, *Wait a minute! Those aren't stars! These are lights on the ground. They're street lights in some neighborhoods, and they're rushing at us real fast!*

I couldn't do anything about it. I'm pressed down in the seat—my damn legs are paralyzed from the g-force, and all my blood is in the bottom of my ass … my face is pushed back into the seat, my eyeballs feel like they're going to pop out my head, and my mouth is forced open and resting on my shoulder—I'm slobbering all over myself. I can't move my head, but I can open my eyes … and I look back in the cabin and see Jim Wallace. He's got his eyes shut, too … but he's got this big ol' smile … got his earphones on, laying back there listening to some rock and roll, and he's holding the Scotch and water in his lap—but the tremendous g-force is keeping every drop in the glass, even though he's upside down. Jim thinks we're playing around in the cockpit.

And the plane is banging, and I'm thinking we're about to tear off the wings. We're fixin' to have structure failure, but Bob slowly raises his arm up on the console, and I look at his hand … he's got the tips of his fingers crawling up the length of the console, pulling his hand as he walks his hand up the console and finally to the throttles. We're seconds away from death.

And I start thinking … if I could just get my arm up outta the seat … the first thing I would do is whup Bob's ass before we hit the ground! The son-of-a-bitch is fixin' to kill us just because he wanted to show me how good the Jet Commander rolls!

And even though it seemed like forever, Bob finally gets a hold of the throttles, and he snatches the throttles back. At the same time, he hits the air brakes, puts the flaps down and drops the landing gear. It was almost like in the cartoons where the characters skid to a stop with a screeching sound effect. The air speed immediately started dropping and the altimeter starts to slow up. We're still half the way over, and by that time, I got my hands on the yoke, and we're both pulling the damn yoke up in order to get the plane cleaned up and under control.

He levels out, and I look down at the houses and treetops. We're at about 5500 feet, but in seconds, we would have hit the ground. My armpits are wet with sweat … my face is clammy, and my knees are shaking … it scared the hell outta me! And Bob, too.

He gets the plane cleaned up and hasn't yet said a word. I didn't say anything either, but in my mind I'm saying, *You son-of-a-bitch!* Then he starts climbing out again slowly, and we get up to about 10,000 feet before we reached Atlanta. By then I was cooling down a little bit, and he starts talking over the radio like everything's calm.

I waited until we got on the ground, but when we got outta the plane I said, "Damn Bob, what in the hell were you thinkin'?"

Bob said, "Hell, I've rolled it several times before. I just wanted to show you what a slick plane this was and how easy it was to roll."

"Damn right, *it's easy to roll!* You just about rolled us right into downtown Madison, Georgia!"

But Bob was really embarrassed about it, but at the same time, it took a helluva pilot to clean the plane up and to get us outta that mess. Bob did such a good job that Jim Wallace, who hadn't even spilled his drink, didn't even know what had happened until we talked about it the next day!

After that, the incident became a good bar story … the ladies seemed to enjoy it … the only person never to have gotten a good laugh out of it was Mr. Brown … and he would have shit if he had known that his plane nearly got the damn wings ripped off!

* * *

I don't know how I was always getting into these situations. Even when things looked cut and dried—something would happen like all the little showcase dates we played at little boutique, hotsy-totsy places.

One time we got booked for three shows in Jacksonville, Florida at a supper club named Peter Abbott's. Terrible name—we kept calling it "Peter Rabbit's." I had never seen a supper club like this … it was a ritzy, dress up place, and the showroom would hold maybe 300 to 500 people. Had two bars in it, and it reminded me of the movies from the 1920s with all those glamorous speakeasies.

But this was "the club" in Jacksonville where the pretty people come go to party … the doctors and accountants, and all your young professional people … and they served them gourmet steaks, lobster and champagne. On the surface, it seemed real elegant, but Mr. Brown was kinda leery of the guys running the place. They weren't really gangsters, but how could they pay an entertainer $50,000 a show for 300 to 500 people? The math just didn't add up.

When I got to the club, Peter Abbot was trying to impress James Brown with a tour of the place and was saying how honored they felt that, *James Brown is playing my club.* Hell, it wasn't an honor for James Brown … it was an easy $150,000! … $50,000 a show for Friday, Saturday and Sunday night! But as Mr. Brown was peeking out from behind the stage curtain, the first thing I noticed was about half a dozen beautiful hostesses flitting around the supper crowd and openly flirting with the male guests in front of their wives.

Peter Abbott was trying so hard to impress Mr. Brown. He said, "Mr. Brown, we have all the lobster you can eat … and you can get anything you want in your dressing room." Then he turned to a waiter and snapped his fingers, "Get Mr. Brown some Dom Perignon!" Everybody was just kissin' James Brown's ass—then Peter Abbott added suggestively, "*Anything else* you want?"—but Alfie was standing next to him, and Brown just turned to me and rolled his eyes.

Peter Abbot continued, "Mr. Brown, we have beautiful girls", like *take you pick.* There was a girl standing there who was really built and had this sexy-looking blouse on. Peter introduced her to Brown and asked, "Do you like her?"

But Brown was real leery of all this, and he glanced over at me a couple of times like, *These guys are slick, better watch 'em, Missa Daviss!* The girls were trying to impress me, too—they knew that they were going to have to do business with me, and I was all business. I had a job to do, so I turned to one of the club's managers and said, "Let me get started with your deposits. I hope you understand, Mr. Brown gets paid in cash."

But as I was talking, I couldn't keep my eyes off of all these classy looking women.

The manager looked one girl up and down as he asked me, "How do you like her?"

I said, "She's an attractive lady."

Then the manager turned to Brown for a response. "Look how she's built, Mr. Brown."

The girl had a great body … and had a great smile with pretty teeth. Then she turned her back to me, smiled at Brown, and then reaches into her blouse and proudly displays her breasts. "How do you like these tits, Mr. Brown?"

Brown muttered, "They're nice."

But I'm standing behind Brown, squirming around like a teenager, and thinking, *Hey! Wait a minute! Don't close up your shirt. Let me see 'em. I want to look at 'em!* But it was all a big game, setting up an attitude like, *We're really out to please you.*

After Brown went on stage, I went back into the office and started on my paperwork. I was real determined to get it finished so that I could go out and watch the rest of the show from a ringside table. But the next thing I know, one of these good looking hostesses came back, and she sits down on the edge of the desk. She wants to know if there is anything she can get me. I told her I was fine.

But she said, "*Anything* … I can get you *anything*." About that time, two other girls came in. The first girl said, "Have you met Cindy and Crystal?", (or whatever their names were), and so there were these three beautiful girls hunched up over my desk, and one of them said, "Mr. Daviss, we can take care of anything to make you comfortable."

And I said, "Naw, I'm just trying to finish these figures," and at that moment, it dawned on me what she was getting at! *Damn I'm naïve … I'm just an ol' country boy!*

But she wouldn't leave me alone! Next thing I know, she asked, "How would you like a nice blow job?"

That sure 'nuff made me stop my paperwork, and I thought for a moment, *Did I just hear what I thought I heard?*

Then she flops her top open and flashes her breasts in my face. "Would you like some of this, or do you think you can handle three of us? You know, we can clear this desk off and lock the door-it's that easy … and you can have any one of us … or all three."

And I started to stutter, and I was choked up. "Well, uh, well …"—it caught me so off guard, and I was thinking, *Let me think about this … maybe we can find a better time and a better place…*

So I feebly mentioned, "I've got business to do … and we can't do it here … "

But she snapped back, "Oh no, we can lock the door, it's no problem … here, let me do a little warm up … a little quickie to give you a little preview."

Then I gave her an *aw shucks* sort of rejection, "Naw." But then I started to get a little leery. I was thinking, *Somebody is gonna trick me—and I damn sure don't want one of them to tell Brown later that I was back here getting a blow job!*

Brown would have gotten so jealous of me. He never liked to see his employees enjoying themselves or benefiting in any way, shape or form. Plus, he'd tell me that I wasn't taking care of my business. *You're back there playing. Missa Daviss, these slick people just ran a game on you.* I can hear him now, so at that point, it hit me—I've got to be cool about this. Finally, I told them that. "We'll talk about this later. It's business time now, and play time's later."

So she said, "You just call us anytime at night, if you think about it … or get a little horny… all you have to do is snap your fingers, and we'll be back. We can go out in the car if you want to."

I laughed and said, "I appreciate it. Y'all are beautiful women, but right now's not the time." That was on Friday night.

I must admit, the club was really rolling out the red carpet. Just like the next day—I went to the club during the lunch hour to discuss some business matters, and they wanted me to have a lobster that they had flown in from Maine. I really didn't care anything about lobster. But they made me eat the damn lobster. They even introduced me to Chuck Norris, and we spent an hour and a half talking during lunch. I wonder if the club flew in Chuck Norris just to impress me. I wouldn't doubt it.

On Sunday night, we were supposed to get the last payment. The club had already paid over $100,000 for two nights, so we needed about another $40,000. Unexpectedly, Peter Abbott disappeared on some urgent business after Saturday night, and there was nobody in charge. But all the staff members tried to reassure me, "Mr. Abbott is gonna pay y'all on Monday morning."

But I said, "Naw, we need money! We need cash tonight!" James Brown had been hustled many times in the past and wouldn't put up with this nonsense. He would have walked off the stage in the middle of the show, but in this case, I kinda halfway convinced him that we'd get the $38,000 on Monday. Brown left it up to me. He flew off in his jet but assigned his bodyguard, Mr. Stallings, and two other guys in case I ran into any problems.

And there were problems … especially when we started to get the runaround. And all of a sudden, I couldn't get a hold of anybody except for a skeleton crew running the bar. Finally, I got a check, but it had some bugs in it. Then they gave me a smaller check to cover the first check, and I did a little swap at the bank so that I ended up getting about $25,000. I felt pretty slick about that … if I hadn't worked for a bank and knew what to do I never would have gotten that much money. But they still owed us $12,000 to $13,000.

I told Brown about it on the phone, and I'm sticking my chest out. "I ain't putting up with this shit, Mr. Brown. I'm gonna go down there and whup somebody's ass."

"Missa Daviss, these guys are gangsters."

"Naw, these are businessmen. They're just running tight on money. They just let their mouth overload their ass—all they got is cash flow problems."

"You need to get in the car and come on home."

"Mr. Brown, do you mind if I stay a few more hours tonight, and I'll put some pressure on the manager, and I will get some more money, because they're a little bit too jumpy. They're scared of us now."

I knew they were. I could look at the guy's eyes. Even Brown's goons looked at me like, *This ol' boy is crazy. I don't care how good he dresses up ... he's crazy.* Maybe it was because I kept on talking about an ass whuppin'.

Mr. Brown said, "Missa Daviss, don't get in trouble. Don't get yourself arrested."

I said that I wasn't gonna get arrested, and I'd be back home on Tuesday. On Monday night, I went back down to Peter Abbott's. They had a pretty good crowd, but no show, and all the pretty people were eating dinner. That's when I ran into the manager and said, "Hey, I'm here to get the money, so you'd better call your boss, wherever the hell he's at!"

Then I walked through the supper club, and you'd think I was the gangster. I went down there with Henry Stallings and his two goons, and I went down this long bar and said, "Get your cash registers open!" and I was dumping all the money in a bag.

One of the bartenders said, "Hey man, we need some change!"

And I said, "I'm gonna leave you $50." And I took all the damn money and the people at the bar were looking like, *What in the hell?* They probably thought I was the Internal Revenue or somebody.

I cleaned out about five or six cash registers while some of these hostesses were running around, cramming hundred dollar bills down in their bra. And I backed one of them in the corner and said, "Gimme the money. You want me to undress your ass? All of y'all have been trying to get undressed in front of us—now you can get undressed and give me that money."

And she said, "I don't have any money, Mr. Daviss."

"I just saw you stick $400 or $500 in your bra. Now you want Mr. Stallings to rip your top off of you? Naw, I ain't putting up with this shit!"

She thought for a moment, but stood there defiantly and said, "You're cold."

"You just don't know, baby."

She looked at me and said, "You could have had all the blow jobs you wanted. In fact, I'll still give you a blow job."

"We're beyond blow jobs, baby. I want the money." Then she pulled down her bra a little and reluctantly gave me money.

Out of the corner of my eye, I saw this little pipsqueak manager hunting for a place to hide. I had positioned one of Brown's goons at the front door and the other at the back door ... there was no way out, so the manager ran back into his office. I walked back there and kicked his damn door open.

"Hey pal, we need to open your safe."

"I-I-I don't have the combination ... "

"Well you better damn start gettin' it, 'cause I'm fixin' to slap the shit outta you. And when I'm through, I'm gonna let Mr. Stallings do some serious shit to you. Mr. Stallings will break your knees. He loves to break people's knees ... he don't like white people anyway."

Henry locked the door behind him and he grunted, "I don't like white people."

And this guy was about to shit. And he said, "I don't have the combination."

"How in the hell do you get in and outta the safe?"

"Well, I'm not the person who opens the safe ... it's not my job ... "

"Hey buddy, ask yourself ... is that money in the safe more important to you than an ass kickin'?

He thought for a moment and said, "Wait a minute, I think we have the numbers right over here." And he finds the numbers, and he was so nervous and his hands were shaking so bad that he couldn't get the damn safe to open.

I said, "Gimme the damn numbers. I'll open the safe." Henry was leaning up against the door and this guy was just wringing his hands, but when I got it open there was some packs of 10s, 5s and 1s ... then there were rolled quarters, dimes and nickels. Small change, but I took it all—tied the bags up just like I used to do at the bank. It wasn't the kind of money they owed us, but every little bit helped. Next, I got to opening up all the desk drawers looking for money.

The manager said, "Hey man, you can't do that!"

But one drawer had a brand new .357 Magnum in the desk. I said, "Whose gun is this?"

He said, "I don't know, I've never seen it before."

"Hell, that thing's probably worth $450", so I put the pistol in the bag and mentioned in an offhand way, "I wish I had some bullets … then I'd shoot you in the kneecap."

He pleaded, "Please, y'all just take what you want, and please let me go."

About this time, I felt like leaving so I made one more run down the bar, after all, this was suppertime and the patrons might have bought some more drinks in the meantime. As I rifled through the cash registers, I'm cussing and ranting and raving and ol' Henry Stallings said, "Mr. Daviss, you're bad … you're bad."

We had squeezed Peter Abbott dry, but we still didn't have all the money. Later, as we made our departure from our hotel, I saw the headlines on the newsstand that the FBI had been running some sort of clandestine investigation on the supper club for months. Apparently, Peter Abbott was a felon who had become an FBI informant.

The Feds closed the club the next day. They put yellow tape around it, and went in with search warrants. Later, I learned they had cameras planted in the manager's office and had the phones tapped—some pretty heavy surveillance!

And I thought, *Oh thank the lord! Even though the FBI has tapes of me looting the cash registers, kicking in the office door, taking money out of the safe, liberating a .357 Magnum and threatening to shoot the manager in the kneecaps … the one thing they didn't have was a X-rated video of Crystal, Cindy and me in a variety of sex acts on top of the manager's desk! Thank god for my moral strength!*

The worst part would be knowing that all those FBI investigators would carefully scrutinize the videotape over and over and over …

* * *

We were always on the edge of the law … and sometimes we almost went over the edge. It was not the way I was brought up, after all, I was a banker … I had integrity. But James Brown's whole life was a hustle, and I got sucked into keeping him out of trouble.

He was always trying to circumvent the tax people. One way was to set up a bunch of living trusts for Deanna and Yamma concerning musical publishing and song writing. That's where the big money was! Many times James Brown took credit for songs he didn't write. He put his own name on the record label and paid the royalties to the songwriter. The guy wouldn't dare object to the arrangement.

Polydor knew what was going on, and the scuttlebutt around the record company was that James Brown would be putting some of the songs in his dog's name—Pudjy. But one time, it turned around and bit them—not Pudjy … Polydor's own arrogance.

After putting an album together, James Brown gave Polydor a list of the album's songwriters. One of the writers, a guy in Texas, had a strange name … kinda like a dog's name, and the people at Polydor had just assumed James Brown was being cute by giving writing credit to one of his dogs. But when the album came out, and started to make a good bit of royalties, this guy came outta the woodwork and sued James Brown and Polydor because his name was not on the credits.

With a little arm twisting, Polydor produced a memo from one of the top executives that said something like, *Hey, don't go along with James Brown … he's just putting one of his damn dogs' names on the label—put James Brown's name on there.* But the songwriter in Texas busted their ass and got all his royalties. Then Brown stepped in and laughed and said, "That'll teach you guys. When I tell you to put a name on the album, put it on, and don't be second guessing me!"

So even when things seemed weird, sometimes they were true. Fact and fiction with James Brown were often the same thing. His plan was really brilliant. He had formed such a maze of corporations and trust accounts that the smartest lawyers would take a year just to get to the bottom of it … and by the time they started to turn up the heat on us, we'd done transferred the money to another place. It was like chasing a ghost.

The classic example of that was when we were both standing before a judge fighting a judgment resulting from a lawsuit. James Brown didn't want to pay and was doing everything he could think of to wiggle out of it. In this case, Brown was trying to say that the money in question belonged to his daughter because she had earned it as a songwriter.

The judge was very impressed with himself—his golf course suntan and deep radio voice. He wasn't about to put up with any of this James Brown monkey business. As he was peeping down over his glasses, he said in this baritone, radio announcer-type voice, "Mr. Brown. Do you expect me to believe that your daughter, Deanna Brown, wrote this song that is earning you millions of dollars in royalties? And how old is this child—seven years old?" (or however old she was at the time) "Do you expect me to believe this, Mr. Brown?"

"Yes, your honor," he said with an expression just as serious as could be—but I'm standing there in front of the judge just rolling my eyes.

Brown continued, "Well, she didn't exactly write the song, but she came up with the concept, and I helped her with some of the lyrics … but it is her song … she actually came up with the concept and wrote it."

The judge said, "Really? From this list of songs, can you give me an example of her songwriting ability?" I was just waiting to see what Brown was going to say—I'm sure the judge was, too.

Brown thought for a minute, and said, "I'll give you a good example, your honor. I came in one day from New Yawk, the kids were playing, and they hugged my neck … they were glad to see Daddy home. Missa Daviss was there, he'll tell you the same thing … but the kids had their toys strewn all over the den. I was tired, so I plopped down on the sofa, but then Deanna came running up, telling me I was sittin' on her toys, and she yelled out, 'Daddy, get up offa that thang'."

And the judge sat there and rolled his eyes while Brown wrapped up his story, "And judge, that was the beginning of that bit hit, *Get Up Offa That Thing*, and Deanna, Yamma and Deedee helped her write it. But Deanna was the very nucleus of that song."

Brown and I would always tune into each other, just like Al Garner and I would. We knew what each other was thinking, so I turned around and said, "Yeah, Mr. Brown, tell the judge about your daughters writing that other song."

"What other song was that, Missa Daviss?"

"The song when you sprained your ankle?" But I saw that Mr. Brown was a bit confused on my lead, so I said, "Remember the time when you sprained your ankle, and you tried to get your boot on and couldn't get it zipped up. And Deanna was worried that you might have to cancel your show, and you're trying to figure out how you're gonna do your show … don't you remember what Deanna said?"

"What was that, Missa Daviss. What did she say?"

"Well, Deanna looked at you and said with the innocence of a child, 'Daddy, all you gotta do is *Get On The Good Foot*.'"

Brown yelled out, "Yeah, Missa Daviss!" as he started to laugh, "Awawawawawaw!"

That pushed the judge over the edge. He simply rolled his eyes and ordered the bailiff, "Take these people out of here! Take them out of my courtroom, now!"

Once again—we got away with it. James Brown successfully played the part of the innocent victim, like, *Hey, y'all are attacking me, and I've only got a seventh grade education. You need to ask Missa Daviss about all those complicated legal matters … I don't know nothin' 'bout that.*

* * *

James Brown was an international celebrity, and his name could open doors on any continent around the world. He was not only a star in America, but in Japan, Europe, and South America, he was a legend. In Africa, James Brown was a god. Naturally, as *James Brown's Money Man*, it was my job to pursue his financial interests there—Africa was open for business.

James Brown used to laugh and tell people, "Yeah, Missa Daviss is the only white boy I know to go to Africa by hisself … and he always brings back money." All I'm gonna say is … airport security was much more relaxed back then.

My business deals lead me from Monrovia, Liberia to Libreville, Gabon and Lagos, Nigeria to Dakar, Senegal. It was a whole new world for me, and before I had ever gone to Africa, James Brown used to tell me how black the people in Senegal were. He said, "Missa Daviss, those peoples' skin is so black that they got a bluish tinge to 'em. They kinda put out a glowing blue look … like a neon light." And sure enough, that was the first thing I noticed when I got there … a guy in shorts and a Jungle Jim hat on—and his damn legs were blue looking! He was the blackest black I've ever seen, and when I mentioned it when I got home, James Brown said, "I told ya."

I always dreaded going to Africa … even when I enjoyed the fabulous wealth, luxury and privilege of Omar Bongo, one of the richest men in the world. He was the President of Gabon, and when James Brown first met him, Bongo's teenaged son requested that Brown play for his birthday party. Bongo paid beaucoups of money for the concert, and he even sent his own personal plane 747 to transport Brown to Gabon. The kid had his own 727 … and his wife, Madame Bongo, had her own Boeing 707, or some other big jet.

In all, President Bongo spent about $250 million dollars for a big three-day birthday party. That may sound like a lot of money, but he even had this big vault in his palace full of currency … including German marks, French francs, U.S. dollars and Italian lire. He also planted all these exotic trees lining the road from the airport to the palace. Then he bought about 120 limos to transport all the dignitaries coming in to his party. I wondered what he did with all these limos after the party … apparently, he gave them away to his friends.

My experience in Liberia was equally bizarre. I went there to meet President William Tolbert in his palace in Monrovia. I'm not sure if Tolbert was such a big James Brown fan, but the business arrangement was set up through Winston Childs, a prominent black attorney from Washington who had gone to school with Estrada Bernard, the Liberian Minister of Finance.

Part of the time, Winston and I stayed at the presidential palace, but I wanted to get away from all that hoopla so we got a suite at the Décor International Hotel. Even though it was a fancy place, everything was ass backwards there. Everything was so slow, including the telephone service. The secretaries were the worst—they were not set up for business, and everything they did was slow … like typing contracts … it was hunt/peck, hunt/peck on these antiquated dilapidated typewriters.

I got really homesick after a day or two, and I missed some good ol' country cookin'. I was just an ol' country boy … you know, a meat and potatoes guy, and I never wanted to try anything new. Plus, I really didn't want anybody handling my food. Therefore, I ended up eating nothing but boiled eggs, and there was no way I was gonna drink the water … or the beer. They had all this crazy beer that was bottled in every kind of bottle they could find, whatever bottle they could put it in. So I ended up drinking Heineken beer and eating boiled eggs … I even brushed my teeth with Heineken.

One day when we were drawing up some contracts at the bank offices in downtown Monrovia, I decided to get a little fresh air. I had my banker's suit on and my briefcase, and I went out the door and was walking around the block. Even though this was the business district, they had all these tin shanties all up and down the street. Across the street, a group of people were grilling something … kinda squatting down roasting things on their little charcoal grills. I was kinda curious so I walked up to this tin lean-to and glanced down on the grill. I know my mouth dropped open in shock … I saw a human baby roasting on the grill! It was the most horrible sight I had ever seen … the baby was split right down the middle from the skull right down through the rib cage-split in half like a chicken! And its little fingers and toes were shriveled up over the coals, and I was thinking, *Oh my gawd! Somebody is barbecuing a child! Damn cannibals! They're fixin' to eat a child!*

But nobody seemed too concerned … some barefooted guy was basting the baby with this sauce, and he's grinning with these ol' rotten-looking teeth. And a bunch of these guys were drinking their ol' lukewarm beer and talking and smoking and carrying on … but I can't believe it! *They're barbecuing somebody's child!* Then I got to looking over the baby—it had a tiny little rib cage—and as the guy was putting some more barbecue sauce on the body, he pinched off a piece of meat and wanted to know if I want a little bite of it. "Hell no!" I was about to lose my lunch of boiled eggs and Heineken beer. But then I glanced down, and I saw this little stub of a tail … and then it all comes together. It's not a baby … it's a damn monkey! But it still looked like eating somebody's child. Then the guy with rotten teeth got the piece of meat and popped it in his mouth. "Hmm. Bar-be-cue monkey."

I should have never wandered off by myself. I needed a bodyguard or something. Fortunately Winston and I had our own driver, Charles, who was one of the President's top echelon soldiers—like a green beret. He even had combat boots and a little green tam … plus he always had an AK47 hanging on his shoulder.

After a few days, Winston and I had wrapped up our business and decided to go out on Saturday night and chase some women and drink some liquor. We recruited Charles to drive us into town and use his social skills to get the party started. It wasn't easy … we tried to get Charles in a conversation, but he would only answer yes or no. Real proper. Couldn't carry on a personal conversation—he was really scared of his boss, the President.

As Charles was driving along, sitting there very properly, his machine gun was ready by his side on the seat as we headed downtown … like Bourbon Street during Mardi Gras … wall to wall people.

Winston leans up into the front seat and asks, "Charles, my man, where do we find some female company around here?"

Charles talked with an accent, kinda like in the Bahamas, "Don't know, Mr. Childs. I don't understand."

Winston rolled his eyes and looked at me while hunching up closer to Charles's shoulder. He said, "Mr. Daviss and I … we want to know where the women are at."

Charles said, "Oh women. Yes, we have plenty of women." But he wouldn't get to the point.

Winston was kinda tippy-toeing around with Charles, but under my breath I was whispering in Winston's ear saying, "I want a white girl. I want to know where the white girls are, Winston." So this goes on for three or four minutes and finally I raised my voice to Winston, "Just tell him! Tell him what we want!"

Then, Winston taps Charles on the shoulder and said to him brother to brother, "Charles, hey bro, where's the pussy?" Charles's eyes instantly grew real big … and if he hadn't been so black, he would have blushed.

He said, "Oh yes, yes … pussy, yes, yes … " And about that time, we had just entered into the main street, and we came into an intersection. Charles abruptly stops the car right up under the traffic light, and all these other cars screech to a stop 'cause we're in this government vehicle. Everybody is holding their breath as Charles gets out and struts around with his machine gun hanging on his shoulder … and all these people back off in fear. Then Winston and I get outta the car to see what's going on as Charles waved his machine gun around the crowd and said to us, "Take your pick, mon."

I'm standing there telling Winston, "I don't see any white girls. Where are the white girls?" So we get back in the car and stop at a bar … of course, Charles has to go in with us. As Charles enters the bar with his AK47, everybody in the bar steps back in fear, but we sit down and order some drinks. Winston starts encouraging Charles to have a drink with us. We could both see how Charles was licking his lips … he really wanted a drink, and finally, somehow or other, we talked him into it. We gained his confidence and swore that this would never get back to the President.

After Charles started drinking, the next thing I know, women were crowding into the booth with us … but Charles still has this AK47 hanging by a strap on his arm. It didn't take long until we all get drunk as skunks, and the damn women were coming out of the woodwork! But I'm still asking, "Where are the white girls?"

After that, we wandered around and hit a few more bars … eventually, we couldn't remember where we parked the car—we had lost the damn car! Then Charles came to the terrible realization that he was drunk.

He said, "Mr. Childs, we be in much trouble."

I looked at him and I said, "Charles, what's this *we* shit? We're not gonna be in trouble. *Your ass* is gonna be in trouble. And you're really gonna be in trouble if you don't find me a white girl!"

So we stayed up until the wee hours of the morning and finally found the car. Charles took us back to the hotel, and I'm kicking these big cockroaches outta the way in this damn fancy hotel. I was sick of this place ... I had a tremendous hangover ... and I wanted to leave Africa immediately, but we weren't scheduled to leave until the next morning at 3 AM! How did we get booked on a 3 AM flight? I wanted to leave as soon as I could, so I walked five blocks to the nearest airline office—I couldn't get the crazy woman at the damn hotel desk to get a call through to an office five blocks away! It was awful trying to communicate.

The best flight I could get was to change planes in Oslo, Norway and pay the ticket price of $3,000. But I stuck it out and stayed in Monrovia until three the next morning. Even then, I had to share the flight with 300 drunks from Caracas, Venezuela ... but it was worth it ... I was so glad to get out of Liberia.

* * *

Later on, I had to return to Liberia. I never saw Charles again, and I don't know what happened to him. It was such a strange place, and it was supposed to be a civilized country, but I could always tell that there were undercurrents there. There was so much poverty there and yet all the ministers lived in their private compounds ... and of course the president had his big fine palace there. With that much difference in wealth and privilege ... there had to be conflict.

A few days after I left, Liberia had a coup. A militant-type guy named Samuel Doe came into the palace and cut a bunch of peoples' heads off, and from what I understand, they dug holes out back and buried the bodies with the bulldozers. I knew they killed the President, William Tolbert, but somehow Estrada Bernard escaped the bloodbath.

On my return trip to Liberia, several months after the coup, I was back doing business with Samuel Doe, like nothing happened. And the first thing I asked him, I said, "Did y'all know that I was over here doing business with William Tolbert?"

And he said, "Oh yes, yes, Mr. Daviss—James Brown, James Brown, James Brown's man."

"So, you knew I was just visiting here on business, right? … so if I had been here during the coup, and y'all had come in killing all these people while I was here at the palace … what would y'all have done with me?"

Samuel Doe looked at me with this big smile, and then he turns and looks at all the members of his entourage … he looks at them back and forth at them in agreement … and then he rolls his eyes and points his finger at me and announces, "We'd cut your head off, too, Mr. Daviss."

And the whole time I was doing business with this guy, I'm thinking, *You son-of-a-bitch!*

But ol' Samuel Doe didn't last long. There was another rebel, Charles Taylor, who came in and overthrew Samuel Doe. They not only executed Doe, they tortured him first and made a videotape of it! So Samuel Doe suffered the same fate as William Tolbert … then Charles Taylor got his … and so on.

One thing I know, you won't catch my ass back in Liberia ever again!

* * *

How did I get in these situations? I'd be doing my job, minding my own business, and some unbelievable stuff would happen—something I would have no control over. Well … I may have been responsible for *some stuff…*

One of the perks of my job was travel, and since I owned a six-place twin Comanche I was able to take along a few friends. I had some business down in the Bahamas so I took a friend of mine to stay at Paradise Island at the old Lowe's Hotel—it's now the Atlantis.

We had a pair of party girls with us, and they suggested we take the plane and go on a picnic on one of the many uninhabited islands throughout the Bahamas. The girls put on their bikinis, and they packed a nice picnic basket with wine and cheese and even brought a radio for some tunes. It was a nice day … the water and the sky was both so blue

… and we were island hopping over these tiny, deserted spits of sand when one of the girls said, “Let’s land on one of those islands.”

I had never landed a plane on a beach before. I was not a reckless pilot. But I made a pass over the island … maybe the length of four or five football fields and not very wide, but it had a little knoll with some scrub trees growing high on the knoll. I set the plane down on the hard packed sand, and then we were able to tiptoe through the scrub bushes and walk up to the knoll. We got up under this little ol’ tree and laid the blankets out and had a nice little lunch. The only thing I didn’t like was I couldn’t drink anything—I had to fly. But the girls enjoyed my share of the wine anyway.

We ended up spending about half the day up there, and everybody eventually ended up nekked … we were just relaxing in the breeze of the cool shade tree. The girls were knocking off the wine, they were about drunk, when one of the them casually said, “I believe the airplane is in the water … ”

I jumped up and looked at the plane—and sure enough—it was in the water!—and it was like, *Oh my gawd! My plane! … Oh shit! … We’re gonna be stranded!*

The tide had come in and the beach had vanished except for an area about 10 or 12 feet wide … the landing gear of the plane was underwater, and the plane was cockeyed as it was quickly sinking in the sand. As I was running toward the beach, I slipped on my shorts and shoved my feet into my soggy tennis shoes … my friend was right behind me. The girls, however, were still sitting under the tree … swigging the wine—they thought it was a great adventure.

On the verge of panic, I jumped into the plane and fired up both engines. I knew it was a lost cause … the left gear of the plane had sunk down in the sand with water swirling all around it, and I was hollering for my friend to get under the tail of the plane and start lifting it as high as he could. Once I got the engines going, I’m revving up one engine and kicking the rudder, trying to pull the gear outta the sand. I rev it up really high, and my friend’s rocking the tail section up and down with his shoulder. Then, I couldn’t believe it … the wheels started breaking loose from the sand! Slowly, the gear climbed up out of the hole, and I was able to taxi up to some dry beach. I was so relieved! The girls thought it was pretty cool, too, as they sat there swigging the wine outta the bottle.

I started hollering, "Get down here! I've gotta get out!" But they were kinda laughing and waving, and I yelled out, "You better get your ass down here!—I'm gonna leave you! Do you understand? I'm gonna leave your ass!"

Finally, they came running down through the little path, through the shrubs. They left the radio and the picnic basket—but they managed to bring the wine with them. Once they got to the plane, I grabbed them and pulled them up on the wing and into the cabin. Then I slammed the door to, but didn't preflight it or anything … didn't care if anyone had their seatbelts on … I had to get airborne. But it was going to be a risky takeoff on such a narrow strip of sand … there was no room for error because my right wingtip was almost clipping the small brush trees that grew up next to the sand dunes. As I revved up the engines and began to roll down the beach, I'm dancing on the rudders trying to avoid disaster. This was a scary situation … if I had clipped the trees, we could have cart wheeled down the beach and probably died. Worse than death, we could have been rescued and our whole stupid misadventure could have become a news item, something about *James Brown's Comptroller Loses Aircraft During Lurid Picnic.* I was gonna be in a world of shit—Mr. Brown would have hit the roof, and I would have deserved every bit of his criticism.

But I was lucky that day … I successfully took off from the beach and soon we made it back to the Lowe's Hotel on Paradise Island, and as you know, it's a pretty slick, classy place. The only problem was when the girls ran and got on the plane, they were buck nekked. Not a stitch.

Once we got in the air, we dug around in the plane and found a beach towel and a T-shirt that was wet. One girl puts on the T-shirt and pulled it down over her ass—but you could still see clean through it. The other girl wrapped the towel around herself to cover the essentials. Once we got to the hotel, we tried to look inconspicuous as we were traipsing through the lobby … and we were all grinnin' at all the tourists checking in at the front desk. I don't know what they must have been thinking about these two guys in shorts and tennis shoes, no shirt … and two, drunk, near-nekked girls swigging on a bottle of wine as they were staggering around, giggling, and trying to adjust the T-shirt and towel to avoid even further attention.

I was so pissed off—and I'm thinking. *Y'all shut up!* And I'm looking at all these people staring back at us, and I'm thinking, *I don't know who these crazy girls are! They just happen to be following us … they don't belong to us!*

I tried to forget that the whole thing ever happened … and I sure as hell never told James Brown about it. In his mind … I'm still a genius.

CHAPTER 15

The Fight For What's Right

I admit I made some bad decisions. At the time, they didn't seem to be bad decisions—they just turned bad ... but I always tried to do the right thing ... it was the way I was brought up. And I was brought up to respect my elders, and that included Pop. I was also taught that if something was right, you should stand up and fight for it.

One day in Augusta, Pop had called and asked me to pick him up and bring him to James Brown's office. It was about 5 o'clock in the afternoon, and I had Pop in the car, and we got stuck in the rush hour. Traffic was jammed-up so bad at I-20 and Washington Road, I pulled in a service station to use a payphone, just to let Brown know I was on the way. This was before cell phones.

The service station was right next to the on-ramp, just south of I-20. Brown's office was just on the other side of I-20-just within sight—but in traffic, it might take me another 20 minutes. As I was standing there, talking to Brown on the phone, (the pay phone was still there at least until 2012). Pop was standing out there next to me with his felt hat on.

While I'm talking on the phone, this carload of four white guys was pumping gas about 20 yards away. One of the guys picked up a rock and hollered out, "Hey! Hey nigger!" Then he reared back and threw the rock at Pop. Pop kinda ducked down, but the rock hit him with a slight glancing blow, knocking off his glasses while clipping the rim of his felt hat.

It was late afternoon … it was about 100 degrees … and I blew a damn fuze! They were fixin' to get an ass whuppin'! This was a personal thing to me … I mean, it was almost like they were throwing a rock at my own Daddy, and I'd take up for Pop quicker than I would for myself 'cause he's an old man!

I threw the phone down, and I started running toward the car. The guys quickly piled into the car and started fishtailing through the parking lot, trying to avoid the pumps and the other cars.

As I was chasing the car around in my suit and tie, Pop picks up the pay phone and started giving Junior a blow-by-blow account of the event. About that time, James Brown came to the window in his office trying to look over the interstate to see what was going on. I'm mad as hell, and the car exits the gas station, it turns right onto Washington Road. These guys were acting so cute, and were shooting birds at me and laughing.

But they didn't laugh for long … as they turned right onto the entrance ramp and got stuck in traffic, I started running up the entrance ramp, too, and I was on the verge of catching up to them. Pop had followed the action and had twisted around with the phone in his hand, giving Brown a detailed description of things … I guess the best he could with his stutter …

I was slowly gaining on the car as it crept along in traffic. Then, I was barely able to grab the back door handle and pull myself toward the moving car. With a big lunge, I snatched the door open and started to reach for one of the guys, but he scrunched himself up at the far side of the seat, but I got a hold of his sleeve and tried to pull his ass out of the car. About that time, traffic cleared and the car started gaining speed. I couldn't keep up and as they pulled away, they continued to shoot birds at me and laugh.

So I'm standing on the entrance ramp, sucking air trying to get my breath when I notice a brickbat laying on the grass. I quickly pick up this half brick and cut loose with it—send it hurling through the air, and it goes and shatters the back window of this ol' car they're in! And James Brown could see all this from his office window across the expressway on I-20.

When Pop and I get back over at the office, Brown gets the biggest kick out of it. He started retelling me Pop's blow-by-blow account. And Pop was funny, too, adding, "Miss-miss-miss-Missa Daviss gonna whup-whup-whup some ass … whup the white boy!"

James Brown told that story to so many people over the years. "You know how hot-headed Missa Daviss is … he was gonna jump these ol' boys," and he said, "You were just like a damn dog chasing a car … Missa Daviss, what would you have done if you had gotten the car to stop?"

And I thought about it and said, kinda embarrassed, "Well, I guess I would have gotten my ass whupped, Mr. Brown."

But Pop added, "No, no, Missa Daviss … his-his-his neck had got red," you know, like once I get mad, there was no stoppin' me.

Mr. Brown knew what Pop was getting at, but took it as an opportunity to give me a little jab and said, "Yeah, he's a redneck, too."

And I snapped back at him proudly, "You got that right, bro."

* * *

In later years, Pop had a stroke and ended up in the nursing home. I was totally unaware of what had happened … I hadn't seen him in several days, and when I asked where Pop was at, Brown told me. He said, "Well, we had to put him in a nursing home three or four days ago … he had already been to the hospital … they did all they could do … "

I said, "I didn't know that! I would have visited him if somebody had told me!"

Then James Brown said, "Why don't we ride over there now to see him?" So we drove over to the nursing home. It was late afternoon/early evening and during the drive, Brown was kinda upset, and he was telling me, "Pop is just like … in a zone, ya know … he just has this blank stare … just laying up in bed with his glasses on … not responding to anything."

When I walked into the room, it was so sad to see ol' Pop. He looked so strange, then I realized what it was … he didn't have his hat on … he looked different without that old felt hat. I guess it was a fedora, but it looked like a gangster hat to me … it had a dark gray or black band on it that was always stained by a permanent ring of sweat.

The only time I had seen his bare head was when he rolled the lawnmower off into the lake … and the time when he got knocked off into the swimming pool, and I had to jump in and rescue him. That was it. The day he had the rock thrown at him didn't knock the hat off … it just knocked off his glasses and tipped the brim of the hat, knocking it off center. So I spent a long time just looking at Pop. I remember when he talked to you, he always scrunched his face up … he was a little skinny guy. Had a little pug nose.

And even though he looked so frail in the nursing home bed, it was hard to imagine Pop in a time before his son became rich and famous. In earlier days, Pop was just what we'd call an "ol' fillin' station nigger" … you know, worked there to pump gas and change tires and stuff. He had a hard life, and he did his best to raise James and teach him about the world … and looking so weak it was difficult to think that Pop used to beat the hell out of women, just like James Brown did.

Pop was a grumpy old man, but he liked me. You could see that little twinkle in his eyes … and I knew that Pop never had a white boy genuinely looking out for his interests … someone who would pet him a little bit and give him attention.

As Pop was laying up in the hospital bed, Pop was just staring into space. James Brown and I moved closer to the side of the bed, and he said, "Pop? Pop? You know who this is?"

Pop rolls his eyes around, slowly raised his head, pointed to me and said, "Miss-miss-miss-Missa Daviss … "

I held his hand and said, "Pop, what are you doing up here?" But he didn't say anything after that. He just lay there and smiled a couple of times at me, and I tried to encourage him. "Pop, you're gonna have to get yourself well, Buddy."

Then I looked over and saw that James Brown was standing there with tears running down his cheek. Pop had not uttered a word to anyone since the stroke … no one except me.

After Pop's death, James Brown proudly told everybody that, "Yeah, Fred Daviss was Pop's buddy, and I'll always love him for looking out for my dad."

* * *

James Brown's life was always in a state of flux … personally and professionally. And when he'd plunge off into something, it was always my job to rescue him. There was a time when Brown was between record deals. After he left Starday King in 1971, he went with Polydor, and after that, we'd make one-record deals with other labels—Mr. Brown would usually drive them all crazy, and we'd go on to the next company.

We even talked with Richard Branson of Virgin Records. Through Cyril Van Vanhemmille, we set up a meeting at the Inn on the Park, a real exclusive hotel there at Hyde Park in London. Richard came into the hotel, and he wore a wrinkled long sleeve shirt with his cuffs rolled up … real shaggy-looking hair, but real likeable … a big smile and a mouthful of teeth. He looked like a guy who had just come in off the street … with tennis shoes and had jeans with the knees worn out on 'em.

James Brown wanted him to hear a demo of a tune he had just recorded, so he put this cassette player on the coffee table and said, "I want you to hear this." As Brown pushed "Play", Richard lay down on the floor on his stomach like a child, wallowing on the carpet while he listened to the music. Then, he'd roll over on his back and stare at the ceiling, listening very intently.

Brown said, "Isn't this great? Listen to this," and then he'd play another cut. Branson looked back at him like, *That's great, Mr. Brown,* but I could see in his eyes that this was not a hit record he was looking for. James Brown thought that any tune that came outta his mouth was a hit record, but unfortunately, we never made a deal with Virgin

Records. Maybe it's all for the best … I'd hate to have such a nice guy like Richard Branson mad at me.

I can't say the same thing for Chris Blackwell at Island Records. I'm sure he still hates me. We made a deal with his record company, and Blackwell sent his son to Augusta to wrap up the deal. He was probably in his late 30s, and I picked him up at the Augusta airport. Brown and I had already discussed the terms of the deal so now it was just a formality to sign the contract. After we settled in James Brown's office, we sent out for coffee and sandwiches. Then Brown said he had to go somewhere for an hour … then he'd call me back and give me a list of addendums for the contract.

Then, I'd have to renegotiate another part of the contract. The Blackwell kid was trying to be cordial and tactful and civil, but Brown would return and negotiations began again. James Brown was the good cop, so I had to be the bad cop. I was really hardheaded about Brown's demands, so every 30 minutes to an hour, the kid had to call his Daddy in New York for approval. As he was on the phone, Al Garner and I were snickering in the corner about what a little pantywaist he was, just because he couldn't close a simple $2 to $3 million dollar contract. We could hear his Daddy's voice across the room … he was raising hell, but his son was standing there smiling like nothing was going on, but you could hear his Daddy screaming on the phone, *The son-of-a-bitch wants what?*

This went on for hours, and after we had dinner, it got past 1 AM, and we got down to the point where Brown wanted to discuss royalties. Brown finally got things wrapped up about 3 AM and said he'd go to bed and get some sleep. As he left, he mentioned to me for Island Records to throw in a two-year lease for two cars—two Cadillacs—because we were always throwing something in the deal.

We never bought any cars … we'd always throw them into a record deal. We're southern boys, and we like cars … like Elvis. People out of New York never even owned cars … people like Blackwell took taxis. So as Brown shook hands with Blackwell and left for the night I mentioned, "By the way, Mr. Brown wants to add one other thing to the contract." But Blackwell was so wore out and whupped … his Daddy had cussed him out … and the boy looked like he had been through the damn mill. He was craving sleep, and he looked at me with this bug-eyed, blank stare.

I continued, "Mr. Brown always likes a little icing on the cake, so we've got to please his ego. We just need two automobiles … "

Blackwell exploded, "What??? Hell, we've already given him the store!"

But after I mentioned that we didn't want to buy the cars, we just wanted a two-year lease, the kid warmed up a little bit.

I added, "You don't have to call your Daddy again, do you? This ain't much—you're not worried about something like a car lease in the middle of a multi-million dollar deal, are you? Do you really want to blow the deal on some little bullshit deal like this? It's nothing but a damn lease … after all, it's just to satisfy James Brown."

Blackwell called his Daddy again, but I convinced him it was no big deal. The next step was to fly to New York and meet with the Island Records attorney to sign the contract. We met at one of their corporate suites at the Four Seasons Hotel on Park Avenue. Very expensive. Flew us in there. Paid our expenses. Their attorney, a typical Madison Avenue Jewish attorney, had his secretary there to get all this down in writing. But he had the flu and a 101 degree fever, so he was eager to get out of there … which was making it easier—especially when it came down to the car lease. The lawyer didn't know anything about cars, so when I added that Brown and I wanted the Cadillac "Elegante Seville," the most expensive, limited edition model, it was no problem. Plus, it was two o'clock in the morning, and the lawyer really wanted to resolve the contract.

I spoke with Mr. Brown on the phone, and he told me that he could have his car delivered, but said to me, "Missa Daviss, before you leave New York, I want you to go down there and get your Cadillac and drive it home … you don't know about how slick these people are up there."

The next day, I went to Potamkin Cadillac in downtown Manhattan to get my car, and as I entered the showroom, I saw it glistening on a revolving stand … a beautiful silver and black Elegante with wire wheels and all the latest technology. It looked like a Mafia car … the baddest car I had ever seen. All Mr. Brown wanted was a black Seville.

But it wasn't that easy to lease a car and drive it out. I started the process about 10 o'clock that morning, and before it was over, it was about 9:30 PM before they would release the car to me and get it completely insured. Then they put an actual hard tag on it, not a paper tag, and it was orange with blue lettering, but it had no expiration date on it … just said "New York." Once I got the keys, I picked up my briefcase with several hundred dollars of up front cash and began haulin' ass through New Jersey … went through Washington before running outta steam in North Carolina. I had to sleep. When I got back to Georgia the next afternoon, I got a shower, changed clothes and jumped on a flight from Augusta to Chicago. I was worn out and hadn't been to bed in three days. I went straight to Brown's hotel suite.

He was sitting there eating his supper. I came in smiling, thinking I had really done something, but Brown was in one of his shitty moods. He would always get that way after signing a contract, no matter how big it was … he always thought I could have screwed them some more.

Al Sharpton was there in the suite while Brown was sitting there in his bathrobe … he was slopping food in his mouth and getting ready to do a concert at the Parkwest Theater. As I dumped a coupla hundred grand on the coffee table, I stood there, dead tired, but smiling. Mr. Brown leaned back and said, "Uh huh." Then he turned around at me, and I could tell he was in a shitty mood … never thought he was mad at me. I had really screwed Island Records … plus I got him a new Cadillac and presented him with several hundred thousand dollars in cash. Now that it was time for me to get paid, Brown started to play his little games. He said, "Missa Daviss, are you on vacation?"

I knew something was up. I said "No." Then he asked me if I was working tonight. I said, "I work 24 hours a day."

"Missa Daviss, where is your tie?" Then I remembered that I had forgotten to wear my tie with my suit. I explained that I was in a rush, but he didn't want to hear my excuses. "You've got to look like a businessman … act like a businessman."

Then Mr. Brown instructed me to give Al Sharpton $5,000 and make him sign a receipt, but he didn't want to give me my cut of the cash. He was playing me because he knew I was tired—he knew all the little tricks. He was a master of intimidation ... one of his tricks was to open the blinds in his office so that the sunlight blinded you and wouldn't allow you to see his eyes. He knew all the little tricks to keep your britches down, and he had a way of cutting you off in order to maneuver you. It was like pulling teeth to get my share of the Island Record money.

About 10 days later, Island Records sent him to the recording studio in the Caribbean where they had a compound with villas and a recording studio. I didn't go with him, because I had other business and was scheduled to join him later. In the meantime, Mr. Brown made a lot of unreasonable demands ... he took his maid, took Pudjy, and had to fly in his own food because he believed that Island Records was poisoning his food.

I learned how James Brown was eat up with paranoia when he confided in me, "Missa Daviss, you don't know these people—they're notorious gangsters. They've got a conspiracy goin' on with the government, they're intertwined with AT&T and all these spies." About two days into this recording session, Island Records started calling me saying that Brown was so obnoxious, and that they couldn't work with him. I asked Mr. Brown what the problem was. He said, "Missa Daviss, these people are trying to make a Bob Marley outta me. I ain't doin' no damn reggae music."

Eventually, the album was finished, but by then, he had pushed them over the edge until they said, "Just keep the money! Keep your album! We don't want to see you anymore. We can't deal with some obnoxious son-of-a-bitch like this!" The multi-million dollar album deal was abandoned, but what was ironic was ... they wanted the two cars back! In other words, they didn't want us driving those Cadillacs while they continued making lease payments every month ... and trust me, the lease payments were outrageous! They demanded the return of the cars, but I kept arguing with them. "I got my paperwork! You can have your cars back in two years!"

Brown and I continued to drive the cars for about three months until one afternoon when James Brown came into the office about 4 o'clock in the afternoon and parked next to me. He was in the office for about an hour, and as he was headed out, he comes running back in the office saying that both the cars were gone. But Island Records had simply taken the cars to a repo lot in Columbia, South Carolina. When they told me where my car was, they allowed me to remove my personal stuff outta the trunk and glove compartment. I talked to a friend in the sheriff's department, and he said that since I had a contract, it would be okay for me to remove my car.

I took that as a go-ahead, so I got some bolt cutters and went over to Columbia on Sunday morning during church hours. Actually, I had the money to buy 10 of these Elegantes, but it was the principle of the thing. It was not in my nature to steal cars, but I cut the chain and drove the Cadillac back to Augusta.

As I went to work the next morning, my secretary, a little cutie pie with short hair and big bright eyes, was all in a tizzy. She said, "Mister Daviss, these people from Island Record Company, they're so mad! They've already called six times, and they're hollering and screaming that they want to speak with Mr. Daviss. And I told them you weren't here yet. And they told me that they didn't give a damn whether you were here or not, that they wanted to speak to you. They're gonna call back in a minute. What shall I tell 'em?"

I said, "When they call back, Cathy, tell 'em simply 'Fuck You'."

And she put her hand up to her mouth in shock, and said, "Oh, I don't know if I could say that … "

I said, "No, you *tell them exactly* what I said!"

When the telephone rang, she was all in a tizzy, nervously screwing around in her swivel chair. After she answers, she said, "Yes, let me see if he's in." And as she pushed the button down and put the call on hold, she's all panicky and said, "Mr. Daviss, it's them! … and he's hollering and screaming. What do I tell 'em?"

I said, "I told you. Pick up the phone, and say 'Fuck You!,'" but she just started stuttering. And I said, "Look, it's real simple," and I wrote it on a little pink pad. I repeated it as I scribbled, "Say, 'Fuck You!' … Mister Daviss says, 'Fuck You!'" And I got up in her face and said, "Do it! You tell 'em that, or I'm gonna run your ass off!" Then I picked up the phone and handed it to her while I held my finger over the hold button. I said, "Read it … just like I said!"

So she gets on the phone, and she begins to speak, obviously reading the words on the pad, "Uh, uh, Mr. Daviss says … uh … 'Fuck You!'" And in a cheerful secretarial voice ends with, "Bye!" as she abruptly hangs up the phone. The whole office was just standing around laughing.

Of course, they called back. This time, I got the phone, and told them that I got my car and, "If you ever even think about getting within 50 feet of my car, I got some shit for you that you don't know about. Don't even let me catch your ass in Augusta, Georgia! You better forget about this car! You done played hell with me! Now I know what y'all are capable of, and you're in the wrong part of the country coming after me. Forget about the car and take your medicine!" Boy, were they irate!

I immediately took my car to the Cadillac place and had my locks changed, and nothing more ever came about it. I reckon they figured, *These people are crazy!* But I was young and hardheaded and could not accept somebody in that slick world of record executives and lawyers getting the better of me! I couldn't accept defeat. And I'm surprised to let something like a car eat at me so much … I could have bought all the cars I wanted.

I kept the car for years, and found out that a New York tag with no expiration is a handy thing. Eventually I got a Georgia tag and title for it, and I kept it more or less as an ego thing. And years later, when I didn't drive it, it was such a good conversation piece.

I bet Chris Blackwell shudders when he hears James Brown's name. But I hope he can laugh about it now, and I hope that he realizes that I'm not a bad guy. I'm misunderstood … like Richard Nixon told me at the White House. Chris Blackwell has to understand that James Brown was the catalyst that precipitated this problem … the problem for Island Records and for me. That was just the way he was … that was his mode of operation … piss everybody off … run off with the money … and then drive everybody to the point of giving up.

The difference is … I never gave up on Mr. Brown, personally or professionally. I fought for what I thought was right.

* * *

During the first year I worked for James Brown, every time I went to New York City, I got ripped off by taxi drivers. I'd get so aggravated, and I knew as soon as the driver heard me open my mouth that he was fixin' to take me for a ride—*dumb ol' southern cracker!* It wasn't the money so much; it just pissed me off to know that that guy is taking advantage of me not knowing where the hell I'm at and not knowing how to get there. They would ask you a question like, "You wanna go over the Triborough or you want to go such and such?" And I wouldn't know what to tell them. Finally, after riding with somebody who knew their way around the city, I started finding my way around, and I knew where I was at.

One time I had to meet James Brown in Newark, New Jersey. It was my usual Saturday night meeting. So I come out of the terminal with my bag in one hand and my briefcase in the other hand, and I get in the cab, and the guy wants to know where I'm going. He puts his meter on, and he starts easing down the curb in front of the Newark terminal. I told him I was going to the James Brown concert at Symphony Hall, and I asked him if he knew where it was. He said that he thought he did. And I said, "Wait a minute. You don't know where you're going? You let me outta the cab." And he starts arguing with me, and I knew then that it was going to be a hassle. I said, "Stop!" And so he stops the cab 100 feet from where he started from. I opened the door, and I slammed the door getting out.

Then I go back to the next cab. And I'm pissed off! There was a policeman standing against the wall with his foot propped on the wall, fiddling with his ticket book. I mumbled to him something to the effect, "What is it with these guys? I'm from the south, and they want to rip me off every time I get in a cab. I'm trying to go to the James Brown concert at Symphony Hall. What do you do with guys like this?"

And the cop looked at me and laughed. He said, "You just knock the hell out of them." An off the wall comment—just a matter of speech—I didn't think too much about it. So I walked down to the next cab and the cab driver sounded like he was from the islands. But he's leaning against the cab and ignored me. No eye contact.

I said, "Hey, do you know the way to Symphony Hall?"

And without any eye contact, he's got his nose up in the air, and he said, "Hey mon, you just get outta that hack?"

"Yeah, I just got outta the hack," I said as I opened the back door of his cab. And still no eye contact.

"I ain't taking you nowhere, mon."

"You whaaaatttttt?" And I'm getting pissed off! I'm in a hurry, and I'm looking at my watch, and I'm running late, and Brown's gonna be on my ass if I show up late. Then I glanced down at the door where they got the sign about disorderly passengers, and I make a remark to him. I said, "Hey, you're gonna haul me any damn place I want to go unless I get disorderly … that's what the sign says here on the door. And I'm fixin' to get damn disorderly!"

"I'm not going to take you nowhere, mon." And he spits out on the sidewalk. Like, *Fuck you!*

I just lost my temper. My hair stood up on the back of my neck, and I just lost it! He's leaning back on the hood of his taxi with his chin up in the air, so I swung my briefcase right across his head hitting him directly on the bridge of his nose! Blood started spurting out everywhere! I hit him so hard, it knocked his ass back on to the hood of the cab … and it busted the hinge on my briefcase and my papers started blowing all over the place. If that wasn't bad enough, my damn .38 revolver pops out of my briefcase and is bouncing across the sidewalk. This is bad! The Sullivan Laws in New York restricted carrying guns. Sure, you could get on a plane with one … nobody ever checked you, but carrying a gun in New York was a damn felony! And the cop was standing right there looking at me!

But that didn't stop me, I was reared back fixin' to bust this guy's ass as he was coming up off the hood, but before I could take a swing, this cop comes out of nowhere and grabs this guy from behind with a choke hold. He's got him on his tiptoes and just kneeing him in his ass as he walks him all the way around to the driver's side and kicks his ass into the cab.

Wow. That cop saved me a lot of trouble, and now he's writing down the cabbie's name and number, and he's getting his medallion number. I'm squatting down on the sidewalk, collecting up my papers and trying to discreetly pick up my gun up as the cop finishes up with the driver. Blood was still spurting out his nose, and I could see the bone in his nose where I hit him. He's trying to crank his cab with one hand while trying to stop the blood flow with the other.

The cop slams the door and tells him to get his ass out of there, "And if I see you back over here, I'll have your medallion pulled, and I will put your ass in jail! And the guy tore on off outta there. All these other cab drivers were lined up behind him, and they were all looking. Got everybody's attention. And then the cop is walking up to me, and I know he sees my gun on the sidewalk. He's in a huff, and he's got his book turned backwards, and he said, "What is your name?"

"Fred Daviss."

"Where are you from?"

And I think earlier I said that I worked for James Brown, and I was just trying to get to the concert hall. And I'm nervous because I thought I was going to jail because he asked me all these questions. And I asked him, "What are you going to arrest me for?" 'Cause I'm very aware of the Sullivan Laws. The lawyers had told me several times that "Freddy, don't get your ass caught up here with a gun in New York or New Jersey." So I'm standing there trying to hold my briefcase together.

"Oh Mr. Daviss, I'm just getting your name and address. We don't like this kinda shit in our city. I see what the guy's doing, and don't worry, I'll get you to the concert hall on time—I'm not arresting you, I want to see that the city of Newark sends you a letter of apology for what happened." And then he made a remark out of the side of his mouth … "You be careful with that gun. I'm glad you didn't shoot the guy."

The policeman walked me to the next cab, and the guy has got the door open like a chauffeur holding his hand out, *right this way.*

The policeman asked the cabbie, "Do you know your way to Symphony Hall?"

"Yessuh, yessuh!"

"And do you think you can get this man here with no more problems?"

"Yessuh, yessuh. I'll take him straight there, boss."

"You make sure you do 'cause I got your damn cab number." Then the cop turned to me and told me to have a good day.

I told this story to Brown and he shook his head and said, "Missa Daviss, Missa Daviss … "

After that, there was a lot of talk about me among Brown's entourage. I got labeled as *the crazy man who will jump on anybody and not think about it until the smoke clears.* In other words, I was so naïve that I could get into stuff and not even know that I was in it!

That day in Newark, the good Lord must have been watching over me … I always seem to stumble into good luck. But it bothers me now … I can't remember if Newark ever sent me the letter or not.

* * *

Newark, New Jersey may have loved me, but I don't know if Knoxville, Tennessee ever will . In the course of working for James Brown, I ended up spending a lot of time in Knoxville … and my first introduction to the town wasn't too favorable. While I was still working at the bank, Brown was doing a concert in Knoxville.

After the show, some redneck people were trying to clear the building by midnight. Brown was still in the dressing room, and some of his band was outside in the alley getting stuff on the bus, and they had fans outside waiting for autographs. They also had the limos lined up ready to leave when a guy knocked on the door a couple of times and said they had to clear the building. Brown told him, "Yessir, I'll be right there. We'll get out."

That's when one of the guys working at the theater was a bit impatient and called the police. He was overheard saying, "I want you to come over here and get these niggers out." Immediately, the Knoxville police came in like gangbusters, and roughed up James Brown ... but Freddy Holmes, one of his road managers, got the hell beat outta him pretty bad—his face was busted all up. Freddy told me later, "That damn hillbilly hit me upside the head about six times with one of those batons!"

Freddy was kind of a funny guy ... kind of a sad sack, too. I remember one time when he looked at me real hard and said, "Missa Daviss ... Missa Brown done fired me *eleven times* this week!" Freddy talked like he had marbles in his mouth ... he had teeth problems ... but he was so serious about getting fired. *Eleven times! ... that's about normal for one week, Freddy!*

They arrested Brown for some trumped up charges ... disturbing the peace and inciting a riot, and all these charges they had, but after he bonded out, he went straight over and got on the air at his radio station, WJBE. He started raising hell! I don't think the local people took kindly to James Brown—they even tried to shut his radio station down. Remember, this was back in the '60s, and there was a lot of unrest in the country before Martin Luther King got shot ... and a lot of stuff was going on ... particularly in southern towns like Knoxville.

One of the first things Brown did was to call me at home in the middle of the night. He told me about the brawl and told me to meet him at the airport ... and bring the lawyer he had recently met. As I hung up the phone, I couldn't believe it ... I mean, *This happened to James Brown?* I was really in shock that the police jumped on him. James Brown was an icon! I could understand how his bodyguards might have gotten involved in something like this, but the police were really after James Brown.

The Learjet arrived at Hartsfield in the wee morning hours ... about 4:30 or 5:00. After it taxied up, we gathered on the tarmac at Hangar One-Brown was sitting on the steps of his plane ... the lapel of his jacket was torn off … he came just the way he was. As we sat there with the attorney, Joel Katz, we discussed a course of legal action, but in the end, we never pursued a lawsuit. Brown let it slide … he didn't want to make a big issue of it. Eventually, James Brown met with the mayor and some of the city officials, and they calmed it down. Everybody got over it. And even though it may have been the end of Brown's Tennessee brawl … mine was comin' up!

* * *

Al Garner and I, the other token white boy I worked with, were sitting in a Knoxville bar killing time about 5:30 or 6:00 in the evening … waiting to pick up somebody at the airport. I believe the name of this place was the Senator's Club … it was just a nightclub on the Alcoa Highway, up on a hill with an old gravel parking lot. And we were sitting in the bar having a cocktail—the place was kinda empty except for a back room poolroom. They had this big plate glass wall separating the bar from the pool tables, and through the glass I could see about 10 to 12 guys shooting pool and drinking their Budweiser. These were typical construction boys … raggedy-ass looking ol' boys who had their trucks parked out front.

Al and I had our banker suits on, and we're just sitting there casually talking and having a drink. Every once in a while, I could see the guys looking our way and talking about us. I was conscious of them staring at us and hanging on their pool sticks. I turned around on my swivel stool, and I saw the bartender behind the bar, wiping the glasses with his old snotty-ass rag. He was cutting his eyes around, trying to figure out the situation.

While I'm focused on the bartender, the next thing I knew, I turned around and these guys had gathered up around us … kinda sidled up to us. There were probably a dozen of 'em … some of them were jamming Skoal in their cheeks up next to their ol' rotten teeth … some of them were holding a beer mug in one hand and a pool cue in the other, like a weapon.

One ol' guy stepped outta the crowd … and he's got such a big ol' wad of Skoal in his mouth he almost choked as he stuttered, "I … I … I … don't like you."

Several of the guys raised their cue sticks almost like, *Batter up!* That didn't scare me as much as the bartender … when he brought out his own little bongo bat from under the bar! He was gonna have his fun, too, like, *Hey look at them sissy boys. We're fixin' to kick their ass.*

It was obvious—the bartender was in cahoots with the boys, and at that point, I knew that nobody was gonna call the police to rescue us. There was nobody else in the bar except us—Al and I were in this by ourselves. I looked at Al, and he looks at me like, *Yup… we're fixin' to get an ass whuppin'.*

So I look back at the guys, and I says, "Hey buddy, I'm sorry you don't like us, we were just getting ready to leave."

And he laughs, "Ha, ha, ha, ha. Naw, naw … y'all are not going anywhere. I'm fixin' to whup your ass!"

"Ah naw, man. You don't wanna whup my ass. Won't ya let me buy y'all a drink?"

"Naw, naw. I'm gonna whup your ass." And all his buddies are laughing, and they're all spiting their Skoal on the wooden floor. Al hasn't said a word yet … he's kinda cool … he knows I'm fixin' to swing on somebody 'cause my theory is, *If you're gonna get your ass whupped, take somebody down at the front end of the fight.*

I'm trying to be cool, too … I've got my drink in my left hand, and I took a drag offa my cigarette. I locked eyes with this guy trying to size up the situation … and I noticed that every time the guy said he was "gonna whup my ass," he'd throw his head back and laugh with this great big open mouth full of ol' rotten teeth.

For some reason, it crossed my mind that the next time he laid his head back, I'd just run my thumb up in his jaw, just like you'd pick a bass up outta the lake. I waited and waited, anticipating him saying he was "gonna whup my ass" … then as he rared back and started to laugh, I instantly jumped up from my stool and jabbed my thumb up between the skin of his jaw and the outside of his teeth … then I grabbed a chunk of his jaw in my fist, and I squeezed and twisted it as hard as I could! The ol' boy instantly fell to his knees, and he was about to strangle on his Skoal as I twisted all of his face I could grab. I'm a wild man!

I decided to push things to the edge. It was all or nothing now, so I got this real wild look in my eyes—like a rabid dog—and I started slobbering. You know, when you look crazy, people will pay more attention to you … it's basic psychology. So, I was slobbering and looking crazy, and I got this guy's jaw in my hand, and I said, "You better back off! Back off! Back off now! You better back your buddies off or I will rip your fucking face clean off your skull!"

So the guy's on his knees and motioned for his buddies to back off. I reached into my pocket and threw my car keys to Al and said, "Get the car open!"

As Al ran outside to the parking lot, I was all alone and looking scarier than ever! I kept saying, "I'll rip your damn face off!" All the other guys kept backing up, forming a small circle around me, but I started walking the guy to the door on his knees. I got through the front door and out on the porch of the bar … and he's on his knees, hobbling like a duck. I kept him moving even as I directed him out on the gravel parking lot toward my white '72 Mark IV Lincoln. Al opened the car door, and I fished around down between the seats where I found my .38 Smith & Wesson revolver. By this time, all the guys were hanging onto the front porch … the bartender still had his billy club in his hand.

Now that I have the gun, I turned my attention to the boys … I started to slobber even more while threatening to blow everybody's ass away. And I got this wild damn look in my eyes, and I look at this guy on his knees and say, "You punk. You're gonna whup my ass, huh?"

And the boy puts his hands up in a prayer position and said, "Please mister, please don't shoot me."

I could see him quivering, and I said, "It's too late! I'm fixin' to blow your shit away!"

"Please mister, please don't shoot me. I've got a wife and two kids at home."

"You bad motherfucker! You didn't think about this a while ago. And now you're nothing but a little pussycat." For some reason, I cocked the gun and pressed it up in his eye socket.

He closes his eyes and scrunches his face up as tight as he could. He's still got his hands in a prayer up under his chin, and he says, "Please, please don't shoot me." And I looked down, and all of a sudden he's pissing in his pants.

I thought about pulling the trigger, but I didn't. I shoved him back away from me on to the gravel, and I started to get in the car. Then I was waving the gun all around in the direction of the bar, and I yelled out as slobber ran down my chin, "Y'all better get the fuck inside! Y'all done scared me—and when I get scared, I'm fixin' to kill somebody! Y'all done scared my ass! I'm scared! Y'all understand that? When you scare me, I will shoot you!"

The guys were hanging on the porch … nobody was gonna step away from the porch and risk getting shot. And they were looking at me like, *Damn, this guy has lost it. He's crazy.*

Al and I got in the Lincoln, and I did a quick lap around the parking lot, holding the pistol out of the open window and waving it wildly around in all directions, and screaming, "Y'all better back up … you done scared me now." And I was scared … I thought they were gonna call the cops and twist the story around. After all, this was Knoxville.

Later, Al and I laughed about the story many times, and Al mentioned, "Damn Fred, I thought you were going to shoot that guy."

I said, "When I cocked that hammer, I almost did."

I had such a damn rush, and I really wanted to blow that son-of-a-bitch's head off. Who did he think he was—come out there and think he's gonna kick my ass around.

* * *

Why do I always get caught up in some fight? I don't go lookin' for fights, but when it comes down to it—I'm the guy who has to make things right.

James Brown had a strong sense of right and wrong … he didn't always follow his own code of behavior, but he did know the rule … that's because he made the rules. One rule included fines for infractions of his rules, and he was notorious for issuing fines for various reasons … a button off your coat, not shining your shoes, or missing a note. Then, Brown would fine you $100 for this—$200 for that.

During one gig, I was instructed to take some money out of James Pearson's pay. Nobody called him by his name—we all called him "Baby James" and Mr. Brown often called him, "Babe."

Baby James was more or less a go-fer, bodyguard type guy who would guard the stage door and run little errands for Mr. Brown. Baby James made a perfect bodyguard … he was a big, tall, black guy who could threaten you with just a look … he had this psychotic look in his eyes and a big gap between his teeth when he smiled. And his hands were so big that he could wrap them around a basketball and pick it up with one hand … and he was so scary-looking you wouldn't want to meet him in a dark alley … *you wouldn't want to meet him in a lighted alley either!*

Also, Baby James didn't like white people and didn't make any bones about it. Brown used to kid him about it, but he'd grin and tell Mr. Brown in his stuttering way, "I—I—I—I—like Missa Daviss." I'm really glad he liked me, and I tried to convince him to like other white people, but he never did … he particularly didn't like Mr. Garner. He said Mr. Garner was "too slick."

After the show, Baby James walked into Mr. Brown's dressing room. It was actually in a locker room of a stadium and there were multiple rooms connecting the dressing room and the showers. It was a large space, and Brown had his dressing table and racks for his clothes and shoes and baggage set up along with a variety of his favorite snacks and drinks.

I was aware that Baby James was there discussing his fines, not in a heated argument, just a normal conversation. Miss Sanders, the wardrobe mistress, had stepped out and gone down the hall, and Al Garner and I had to run outside for a few minutes to take care of some business … so Brown was alone in the dressing room with Baby James. When we returned, three or four minutes later (five minutes at the most) I didn't see James Brown at his dressing table ... in fact the dressing room was empty.

I thought James Brown had just stepped around the corner of an alcove to hide himself for 30 seconds to slip his pants on. I called out for Mr. Brown, and I could vaguely hear something ... a sound in the distance ... and it sounded like somebody in trouble. Then I thought ... "Where's Mr. Brown?" And I started peeking around the corner looking for him and got kinda panicky ... and the further I went back into the dressing room toward the showers, the sound got louder and louder ... then we realized what was happening!

As I stepped into the showers, Baby James had Mr. Brown slammed up against the wall like a rag doll ... and his little feet were dangling about knee high off of the wall. Baby James had his enormous hands wrapped around his throat and was shaking him violently and threatening him about his money. But James Brown could barely get a sound out ... just a weak, "Hep! Hep! Hep!"

Man, it scared the hell outta me! And I don't remember how I did it, but I ran and jumped up on one of the benches, and I took a big leap and landed on Baby James' shoulders. Al ran out the room to get security, and like a 140-pound fool, I started pounding Baby James on his head trying to get him to turn James Brown loose.

As hard as I was hitting him, all I was doing was busting my knuckles on his ol' hard head, and he was swatting at his head—like I was a fly bothering him or something. I'm beating the hell out of the top of his head with both knuckles and had my legs locked around his throat. Within 30 seconds, six security people, a gang of policemen and some bodyguards and roadies were able to pull James Brown from his grasp ... but I'm still up on top of his shoulders, just beating the hell out of him!

Finally, they got me down, and I've got blood all over my suit. But Brown is staggering around holding his throat, sucking air trying to get his breathe—gasping. Brown called everybody off Baby James, and he came to his senses ... meantime, I'm standing there looking at my knuckles thinking, *Damn, I have destroyed my knuckles. All the skin was gone.*

Everybody knew that Babe loved James Brown, and he wouldn't question anything that Brown asked of him … he'd put his head through a brick wall, if that's what Mr. Brown told him to do. But on that night, Mr. Brown pushed Babe too far, and he became blind with rage.

Later on, Brown started braggin' about me. He said, "Yeah, Missa Daviss jumped on this big nigger … Missa Daviss was out to save my life, and he got enough pressure off my neck … who knows, this crazy nigger might have killed me before security got there!"

Brown was real appreciative to me. He realized that I would even take on Baby James without thinking about my personal safety—something that *really was crazy!*

I'm just so glad that Baby James liked me … I shudder to think if he didn't.

* * *

James Brown is known for two things: his music and his tax problems. I didn't have much influence on the music—but I was intimately involved in his financial affairs, and I spent a lot of my time and effort fighting with tax people. Everybody was after James Brown! … regional IRS directors, social security people and state revenue agents … so I ended up knowing a bunch of agents throughout the United States … we even had tax problems in England!

I'd spend a certain amount of time with each agent before being passed on to another one … and they would either get transferred … retire early … wear out … or die. There was one man in the Baltimore area named Azarella … a real laid back guy who was proud of his collection of pipes—he had a big ol' curved one that he seemed to favor. We seemed to have a good relationship because he met me in the early days, when I was just getting into Mr. Brown's books … I guess he took pity on me and didn't give me a lot of pressure by putting deadlines and ultimatums on me. But the longer I knew Azarella, the deeper I got into his head.

He used to go around and around because he could never get the corporate names for the three radio stations right in his mind. The first station in Knoxville, WJBE, was called "JB Broadcasting Limited." Supposedly, JBE stood for "James Brown Enterprises." The next one was WRDW in Augusta, and it was called "JB Broadcasting of Augusta Limited", and the one in Baltimore WEBB, was "JB Broadcasting of Baltimore Limited."

When we were launching the Baltimore station, I was interviewed by the local TV news. The reporter asked, "Mr. Daviss, if WJBE in Knoxville stands for James Brown Enterprises, what does WEBB stand for?"

I had never really thought about it, but there were a whole mass of black people standing around me at the time, and I knew I was being looked at him, so I grinned as big as I could, and said, "WEBB … We Enjoy Being Black." Later on that evening, in James Brown's hotel suite during the 6 o'clock news, he saw the interview and erupted with laughter, "Awawawaw!!!" as he rolled around on the floor. He was gasping when he said, "Missa Daviss, Missa Daviss, you're a genius!"

I knew all these radio call letters and corporate identities drove Azarella to the point where he would pull his hair out and soon his laid back attitude boiled over until the point where he would begin raising his voice to me. All the time, he'd have his pipe in his mouth … (I really think he was using it as a pacifier). The next thing I knew, we pushed him over the edge and he clenched down on his pipe so hard that he bit clean through the pipe stem … even broke two teeth. I really felt sorry for him, but he just lost his cool, and I think he retired a couple of years earlier than he was supposed to just to get out of this James Brown quagmire of taxes.

There were some other agents I could remember. There were two federal guys, Hinton and Connors, and they were sent down to do a criminal investigation. One was white—one was black, and I believe they wanted to cover the bases—they didn't want anyone to infer any racial bias. I think Connors was the white guy.

These mysterious guys were not Internal Revenue agents or from the Justice Department, but they carried pistols and did their best to threaten us. The white guy would always stand in front of my desk, open his coat and prop up on his big gun with one hand in a casual manner. He wanted me to be very aware of his gun sticking in my face. The gun looked too big for a little guy his size ... probably had a complex. But Hinton and Connors thought they were threatening ... *and they were* ... they had the power to arrest me, and even shoot me ... but one thing I knew, no matter what ... *they couldn't eat me!*

One day they dropped in from New York outta the blue—it was about mid morning, and I was standing there licking an ice cream cone, and I said, "I'm not gonna talk to y'all anymore ... you don't have an appointment with me." I was tired of them trying to intimidate me with the pistol, and I told them to get out of the office. After that, they made scheduled business appointments in order to threaten me.

The federal guys thought they were tough, but the local boys were just as aggravating. When I came to work for James Brown, the Georgia Revenue was trying to collect $14 thousand dollars from the Augusta radio station. It came down to the midnight hour because I had already bought some extra time. But their agent was a typical Augusta, Georgia redneck—little short guy with a paunch on him—little peon type guy—typical tax collector—and he was just chomping at the bit seeing this as his opportunity to put James Brown out of business and shut his operations down.

To James Brown, it wasn't the money—he had the money—he just wanted to push it as far as he could push it ... right up to the deadline. I knew that missing the deadline would result in the padlocking of our doors, so as I walked into the agent's office only about an hour before the deadline, he immediately thought that I was there to beg some more time—he just assumed I didn't have the money.

He said, "Mr. Daviss, I'm not interested in hearing any sob stories about you or James Brown's money ... I know you're not gonna be able to pay us ... all I want to do is close you niggers down."

I couldn't believe it! ... he actually called me a "nigger!" He said, "I'm gonna close *you niggers* down." He didn't say, "I'm gonna close *them niggers* down." He included me!

This was my first encounter with anything racial, and I called him a son-of-a-bitch right in his office. I said, "I wish I had this on tape—I would have your damn job!"

But he laughed and said, "Oh no ... I'm the one who's gonna have your damn balls before this is over with."

That's when I shoved a $14 thousand dollar cashier's check in his face, I said, "Naw, not today." And then he gritted his damn teeth so hard, I thought they were gonna crack! Then I proceeded to tell him what he could do with the check.

When I went back to our office, I told the story to James Brown, adding, "Mr. Brown, this guy told me, *'I'll close you niggers down.*'" Brown just about fell outta his chair laughing—he just about bust a gut.

He said, "Now you know what it feels like to be a nigger."

I said, "Yeah, it doesn't feel too good."

All these stories seem kinda silly and benign, but there was one agent with whom I spent more time with and who got deeper into James Brown's tax matters more than any agent. I won't mention his name, because I have too much respect for him ... (I'll just call him Mr. R.), but at the time, he was tenacious ... like a bulldog that's got a death hold of you.

On first look, he appeared to be menacing ... a big tall guy, about 300 pounds. But he also seemed oafish, more like Dumbo the Elephant ... he wore those conservative, lace-up wing tips with a drab business suit, and when he was peeping over his glasses, he looked like a pretty jolly fella. And he always had his briefcase, the expandable type—I had my Gucci briefcase.

He worked at the Strom Thurmond office building in Columbia-about 70 miles from Augusta, and was your typical civil service employee—a guy who had been brainwashed by the IRS to go out and get you. But to me, he was mostly an aggravation I couldn't ignore ... like a damn fly crawling around in your salad bowl.

However, Mr. R. was different ... he dug deeper and deeper and understood things better than most of the agents—he knew where the money was. And rather than let something peter out, he kept on, inching closer to the day when he could pin things down and confiscate our assets. It was a battle of wills … James Brown continued creating trusts to shelter his money, and Mr. R. continued wading through the paperwork chasing the money trail. It might have been a game to Mr. Brown, but I was the one who had to answer to the IRS—and they were taking up more and more of my time and effort. This son-of-a-bitch wouldn't go away … he was constantly in and out of the office, and I did my best to accommodate his investigation because I believed in the authority of the U.S. government.

I had grown up assuming that our government and our business institutions are *the good guys*—like the bank where you keep your money. But now I know that the bank's out to get every damn nickel they can from you! None of these businesses or corporations are good guys to you, and you just assume they're not gonna screw you. And you also believe that the government's not gonna screw you either! But these IRS agents were actually taught to intimidate you, to trick you, and to not play by the same rules that they expect you to play by.

I found that out the hard way. When I first started making payments to the IRS, I didn't ask for a receipt, I just made the payment. Then several quarters later, we would get charged with penalties because we weren't *filing in a timely fashion*. When I said, "I made those payments on time!"

And Mr. R. would say, "Naw you didn't." And he'd go back, and he'd show me where they had stamped the payment with a later date.

I said, "You are the U.S. government—and I can't even trust you to be honest." That's the way they were taught, and that's what they had to do to out-maneuver us. Not only did I have to deal with dishonest IRS agents, I had to put up with Mr. Brown who wouldn't allow me run his business the right way. His way of doing business was like some guy running a corner hot dog stand.

The IRS didn't treat us right, and they did everything possible to intimidate us. Mr. R. brought out a front end loader and parked it in Brown's front yard and said that he was gonna dig up the entire yard looking for buried money. He knew there was nothing there, he just wanted to harass us—and he was gonna do it too, but we got him to back down.

Another time, the IRS came into Brown's house and ransacked the place … loaded up everything they could take with them … furniture, silverware and personal possessions. They put everything up for auction, and I went there and bought it back and returned it to Mr. Brown. Brown never reimbursed me for it so legally, I guess I own all that stuff.

Everybody is brought up to be intimidated by the IRS. These agents get a big kick out of putting a gun on you, and think they can slap you around whenever they want. In later years, the IRS has changed some of that. I hope so … it just wasn't right.

But back then, Mr. R. was so ruthless, I got my gut full of it, and I realized that he was gonna bust our ass anyway … so why be intimidated by him? He was in Brown's office one day, and I said, "Let's go outside and smoke a cigarette." We went outside the office and I immediately turned on him.

"If I do everything right, you're still gonna bust my ass and make it look like we're not doing what we're supposed to do. So I'm gonna start treating you with no respect—you've backed me into a corner, and I'm not gonna be scared of you anymore. We finally had enough of this!"

I told him how lowdown he was and what a sorry son-of-a-bitch he was. "You're about as low as anybody I can think of, you unscrupulous son-of-a-bitch! Your word is no good. You're just the bottom of the shitter to me—you're just scum. I've tried to do right, and you come in here and you lie, you will pull everything in the damn book to make us look like we're worse than we are! I've had enough of your shit, and I just want to tell you, I detest you, I don't like you, and I wouldn't wipe my ass with you." I felt like I wanted to slap him.

He was in such shock to all this profanity that he was almost slobbering in the mouth. Then he started telling me that he could get me arrested for talking to an IRS agent with this kinda language. But I hadn't threatened him … I just told him what a son-of-a-bitch he was.

After that, we went back to work … until the next time he would breeze into the office and expect me to stop everything to answer his questions. Mr. R. didn't make appointments, he just came anytime he wanted to. Finally I said, "Fuck you. I ain't doing this any more. If you want to see me, make a damn appointment. I ain't got time for this bullshit."

Then it got to the point where I had to go to his office in Columbia-which was an inconvenience to say the least. One time when we got through with our business, we were coming out of the Strom Thurmond Building along with all the other federal employees getting in their cars to go home. As we crossed the parking lot, walking between the parked cars, I told him how sorry he was. I don't recall exactly what I said … I might have said something about his mama … whatever it was, it triggered something in this man, and it shocked me how fast he was for such a big man.

Suddenly he whirled around, and he slammed me so hard in the chest with the palms of both hands that it rattled my teeth—rattled me to the bone! Whoom! It nearly knocked the wind out of me, and he hit me so hard that he slammed me on the hood of the car. He had a look in his eyes of total hate, but he was also shocked, like he hadn't realized what he'd done.

My first instinct was to cold cock his ass right between his nose and his upper lip. His glasses exploded and went flying through the parking lot. I busted his nose and both of his lips … and I hit him so hard I thought I had broken my arm. And when he hit the ground between the cars, I swear, he shook the whole parking lot. He was like a damn baby elephant.

The way I was brought up is, if you have a hassle with somebody, especially with a big guy, when he hit the ground you had to start kicking his ass. You don't want him to get up and hurt you—so I kicked him and I kicked him with my nice Italian dress boots—some kind of soft kangaroo leather. But I couldn't get any room between the cars, and I broke a mirror off somebody's car trying to prop up on my hands. And he was so big I couldn't swing my legs to kick him, so I ended up standing on top of him, stomping him up and down. And I was stomping the hell out of him, and he's trying to get out from under me, and I'm just kicking and stomping and rolling on top of his belly trying to maintain my balance.

Somehow, he proceeded to pull himself up into a sitting position, and his face is profusely bleeding from his nose and his lip. My briefcase was laying open, papers blowing across the lot and as people were walking to their cars, wondering what was going on.

But he pulls himself up between my legs and the son-of-a-bitch bit me on my inner thigh! He chomped down!—I've still got the scar! He took a chunk out of my leg, and it ripped a tear in the pants leg of my suit. When I saw the blood from my inner thigh, I backed offa him, and I'm staggering around, "You son-of-a-bitch, you damn ruined my tailor made suit!"

And he gets up, and he's holding his mouth and bleeding like a pig, and he was crawling around trying to find his glasses. I'm getting stuff in my briefcase, my papers were blowing everywhere, and I'm hopping around trying to stop the blood flow from my thigh.

In all the time I knew him, I never heard him utter a single cuss word. He always played things by the book … that way, you couldn't pin anything on him. So if you really want to analyze the fine points of the law, in fact, he hit me first … I was merely defending myself. But, I probably had it coming for antagonizing him, but he didn't see it that way.

He calmly stated, "You have played hell today, Fred."

"Whatta you talkin' about?"

"You know, you're gonna be tried for this. I guarantee … you will do damn jail time for hitting an agent of the service."

"No shit! Let me tell you something. You know Baby James?" I paused a moment while he gathered a mental picture of Baby James, the scary-looking black guy he used to see hanging out in Brown's office.

"Are you threatening me?"

"You can call it what in the hell you want to, all I did was say, 'Do you know Baby James'?"

"You're threatening me!"

"Let me put it to you this way … go down there right now and get the sheriff. Bring him up here. I'll stand here in the parking lot, and wait for you … then you can put the damn handcuffs on me. Hey, you already know where I live—you know where I work—you know the vehicles I drive … you probably even know when I go to the bathroom. You know every damn thing there is to know about me, and I've dealt with this shit for how long now? You can do whatever you want to—put my ass in jail if that's what you're gonna do. But I tell you what, I don't know when it'll happen, but I wanna let you know that Baby James don't like you. He'll probably come see me in jail. And I guarandamntee you, one of these days while I'm in jail, Baby James might come up on your ass, and he will be the scariest, damn ugliest scariest-looking Brother in your worst nightmare! Baby James don't know but one thing, and that's to break your damn legs off!"

And I was slobbering then. "I've had enough of your shit, and you have threatened me, and intimated me, and you have tried to run my damn life! I've had enough of your shit, and if I have to get in the damn gutter with you, that's where we're gonna go, and yeah, I ain't gonna tell him to do it, but Baby James is gonna go after your ass 'cause he don't like you! He don't like white people to start with, and he damn sure don't like you because he's heard me talk about you, and he's just itching to whup your ass. He's spent enough time in jail that he don't give a shit. So you think about that. I'm fixin' to get in my damn car and go home, and you can go ahead and take out a warrant for my arrest. I'm going home now … and you can kiss my ass!"

I got back in my car, and I was so pissed off … I wish I had whupped his ass a little longer before he bit me. I drove back to the office, and James Brown was having one of his little bullshit sessions while he waited for me to get back. And I walked into the office, he could immediately see that my damn knuckles were busted and the spattering of blood on my shirt and my suit. I can hear him now, "Missa Daviss, Missa Daviss … what has happened to you?"

"Mr. Brown, I just kicked the shit outta Mr. R."

And Brown jumped back and there were about six of these guys sitting in the office and their eyes got real big and Brown said, "Whaaaat? You hit Mr. R.?"

"'*Hit him?*' Mr. Brown, I stomped his ass all over the parking lot. That son-of-a-bitch!"

"Missa Daviss, you need to calm down, you know, I'm a spiritual man."

"Mr. Brown, I kicked that son-of-a-bitch all over the parking lot."

Brown rolled his eyes and put his hands up. "Missa Daviss, oh lawd, Missa Daviss, what have you done? We need to call Mr. Boyce" … he was the attorney who always took care of our stuff.

"Hell, there's no need to call Mr. Boyce. I done told Mr. R. that I was gonna turn that ugly-looking Baby James on his ass, and he would break his ass worse than I did."

"You what???"

"Yup, that's the scariest-looking Brother Mr. R. has ever seen."

And Baby James lit up, and he stuttered, "I—I—I don't—don't—don't like Mr. R. You—you—you want me to break-break his legs?"

Brown said, "Hush … hush Babe … "

Baby James said, "I—I don't like him … "

Brown repeated, "Hush, hush, Baby James." But Baby James is just standing there, grinning with that that gap in his teeth and that scary ol' serious look on his face.

James Brown was in total disbelief. He said, "Missa Daviss, this is serious. We can't have you locked up." He was worried that if I was locked up I couldn't take care of his business. But that fear never came true.

This was a Thursday, but I cooled down and went home and doctored my leg and got a tetanus shot. I was wondering over the weekend if I was gonna get arrested. But nothing happened. The next week, on Tuesday or Monday, Brown and I had a meeting with Mr. R. at our offices. When Mr. R. showed up, nothing was said … we just did our business … the whole time I was staring at his glasses, taped together on the bridge.

I suppose Mr. R. must have taken my threat to heart. But I would have never, *ever,* been capable of unleashing Baby James on him—I would never have done that. It was the only thing I could think to keep from getting locked up. It was just talk … because I was not raised that away, but in some situations, you never know what you may do.

As time went on, Mr. R. and I were still at each other's throat, and I would still get pissed off at him … but I quit calling him a son-of-a-bitch.

In turn, he backed off from me a little bit because he realized that he could only push me so far. Within a few months, Mr. R. got transferred, and I'm glad, because I always felt bad about that episode. I'm almost ashamed to tell it, but it's part of the James Brown story, and I want people to know about the business environment I had to work in. All I tried to do was bring a little peace between the IRS and James Brown and try to get his business straightened up. I meant well ... I tried to pay his taxes, but these sons-of-bitches just keep piling the shit on top of us to where there was no end to it. Hopefully in this day and time, it's a better system, or a more gentle system ... but in those days it was different, and I did everything in the world I could to get these problems resolved, but I had to constantly fight both with James Brown and the IRS. I was caught between a rock and a hard place.

I couldn't believe that the government would do this to you and get away with it. A lot of other entertainers are that way ... they just don't understand that you've got to pay your taxes. But running a business is not as simple as it looks. I can see how entertainers get into tax problems, not so much from just pissing away their money, but from just not knowing what to do. They're not used to handling this big money. A lot of people are scared of big money—it scares the hell outta 'em. You may not even conceive of what I'm saying ... but people are afraid of losing it, and they get to chasing a ghost. Look at how many people win the lottery and then become broke. They're scared of that money—they don't know how to handle it, and the next thing they know—it's gone. And you say, "How did it happen?" But it happens every day.

James Brown's money was never gone. In public, he liked to holler "I'm broke!" ... but he had the money all the time, because he was one of the more successful people I've ever seen in show business. Believe me ... James Brown had a helluva cash flow!

CHAPTER 16

James Brown vs. The World

James Brown never got over feeling vulnerable. In my amateur psychology, I'm sure it had a lot with being black … being abandoned by his mother … and growing up alone doing anything he could to survive. One time he let me examine the palms of his hands—they still have all the scars from picking cotton as a child.

He said, "I've been called 'boy' all my life," and that's why he always called people "Mister"—and in turn, he demanded the same respect from others. This formal attitude got old … calling everybody "Mister." "Mister" this and "Mister" that. Sometimes I just wanted to call him "James"—but never in front of anybody. Every once and a while, usually around Christmas time, he'd get real sentimental, and he'd lean into me, and say, in almost a childlike whisper, "Tonight, let's call each other 'James' and 'Fred'."

And I'd always say, "Mr. Brown, that sounds strange to me … "

Then he said, "Aw Fred, if it sounds strange it's because you just never hear me call you 'Fred'. Let's give it a try."

Then I'd go along with it … but it still didn't feel right … like I had just dropped my pants or something.

I felt vulnerable, but not like Mr. Brown. His early life forced him to develop a hard outer protection that would shield him from people trying to harm him or cheat him. In most ways, it was James Brown versus The World. That's why it was so rare, and weird, when the shield cracked and he would reveal himself to me.

To protect himself, James Brown was very aware of his surroundings, and he was ahead of his time on things that would go past other people. He was very worldly. He had been all over and had talked to different people and could see some of this stuff that's happening now with the Muslim community. Mr. Bobbit converted to Islam … maybe that's where some of his understanding came from. I was not aware of things like this … I had seen some Arabs down on their knees praying to Allah—but I didn't pay any attention to it at the time.

One day Brown came over to my house when Pepper was just a little girl in grammar school … she was standing there with a little dime store necklace on that some little ol' boy had given her at school. James Brown was in the middle of a conversation when he happened to focus on her necklace. He stopped right in the middle of his conversation and he said, "Pepper come here." And she came sidling up to him, and he inspected her necklace … it was something with a star and a half moon or something. Brown asked, "Where did you get that?"

She said "What?"

"That necklace."

"Oh … Bobby gave it to me … he's a boy in my class … "

"Gimme that."

"You wanna see it?"

"No! Take it off now!" He was real demanding. And it scared her. And he took it and said, "You can't have that," then he turned to me as he stuck the necklace in his pocket. He said, "Missa Daviss, you've gotta be careful of this sort of thing!"

Then he started explaining all this Muslim ideology, and Pepper was standing there just about to cry, like, *You've taken my necklace!* It was obvious that she was upset, so Brown undid the necklace around his neck, bent down, and explained things in a childlike tone … "Pepper … here let me trade you something … you don't need that necklace. You'll have to talk to your Daddy about this later, but this little ol' necklace could get you killed. Do you understand this Pepper? I love you, and I'm trying to look out for you … now I know all this went past your Daddy, and I'm gonna explain it to him, but here, let your Uncle James take care of this." Then James Brown placed his necklace in her hand depicting his astrological sign—Taurus the bull. It was sold gold.

Brown was never the type to give jewelry away, but when he gave it to Pepper, he said, "Here's a real piece of jewelry," and she smiled, not realizing that it was probably worth $1500 or more.

Later on, I talked to my wife, "You know, James Brown is so dramatic about this kinda stuff, I mean, Pepper getting' killed 'cause she's wearing some little cheap necklace! Brown's in another world! … he thinks he knows what's goin' on!" But now, I think he did. He knew more than he talked about.

Years later, in 1980, we had a break-in and lost a lot of jewelry, including the pendant. Now, there's no telling what it would be worth, simply because it belonged to James Brown. But to Pepper and me, its value is worth more than any amount of money … it was a token of very sincere affection and love … and concern for her safety in this mysterious, hostile world that James Brown lived in!

* * *

Mr. Brown worked hard to protect himself from the world, that's why, after he bought his first corporate jet, he seldom flew on commercial airlines. There were rare occasions, like when his plane was down having some maintenance done. One time we flew on Delta Air Lines to visit Hubert Humphrey in Washington. We were about midway in the first class section when I got a rip-roaring headache … probably from tension and eating late. I usually took a Stanback or a BC or Goodys powder, because it would knock out my headache as quick as anything.

I ordered a Coke, and I pulled out one of these headache powders. Brown kinda glanced at me as I rolled the paper up … I made a little funnel to dump the powder on the back of my tongue—it tasted awful!

I dumped the first powder on my tongue and made a face, but Brown just sat there—speechless, until he mumbled quietly, "Missa Daviss, you need to put that down … "

I didn't feel like discussing it … I had probably gotten the headache from listening to him anyway. I said, "That's just a headache powder, Mr. Brown … I got a headache."

"Missa Daviss, you can't be doing that." He looked around in back of the plane and told me that the people would think I was doing cocaine. This was the "James Brown Pre-Drug Days" when Brown was totally against drugs.

He kinda remained anti-drug the rest of his life. In fact, he never thought he had ever done any hard drugs … the PCP that he sprinkled into his reefer was just *a little bit of smoke …* that's the way he justified it. That's why he was getting really upset with me … he didn't want to be associated with any hard drugs, or any kind of drugs at all. And he was very careful about the public perception, especially with photographs. Anytime someone was making pictures back in the dressing room, he'd always set his cup down, no matter if he was drinking water or pop. He thought that if the public saw you with a cup in your hand, they'd always make you into a drunkard … an alcoholic. So he was very conscious of image.

I couldn't believe that people on the plane would think I was openly sitting there swallowing cocaine. I mean, that's ridiculous. Usually I would take Brown's suggestions just to avoid him getting his mouth stuck out … or getting into some stupid debate with him … and I'd normally stop what I was doing. He'd always give me advice like, "You don't do it this way!" … but by this time I had the second powder in my hand, and I said, "Mr. Brown, I don't give a damn what they think—I've got a headache!" I wanted to say something like those Excedrin TV commercials about having "an Excedrin headache" … and I wanted to add to it, *I got a damn James Brown headache! And Mr. Brown, you damn gave me the headache!"*

Brown kinda got quiet after that because he always thought of himself as the leader, the teacher … he knew the best about everything …

he had the best … his old lady is better looking than your old lady … she's smarter than your old lady … my car runs faster than your car … and his jet airplane is bigger than your jet airplane. He always wanted to be the top dog. He was very egotistical, and he wanted to tell you in detail what you were supposed to do. *Don't eat this—don't eat that.* Whatever he did was always the right thing.

Just like with Vaseline. One day I saw him dip his finger into this giant, big ol' economy size jar of Vaseline sitting on his dressing table. He got a gob of it and sucked it off the end of the finger and swallowed it. I said, "Gawdamighty, what are you doing, Mr. Brown?"

And he said, "This keeps your insides greased up. It keeps you healthy. You need to take a little dose of Vaseline every once and a while. It loosens up your insides." In other words, he thought it really lubricated his mid-section from his esophagus down to his behind.

I said, "Naw, Mr. Brown, I see what you're getting at. But that gob of Vaseline you put in your mouth is gonna go straight through your digestive system, and you're gonna shit it out. If you take some vitamin E pills, they may lubricate you and spread out through your system … but that Vaseline won't do it."

Then I saw Alfie get the Vaseline treatment. And she said to Brown, "Oh Baby, you know best," because anything he would do—she would do. Like, *Yeah Baby, I'm glad you came along and showed me all this stuff … how to keep healthy … how to keep pretty … how to do this and how to do that.*

He'd take a gob of that Vaseline and say, "Yeah Baby, let me take mine." In return, she would dip her finger into the jar and nonchalantly swallow it, making sure he saw her sucking the Vaseline off her finger. And I'm sitting behind her looking at all this … and she would turn her back to Brown and stick the Vaseline in her mouth and just grimace. It was all she could do to swallow it. Then, she'd turn back around to Brown, just smiling, like, *Yeah, Baby, you know best.* That's just another example of all the people who were constantly "yessing" Mr. Brown.

But on that Delta flight, Brown was so horrified to see Fred Daviss swallowing cocaine and disguising it as a package of headache powders

… and it was just so unfortunate that James Brown had to compromise his moral values by sitting next to a hardened drug addict like myself! That kinda nonsense would really piss me off!

* * *

It was like the whole moon and stars revolved around Mr. Brown. Even when he knew he wasn't the center of attention—he always turned things around to his favor. I remember being in this big hotel in North Miami Beach. It was an ordinary business day … I got to bed about 4 AM after the best rib dinner of my life! They brought 'em in to the hotel for all of Brown's entourage, and I was starving.

Being an ordinary day, about the time my head hit the pillow, Brown would call me up to gossip and talk about business. It was his afternoon, and I'd say to my self, *Oh lawd, let me go back to sleep.* Brown's habit was to smoke a joint, have his sex with whoever he was with, and then after he was through with that, it was time to lay up and talk to me half the damn night. And if the telephone rang in the middle of the night, you knew it had to be James Brown calling.

After we talked for an hour or so, I had gotten right back to sleep, and by then, the sun was up, and it was about 7:00 or 7:30 when the telephone rings. I felt like I haven't been to sleep but 10 minutes, and when I picked up the phone, I barked, "Hello!"

James Brown was panicked. "Missa Daviss, Missa Daviss, the hotel's on fire! Get out! Get out now!" This was when he was with Alfie, his third wife. He hung up real quick, and I immediately peeked through the curtains to look around. I didn't hear any fire alarms, and the only thing I can think of is that James Brown is high, and he thinks the hotel's on fire. Or he probably saw something on TV and couldn't separate reality from his hallucination. So I thought about going back to bed. It was the middle of the night for me.

But I hear all this commotion in the hall, and it sounds like people are running up and down the hall. Finally, the fire alarms went off. And I thought, *Oh man, James Brown is right! The hotel is on fire, he knows before anybody else did.* So I slipped my pants on and tried to get out. I knew better than to get on the elevator, but since there was no smoke or anything, I punched the button on the elevator, and suddenly, the elevator doors open and there stands Alfie and Brown. They had come down … I was on the second or third floor of the hotel, and they were higher … in more ways than one.

She's got her housecoat on and Brown was in his *morning uniform* … pants, no shirt, open bathrobe, leather slip-on bedroom shoes and hair curlers. I was glad to see them … "Hey, Mr. Brown."

"Missa Daviss, you better be glad I saved your life. I saved your life … the whole hotel is going to burn down."

It took me a moment to notice that he had an unlit joint in his mouth. Apparently, he had run outta his room and not noticed it … so he was standing there so nonchalant while we rode the elevator to the ground floor. I said, "Mr. Brown, you need to take that outta your mouth."

But he glanced down, "Oh man, I didn't realize … " as he tucked it into his pocket.

About the time we got to the lobby, the fire trucks showed up—even though there was no smoke at all. The hotel staff was herding everybody outside into the parking lot—it seemed like a thousand people milling around outside in their pajamas and everybody got talking, "There's James Brown … " and I'm thinking how glad I was that he put the joint in his pocket.

Mr. Brown remained calm and was able to evaluate the situation as an elaborate conspiracy against him. He didn't have all the facts, but he was sure that all the commotion was designed to lure him out of his suite. There was always a conspiracy everywhere we went, but we come to find out later that there was a fire up on the fourth floor of the hotel … it had started in a hallway broom closet. And with that information, James Brown swore up and down that the Puerto Rican guys who had delivered the ribs the night before had participated in the conspiracy … and since the guys were foreign, I imagined that they probably worked for the CIA and not *the usual sinister forces* like the FBI or the phone company. There was always a conspiracy going on … and James Brown was always the target.

* * *

Over the years, James Brown had developed a deep sense of paranoia, a feeling that was no doubt fueled by drugs and his raging ego. No matter what the cause was, his fears seemed absolutely real to him, and the best comparison I can make is during the last years of Howard Hughes' life.

Like Hughes, Brown's logic had gotten so warped, his unreal world began to make perfect sense … especially when it came to his biggest enemy—the U.S. government … more specifically, the FBI and the Internal Revenue along with their agents—The Phone Company. He was absolutely sure that his phones were tapped. It sounds crazy … but I think Mr. Brown was right! There was a time in this country when the government had a dossier on various people, like John Lennon and The Beatles, because they could be dangerous and influence a lot of people—a power that James Brown definitely had. If James Brown ever wanted to get militant, or become anti-war, or lead his followers to riot, things could have turned bad. And that's why James Brown believed that his phones were tapped … at the time, I was just too naïve to have joined in his paranoia.

At first I was a skeptic … even when a New Jersey attorney informed us (on more than one occasion) that the phones were tapped as part of Brown's tax investigation. I just thought the lawyer was trying to be dramatic. However, one time I had some phone troubles at my Atlanta home. While the phone repairman was in the basement, my wife asked him if he could check to see if the phone was tapped. Back then it was more of an antiquated process to tap phones. Now, I'm sure it's just a flip of a switch at some central network. But what this guy did was, he put a meter to the line which indicated some sort of unusual load … like the phone company was working on the line. He checked the work orders and was assured that there was no such work being done in the area. He said to my wife, "If I had to bet money on it, I'd say there's a 90% chance your phone is tapped."

Having your phone tapped was a prestige thing with Brown. It meant he was important enough—and dangerous enough—for the government to take seriously. Brown felt like they were trying to control him—and this just further fed his out-of-control ego.

His paranoia grew and grew as the years went by, and he got this wild idea that a worldwide network run by the Trilateral Commission had ordered the surveillance. In other words, the heads of the countries were just figureheads, and they were directed by a vast secret organization that pulled all the strings. He accepted his own conspiracy theory, but pointed out that the most pervasive and biggest villain was The Phone Company. He began showing me examples everywhere we went—pointing out all the telephone switching buildings … and of course, all over the country, you can't pull into any shopping center or any hotel without seeing a Bell Telephone truck sitting out there. It was all part of a network that was spying on James Brown.

It got to the point where every time we'd pass a telephone truck, Brown would point them out, and in particular when we would come from the airport and pull up in a limousine in front one of the hotels to check in … there was always a couple of telephone trucks sitting out there, and Brown would kinda wink at me and smile. "See Missa Daviss, they're getting my suite all wired-up before we get in. The hotel already told them we're pulling up under the marquee. By now, they've already set up the tap, and they're just clearing outta the room right now."

This paranoia got worse and worse and surprisingly—it all began to make sense to me, too! As an example … the corporate offices of James Brown Enterprises was situated in an Augusta office complex overlooking Interstate 20. It was a nice place … we had an atrium and a courtyard with a little putting green in the middle surrounded by all this beautiful shrubbery. The serene setting was just a distraction to hide the fact that the offices adjacent to ours were highly suspicious.

One neighbor was Worldwide Texaco Oil, and on the other side was The Phone Company—a double whammy of Big Oil and

Communications—but what really put the lid on it, there was a polygraph office right next to us … we even shared a common wall! Brown explained it to me that the government could not only tap into what we were saying, they could also decipher whether or not there were any lies being told in the conversation. And of course, it was all hooked up to the telephone system.

Weird, huh? But conspiracy grew all over the world … even when we were overseas Brown told me, "They have a foreign network over here that's hooked up with the KGB and Scotland Yard … and everybody else! You know, Missa Daviss … we are very popular people!" Every once in a while he'd even pull his car into a service station and put it up on a rack. He'd get us to go up under it and check for bugs—he knew that they wouldn't plant any bombs under the car—he was too important to kill. They had to keep him alive so that they could control him … make sure he didn't get too powerful … but then, he got to the point where he said, "Let 'em listen." And he'd look at me and wink. "We've got nothing to hide. Hell, they know everything we're doing, Missa Daviss!"

He fully believed his own conspiracy theory, and what was really embarrassing was when he got in a hotel room, he would get on a rant about the television surveillance. He was sure the TV was looking at him and listening to our conversations. And of course, all the bathrooms had two-way mirrors … but that was mostly for the entertainment of the government employees so they could see his old lady when she was nekked and taking a shower.

He finally flipped out one time in Jacksonville, Florida. He was in such a rage he called me to come up to his room—the Presidential Suite! When I got there, he had the double doors wide open, and he was standing there in a stance with his legs spread apart, waiting for me, and waiting for security to check his room. Apparently, he found some gizmo on his TV that didn't look right, and he was ranting and raving so much that they got the assistant manager up there … but that wasn't good enough, so they dragged the manager all the way back from his summer vacation home to fix the TV.

While we were waiting for the manager, an unfortunate family on their vacation got sucked into the drama … a black couple and their teenaged daughter in an adjacent room. When the girl found out that James Brown was in the suite, the little 16-year-old got the nerve to knock on his door and ask for an autograph. Oh boy! … Brown started to raise hell! He got the whole hotel security up there to confront this poor black family, and Brown was swearing that the entire family were government spies, and that they had actually gotten this teenaged girl to pose as a fan only to spy on James Brown. He knew she was a spy, and he was so filled with rage that he scared that poor little girl to death! She was huddled up there crying … and I was so embarrassed I didn't know what to do …

Finally I told Brown I could locate hidden microphones and bugs. He already knew I was mechanically inclined … I could fix vintage Rolls-Royces on the side of the road, and I repair broken pool pumps as well. He said, "Missa Daviss is a genius. Let him look at it."

So I got one of the maintenance men's screwdrivers, and I fiddled around behind the TV set, and I couldn't tell him there were no bugs there because he was sure they were there. I remember ripping something out of the TV … a part that didn't amount to nothing, and I confidently showed it to him. "Here it is Mr. Brown. I've cleared it out now."

"Missa Daviss is a genius. Missa Daviss knows about these things." I was pacifying him at the time, but in the long run I was adding fuel to the conspiracy fire.

In another memorable event, the two of us were in Augusta taking a little ride in his Cadillac Biarritz. We just got it a few days before. He wanted to get outta the office where we could talk. It was a lazy kinda day, and we went to a car wash … and then drove through a McDonald's to get a drink. He was in a good mood … it was a nice summer day, the sun was out, and he was a pleasure to be with—mainly because he wasn't ranting and raving about something. Then we stopped at a convenience store to buy an apple and some Hall's Mentholatum cough drops. He liked to suck on them when he was smoking a joint … it cooled his throat so the reefer wouldn't be so harsh.

We were coming back to the office off of Washington Road in the 5 o'clock traffic, and the cars were jammed up six lanes, bumper to bumper. While we were sitting at a traffic light, Brown was eating his apple. But I noticed he was distracted … he kept glancing in the rearview mirror … and he had a hard look on his face. All of a sudden, without giving me any warning, he violently jams the car in park, throws his door wide open and rolls out of the car. I'm thinking, *What in the hell is going on?*

So I opened my door thinking that he was going to pull somebody out of the car behind us and start a fight. Brown is standing at the back of the Biarritz, and wouldn't you know … there's a green and white Southern Bell Telephone truck right behind us in traffic. Apparently that's what caught his eye in the rearview mirror. There were two burly, redneck guys sitting up in the truck—and the driver's got his hairy arm hanging out the window … probably just getting off from work. And Brown is standing there at parade rest … his legs were spread apart and he had his hands on his hips. He's just staring at them, and smiling like he was on stage and the audience was applauding. And all these people sitting there in traffic are pointing, "There's James Brown!" But these two guys in the phone truck are just looking back and forth at each other and shrugging their shoulders, looking like, *What in the hell is going on?*

Then Brown loudly announced, "Aha! Aha! Yep, I just wanted you fellas to know that I know you're there. In case we get lost in traffic, you know we've just been through the McDonald's, and I stopped up at the 7-11 … I guess y'all know that, but in case you lose the tail, Missa Daviss and I are going back to the office now, and I wanted you to know that so you wouldn't get in trouble with your bossman in case you lost us in the traffic. I know about you guys. I know what you're doin'. How you like that?" And he put his hands back on his hips.

And the guys were looking at him like, *What in the hell?* And I think it started dawning on them, *Damn, this is James Brown! What in the hell is he raving about?*

And he turned to me and snapped his wrist and said, "How ya like that, Missa Daviss? They know now." Then he turned back to the guys and grinned and smiled and said, "I just want to let you fellas know that I know that you know that I know—you understand that?" Then he turned to me. "Come on, we're going back to the office. Traffic is fixin' to move." And he went strutting across Washington Road with his swagger, and he got in the car and did a little salute and crawled back into the car. "How you like that, Missa Daviss? I just wanted them to know that we're on top of all this."

And I said, "Yessuh, Mr. Brown. You showed 'em Mr. Brown!"

Brown continued. "I know you didn't realize they were behind us … they used to be slick about it, but they're getting bolder and bolder, ya know. I guess they know I know. If they don't know that I know that they know—they know now!"

I got so damn confused with this *I know/They know* rant, but when we went back to the office he told everybody, "I got those Bell people told off! I know all about that conspiracy!"

He leaned into me and said very directly, "Missa Daviss, you know there's a conspiracy, don't you?" If I had disagreed with him, he would have been pissed off … but if he was putting me on and I "yessed" him, he would know that I was a "yes man." Somehow, I had to keep my integrity … I couldn't insult him, but it was also below me to agree with him! I always found a way to sidestep any issue. I'd say, "I hear ya, Mr. Brown."

I couldn't go against Mr. Brown, and yet I couldn't agree to join with him to fight the invisible ghosts who tormented him so much … and the last thing I wanted to do was get caught in the continuing battle of James Brown versus The World.

CHAPTER 17

Personal Struggles

My job with Brown pushed me into a unique situation. I had a front row seat to all the fame and fortune of celebrity. I shared in the wealth … the privilege of private jets and hotel suites … the power of fame … and the easy access to people and places that were off limits to the mere mortals of everyday life. I had all that, but I didn't assume any of the pressures of performing on stage. I didn't have to deal with the fact that one day, it was all gonna go away. And it does, in one way or another. And even when a performer is on top of the world, drinking in the adoration of fans, and making so much damn money they can't even count it—it's almost certain they'll start to self-destruct … anticipating that all this glitter will soon go away. I never experienced that sense of conflict … I was just an observer to the whole thing.

Kris Kristofferson

The first time I saw this was with Kris Kristofferson. Joel Katz and I had gone to some benefit concert hosted by Roger Miller … it featured a lot of Country & Western stars, including Kris Kristofferson and Rita Coolidge. I had never heard of either one of them. I just remember that

Kris was in jeans and looked grubby. Rita Coolidge was with him, and they were both drunk ... drunk as skunks. Joel introduced me to Kris as *James Brown's Money Man*, and Kris immediately brightened up as he leaned into me and told me that he was such a big James Brown fan, "Man! James is my favorite! I love him!"

Next thing I knew, Kris wanted my autograph! Since I worked for James Brown and was so personally close to the Godfather, *Kris thought I was famous, too!* So he opened his wallet to retrieve a scrap piece of paper to sign. Spreading it apart, he commented, "I only have two dollars." That's all ... along with a Visa card, and two or three little pieces of paper with people's telephone numbers on them. Other than that, the wallet was empty. But what really struck me as funny was the innocence about him. It was kinda pitiful. And as I look back, here was a guy that was supposedly making a lot of money—but he was probably in a drunken haze all the time ... probably didn't know where his money was at.

But he carried his wallet like a kid with his first wallet ... when you get a dollar or two to put in it and you feel important ... just like your daddy, and you try to get little things to put in your wallet like it was your daddy's.

If I knew he was famous, maybe I would have given him more attention, but I found one of my business cards and wrote something on it, and I told him, "We'll have to get together sometime." He was so nice, but I didn't know who in the hell he was. When I got home and told my wife that I had met Kris Kristofferson, she was so impressed. I said, "Who in the hell is he?"

And she said, "Oh, he's the greatest songwriter that ever was!"

And then when I saw him in the movies with Barbra Streisand, I said, "Damn!" Then I really was impressed!

One time when Brown was on Johnny Carson, or some late night show, I ran into Kris again. This time he dressed a lot nicer ... but he was still drunk—pretty well tipsy.

I asked him, "Kris, every time I see you, you're drinking. Are you ever sober?"

Then he put his arm around me and said, "Fred, man … I'm scared. I get stage fright, and these people frighten me … it's the crowd. I like to write my songs, but I don't like to perform … I have to drink to get over my stage fright."

Since that time, I've read interviews where he said pretty much the same thing. And it was so pitiful to know that such a nice guy could ever be so afraid of all these people who loved him so much. I got a good feeling about him … he's a helicopter pilot, and we talked about flying. I really respect Kris Kristofferson. He's a sharp guy … he's got a lot of sense. He's a survivor.

Marvin Gaye

Marvin Gaye's upcoming concert in Augusta's Bell Auditorium was all the talk in the Brown household. Deedee and the two girls were just wild to go, but Mr. Brown took every opportunity to throw water on the idea. Finally I said to him, "Aw, go ahead … let the kids go."

But Brown kept turning them down for no reason. When I pressed him further, he said, "I don't want my kids going there. Marvin is vulgar … I don't want them seeing this dirty stuff." I didn't think his act was dirty, but Brown was about to get in an argument with me … he said he didn't want his daughters "going down there to see Marvin pull his pants down and show his bare ass on stage. Deanna started crying, wanting to go to the show.

But it was really about Brown's delicate ego. He didn't want anybody else on the charts competing with him—especially within his own home. He was jealous of Marvin Gaye … it was an ego thing.

The next day, Marvin called the office and invited Willie Glenn and me to come visit him in his suite at the Hilton on Broad Street. Marvin and I hadn't seen each other in a while, and he said he had *something* for me … like a gift. When Willie and I went to his room, Marvin came to the door in his boxer drawers and stepped out in the hall to hug my neck. It was very obvious that he had been snorting coke … he had powder all over his nose. As we were catchin' up on things, he was kinda rockin' back and forth when an older white couple in their 70s eased their way past us in the hallway. They looked like, *What in the world is going on?* And as they tried to avert their eyes from this large black man standing there in his drawers, I know they must have been thinkin', *Oh my goodness!*

As they went past, I said, "Marvin, you're standing here in your underwear."

"Oh man, I didn't realize it." He was high and didn't realize it, so we stepped back in the room and sat down on the corner of the bed to talk. He wanted to give me a Rolex watch. "Fred, I want to give you something nice. You're a nice guy … " and so forth and so forth …

I wanted the watch. It was worth several thousand dollars, but the significance was that Marvin Gaye was giving it to me. If it was a Timex, I would have been thrilled. The only problem was that Willie Glenn was like a gossipy, little old lady—we wouldn't have been out of the hotel good when he would have called James Brown and tattled on me.

I told Willie, "Don't tell James Brown we're down here because he'd be mad at both of us." He was jealous. He didn't want us to associate with people like Marvin Gaye or anyone else who was famous. Our entire world had to revolve around James Brown.

Brown would say, *You work for me! What are you doing lollygagging down there with Marvin Gaye?*

Willie and I were going to keep our visit a secret … the fact that we had taken off down there and talked to Marvin. But certainly, Willie Glenn would have told. When Willie left the room to make a call or something … that's when I told Marvin that I couldn't take the Rolex … it would make James Brown mad.

He got to laughing, "I don't know what you're talking about—that's so stupid. Tell me, is James really that jealous?"

"Yeah, I'm afraid so."

"I'll keep the watch for you. Next time I see you when Willie Glenn's not around, I'll give it to you. In fact, I'll slip it to you now."

"Naw, I'll get it from you later." But I never saw him again. Not long after that, Marvin's Daddy shot him. Another talented performer, and a nice guy, left us. What a tragedy. Marvin had tried so hard to get rid of the demons inside. I believe he was comin' out of it, and I think he was going on to greater heights in his career and in his life. But it all came to a worthless end.

RICHARD PRYOR

Richard was one of many people I got to know. I mean, *we knew each other* but it wasn't like we were close friends. I did recognize that Richard was a unique talent … I'd like to say he was crazy—but crazy in a comic genius kinda way. The first time we met was at a concert. He came backstage to see James Brown, and we go to talking. I was always meeting people at Johnny Carson or David Letterman or some benefit concert or award show. Then you start seeing the same people over and over and when you happen to be in the same town at the same time, you go over and visit them at their show or you drop by the hotel to see 'em.

One time Richard and I happened to be in Las Vegas at the same time so I went to check out his show. I couldn't believe he was acting so weird on stage. Finally, he stopped everything and looked out in the audience, searching for something. Then he just totally freaked out. He jumped off the stage and ran down the aisle past me. I got up and followed him as he ran out into the casino and jumped up on one of the tables (I believe it was a blackjack table) and proceeded to unzip his pants … and he was swinging his pecker around and just pissing all over the table like a fire hose. Wild eyed.

I was shocked, and I looked up at him and couldn't hardly speak, like, *"Richard? … "*

And he locks eyes with me and kinda stops for a moment like he was coming out of a dream and surprised to see me. "Fred?"

About that time, security and some of his people rushed up to the table. He had pissed on about six people, and as they got him down from the table, Richard was babbling, "I bet these people have never seen a big black dick like this one." And he said, "It's so big … it's scary!"

They rushed him out through the lobby to get him out of there. And that's the last memory I have of Richard Pryor. I don't know what did it … a rough childhood, too much money, too many drugs, too many "yes men" around him … I don't know.

Elvis

A lot has been said about Elvis. I don't need to repeat what's already been said. He was a well-mannered and generous guy and a talented performer. And he became real rich and famous as a young man, and I guess, he never really grew up. And once he got famous, he became so isolated from the rest of the world. It was a dangerous situation.

After I met him at the International in Las Vegas with an unforgettable two-hour private concert with James Brown, I would see him occasionally when he was on tour. Once I went to see him in a hotel suite, and we were sitting at a table, talking. He was real proud to tell me about all the pills he had laid on the table alongside a quart of orange juice. He started describing each pill—they were mostly vitamins and supplements, but I sorta thought that they were really uppers. It was my suspicion … I don't think he could reconcile himself taking drugs … to him, they might have been medications, but nothing illegal or harmful.

I was really shocked, and I blurted something out—I called him a junkie. Man, he jumped outta his chair and got all bent out of shape! He said that nobody had ever called him a "junkie" … and I guess I shouldn't have either.

But I shot back that the reason nobody called him a junkie was that they were on his payroll. They didn't want to say anything that would alienate themselves from Elvis … they didn't want to lose their jobs. You see, I was very aware of this attitude by working for James Brown. Everybody "yessed" Mr. Brown, although I never became his yes man … it was a daily struggle not to become one.

After Elvis got mad at me, he kinda broke down and said that he was so tired. We hugged, and he kinda cried on my shoulder. A few months later, he was dead, and when Mr. Brown demanded that I touch him in his coffin to "feel better" … I didn't. I didn't feel better. I just felt like his death had been such a waste.

Michael Jackson

The first time I laid eyes on Michael Jackson, he was just a child dangling from his arm as his father was beatin' the hell outta him. Through the years, we had a casual relationship … and I don't know that he had a deep relationship with too many people. And I'm not so sure Michael knew who he really was. He kept getting whiter and whiter, and he never seemed to look the same way twice. And he never seemed to grow up … I think he might have been permanently psychologically stunted by his father's brutality. I don't know … I'm sure there will be many books written about the subject.

When Michael got older, I found out that he was looking to buy a castle somewhere in Europe. I knew of a French chateau for sale at $9 million dollars so I attempted to broker the sale and offer my contracting services to modernize and customize the estate to his tastes. When he found out about the offer, he immediately called me on my cell phone for more information.

He caught me at a bad time. I was building about four or five homes in middle Georgia, and it was difficult to carry on much of a conversation with him while I was standing in the middle of a muddy construction site or working out details with my brick masons and framing carpenters. But it seems like every 20 minutes or so, Michael would call me, and he'd be squealing on the phone like a little girl wanting to know all about the chateau. Eventually the deal fell through … and that's maybe when he got the idea to create the Neverland ranch.

The last time I saw Michael was at James Brown's funeral. It was an emotional scene for everybody, and maybe more so for Michael. I think that Mr. Brown really was a great inspiration for Michael Jackson … and when your hero dies, a little bit of yourself dies along with them. I tried to be strong for Michael. I comforted him, and we hugged. He cried real tears on my shoulder as we held each other. I had his makeup smeared all over the shoulder of my black suit hanging in the closet—but I eventually sent it to the drycleaners.

Maybe someone should write a psychological book comparing the personal struggles of Elvis, Michael Jackson, Richard Pryor and Marvin Gaye. They were alike in so many ways, the way they reacted to fame, money and the temptations that often lead to their destruction.

James Brown & Me

I knew about self-destruction—not my own—but James Brown's destruction. When I first met him, he could have been a church lady, those biddies in your church who safeguard the moral and social standards … with James Brown, it was always "Mr. This" and "Mr. That", and he didn't like people who drank too much or smoked too much. Very straight-laced. He had many struggles, but he didn't turn to drug abuse until his relationship with Alfie. And during all our time together, I never saw him drunk.

His drug use escalated during his time with Alfie. He started out smoking some joints, and I'd join him to be sociable. Even then, smoking pot was something he did *after the performance*. His work ethic demanded that he give 100% on stage. After his workday was over, he'd often unwind, and since I stayed up with him until 4 AM, we naturally shared a lot of things in the wee hours of the night … our beliefs, our fears, our dreams.

As his drug use increased, he started experimenting with stronger stuff. It was something I didn't care for, and when he'd smoke a joint, he'd sprinkle some of this green stuff in with the marijuana. I think it was PCP, but he'd call it "Go-rilla." I don't know why, but one time I must have gotten a hold of one of his Gorilla joints, and it became one of the most terrifying events of my life! … I quickly lost all feelings in my body from my neck down! I couldn't even walk! I don't see how he kept doing that stuff.

The difference between me and James Brown was that I never got addicted to any of this stuff. I was a recreational drug user who got into it mainly to be sociable. I was not a regular user, and I was never a big boozer either—fortunately.

I don't think Mr. Brown could have been considered an addict … he just got in this rut of working late, doing drugs and going to sleep as the sun was coming up. The rest of the time, he was all work. I suppose he would have continued in this routine, but Mr. Brown went to prison, and later, Alfie died … and after that, I guess he got that stuff outta his system. It's just too bad that he had to go through all that drama first … but it's a hurdle most entertainers have to face one day or another. Whether they overcome it is another story.

CHAPTER 18

The Biggest Heart Of All

James Brown was such a complex man, it's hard to explain his many inconsistencies. I've mentioned his violent side (shooting his wife and father-in-law and beating up his wives and girlfriends) and I've discussed his jealousies and how petty, mean and stingy he could be. All those things are true. But they don't present the whole picture of the man, because deep down inside he had a very warm and generous nature. Few people ever saw that in him ... and for him to reveal that side of him would make him vulnerable and perceived as weak and sentimental. Fortunately, I was able to see past the protective veil that he wrapped around his feelings.

Back in the 1960s, when I was still at the bank, James Brown was always so impulsive about what he was gonna buy and where he was gonna live. He impulsively bought a house at 119 Linden Boulevard in St. Albans, Long Island, which resembled a castle. It even had a moat. Then he bought his place on Walton Way in Augusta. Then after touring the new Hyatt Regency Hotel in downtown Atlanta, designed by John Portman, the famous architect, he changed his mind once again. He wanted to build a home just like the Regency ... something that would reflect his tastes—something humble. Brown wanted it at least three stories tall with a glass elevator, and he wanted a tree growing up in the middle of it.

I met with Portman about building him a house, and he was honored that *The Great James Brown* wanted him to build his personal house. But Portman was used to building multi-million dollar hotels and office buildings ... he was backed up with work. He was thrilled to design Brown's dream house, and he could get right on it ... in about a year. That wasn't good enough for Brown. He wanted Portman to drop everything he was doing and start on the project the next day. The deal fell through.

Next thing I knew, Brown wanted to find some suitable property with a lake. So I called one of my realtor friends, and I took the Brown family to see several properties. But there was one property in Riverdale that everyone liked. At that time, Riverdale was a sleepy, rural village just south of the Atlanta airport. It's hard to believe how rural it really was. The property had 72 acres and a 3500 square foot log house that overlooked the 12-acre lake, and Brown envisioned himself in this nice home with some horses and cattle and all this stuff he wanted.

So I went out and bought it. But I was the one who fell in love with the place. I thought it would be nice if I could buy a piece of property like this one day ... my fantasy house ... and that eventually I'd even make enough money to make it happen. While I was daydreaming, Brown had done bought four or five other pieces of property and decided to put the Riverdale property on the back burner. I told him I'd keep an eye on the house and property, and I even suggested that he fence the place in and get some horses and cattle.

As soon as I mentioned it, Mr. Brown and I went into the cattle business together. I fenced the place and started buying cattle. He even bought me a tractor and a bush hog to keep the place neatly mowed. It was a nice place to relax after a long day working at the bank, and before long, Brown suggested I move into the house to make maintenance a little easier. I told him that the house needed to be refurbished so Brown paid for the cabinets, new carpet and tile, and some brickwork. The place really looked great!

After my family moved in, I rented out the house we owned in Atlanta, so I was getting a rent check every month and still living rent free. I was living the life! I had horses to ride, a pool, a party house built on the lake, a boat house with two boats and the kids had go-karts and mini-bikes to ride. I shoulda stayed off the mini-bikes … that's how I broke my thumb, goofing around with Brown, and that's why my hand was in a cast when we went to Graceland and when Priscilla helped me sign my name in the guestbook.

Brown really knew that I loved the farm and he said, "If I ever sell the place, I'm gonna give you the house and an acre of land."

Of course, he meant it, but I know he could change his mind. So you always live with that thought in the back of your mind. Eventually, Brown grew tired of owning the property and told me to sell it … and he said, "By the way Missa Daviss, make sure you get that lawyer to cut that house outta there."

I sure did. In fact, I did better than that. I formed a corporation with my father-in-law to buy the remaining property. I even paid Brown twice what he had paid for it so that there would be no implications that I had gotten the property unfairly. I knew Brown's ego … he would not sell the property to me. He was just that way. He didn't want me to receive anything on my own … just like Marvin Gay's Rolex.

I realized I didn't need the whole 72 acres so my father-in-law and I began to develop the property so that we could build some nice, fine homes around us. I cut out six acres for my house and then spent about $300,000 to put in some streets. We named the streets, too … the address on my house was 1 Daviss Court, Riverdale, Georgia!

Years later when I was testifying in Baltimore about Brown's chaotic financial mess, the government grilled me about the corporation that bought the Riverdale property. They thought it was a dummy corporation and that Brown created it to hide his assets. Since Mr. Brown was sitting right in front of me in court, I kept dodging the issue by being coy with my answers. Finally, under oath, I said, "Do you want to know who owns this corporation? I own the corporation!" That's when Brown found out.

Secrets can get you in trouble. I didn't mean to keep the truth from Brown, it was just easier to let him think otherwise … besides, he made a healthy profit on the deal! Another secret got loose in the community right after Brown bought the property. Word had gotten out that this *rich nigger, James Brown* bought this property and that the NAACP was going to build their headquarters down on this property and that James Brown was fixin' to build a *nigger radio station*, too! They were so pissed off about some nigger was buying the property in the middle of their community—this was back in the late 60s, ya know.

Later on, after my neighbor and I got to know each other, he said, "I never told you this because I just met you, but you won't believe the shit that went on when you first moved down here. You didn't know it, but there was a main gas line that ran within 10 feet of your bedroom, and some boys had planned to come down there and blow the house off the damn face of the earth! These dumb bastards were going to blow the house up—with me in it!

When I told James Brown about these stories, he said, "See what I was telling you … Missa Daviss got a lotta guts! You see, he's got it worse that we have." In a lotta ways, he was right. He said, "You catch more hell than the black people, because the blacks don't like you … and the whites don't like you either!"

I lived in the house, blissfully ignorant of my peril, until I got divorced in 1980. But Kelley and Pepper continued to live there and grew up there, and all their friends wanted to come to Pepper and Kelley's Daddy's place to ride the horses and go-karts. A lot of happy memories.

Now, my house is gone. I heard that they took it apart in three parts and made it some sort of clubhouse at a country club in Atlanta. Never found out which one it was. I couldn't give a shit. About 75% of the lake has been filled in … there's nothing but a little pond out there, in fact, it may not even be there anymore. The property was developed by somebody else. They built houses, but not as upscale as I wanted to build … it's kind of a middle class community. Now, all of Riverdale and Clayton County have gone downhill, mostly black neighborhoods that have gradually deteriorated.

The important thing was that Brown gave me this house, and he kept his word. Who in the hell would give you a house that was worth, on today's market, anywhere from $300,000 to $400,000? That's quite a gift! … but James Brown always meant well. He really did. And he knew that by giving me a house (at a time when I didn't have that much money) was the most thoughtful and generous thing he could have ever done. I'll always be so grateful to James Brown.

* * *

If you hung out with James Brown long enough, you'd learn something. Unfortunately, you'd have to filter out a lot of nonsense first … kinda like panning for a gold nugget … you'd have to shovel a lotta dirt, but if you kept your mind open, you'd always find something of great value.

When the time that I got my skull-popping *James Brown Headache* on the Delta flight, we were on our way to Washington to see Hubert Humphrey. After we landed at the Washington National Airport, we went straight to the bathroom … we both had to pee. Back in those days, they had shoeshine stands inside in the bathrooms. This one had four chairs, and the shoeshine boys were jumping around and shining shoes for a bunch of businessmen with wingtip shoes, sitting there reading the Wall Street Journal. James Brown was washing his hands when one of these shoeshine guys started mumbling, "That's James Brown … that's James Brown!"

James Brown walked over there and asked, "Son, you been shining shoes long?"

"Yeah, Mr. Brown, I've been doing it for four or five years."

"Do you make a lot of money?"

"I do pretty good sometimes." And the businessman who was getting his shoes shined kinda peeked over the top of his paper and got to looking like, *Damn, that's James Brown!*

Then James Brown said to the shoeshine guy, "Hey bro', let me have them brushes. Let me borrow your brushes. Let me show you how to do this." And he got a brush in each hand and tapped the businessman on the toe of the shoe and asked, "Hey sir, you mind if James Brown shines your shoes?"

And the businessman looks around to the guy next to him and says, "Hell no, man ... it would be an honor! You really want to shine my shoes?"

James Brown said, "I'm gonna show you how it's done." That's when Brown broke into a rhythm ... he got to swinging these two brushes around, crisscrossing 'em back and forth, faster and faster until he got into a real rhythm. And then he gets to swiveling his hips while he's hitting the shoes ... and all of a sudden, all the people in the bathroom were coming out of the stalls or coming into the door. He's getting an audience. And they're standing around and somebody starts to hum out *Sweet Georgia Brown* ... and Brown starts dancing like the Harlem Globetrotters.

Then Brown's got those brushes, he's clicking them together criss-crossing them behind his back and in front ... and every other stroke, he's hitting the shoes, and brushing, and spiting on the shoes ... then he pops the brushes together, puts them down and grabs the polish.

Now here's James Brown in a $1500 outfit, damn $500 pair of shoes, and he's putting shoe polish on his hands, and he grabs this rag and twirls around like he was on stage, and I thought he was gonna do a damn split in the bathroom, and he whirls around and pops the rag. Whap! Then he starts to hit the shoes with that rag like a madman. He was puttin' that rag on it ... popping that rag and had it going in a rhythm like a guy on a set of drums. Pap-pap-a-pap-pap-a-pap.

And the other shoeshine guy was still humming, and they get to clapping and carrying on, and James Brown danced a little ... he'd hit the shoes a couple of times until the damn shoes looked like somebody had rubbed them down with grease.

The businessman dropped the newspaper down in his lap and was looking in awe as he said, "Damn! Damn! I can feel the heat coming through my shoes!"

But James Brown kept on popping that rag, and everything was done in rhythm. Never missed a beat, and he kept on for about five minutes. Pap-pap-a-pap-pap-a-pap. He was making music—clicking the wooden handles of the brushes together, popping the rags and keeping beat with the sound of the brushes hitting the leather in perfect rhythm. And when he got through, he popped that rag and flopped it over a couple of times, snapping it in mid-air as he folded it one more time and laid it down in a nice neat bundle. He straightened the rag up and patted the businessman on the toe.

And before the small crowd could react, the businessman pulled out his wallet. "How much I owe you, Mr. Brown?"

"That one's on me bro' … you don't owe me a thing. You can say you got your shoes shined in the Washington National Airport by James Brown. Ya know, before I recorded my first song, I was a professional shoeshine boy, and I just wanted to show this young man here that no matter what you do, you need to get your routine down and handle it in a business-like way. I don't care if you're shoveling dirt in a ditch … make it happy. Put a little rhythm in it … a little music. And get your game down. I just wanted to show him how to be an entrepreneur … and because of that, I guarantee—you will make more money."

James Brown turned to the shoeshine guy and pointed to the businessman. "You see this man right here? He was ready to give me $20 for a shoeshine. But it's on me bro'."

The businessman laughed, and said, "Thank you, Mr. Brown."

Then James Brown turned back to the shoeshine guy and said, "By the way, I just beat you out of a shoeshine." Then Brown reaches into his pocket and pulls out a roll of money and peels off a $100 dollar bill. And he said, "Since I took your time, teaching you how to make money, I'm gonna pay you for your time." The shoeshine guy just about crapped, and everybody was oohing and aahing.

Brown looked around at everybody and said, "Well, we gotta go see Mr. Humphrey. Me and Missa Daviss are gonna visit Mr. Humphrey."

And the shoeshine guy said, "You mean, Hubert Humphrey?"

He said, "Sure, that's where we're going. And I reckon he's gonna wonder why I have all this shoe polish all over my hand."

I'm also sure that businessman has told that story many, many times. And I'm sure the shoeshine guy has told that story, too. I just hope he appreciated the $100, but of even greater value was James Brown's advice. It wasn't about how to shine shoes … it was about always doing your best, not matter what you do. Being a professional. Taking pride in your work. Enjoying your work so that those around you will benefit from your attitude.

There's a golden nugget of wisdom in that. And since he was sitting there, maybe the businessman took James Brown's advice as well. Maybe his business started to grow—maybe his attitude started to improve. And why wouldn't it? … he got a free shoeshine … and it was done by James Brown!

* * *

James Brown met thousands of people through the years. Only a few made an impression on him … and their friendship always seemed to endure. One of these people was Hubert Humphrey. Before I began work for Brown, Mr. Humphrey and had been a friend for years—probably through his association as Lyndon Johnson's Vice-President.

Brown had worked with Humphrey through Brown's "Don't Be A Dropout Program," and then Humphrey contacted Mr. Brown after the King assassination to do something about the rioting.

My first contact with Hubert Humphrey came when I was in Brown's suite at the Hilton Hotel across from the Atlanta Airport. I was still working for the bank, and Brown was eating … actually *slopping* his food and talking—which was typical of James Brown. Many times I talked to him on the phone when he was slopping his food with a mouthful of steak and potatoes. Normally, I couldn't understand what he was saying, and you damn sure couldn't understand him with a mouthful of food! As the phone rang in the suite, the person who answered the phone mentioned that it was Hubert Humphrey.

My eyes got big like, *Hubert Humphrey?* But when Mr. Brown got on the phone, he was in one of his shitty moods and immediately began to chew out Mr. Humphrey.

Apparently Humphrey was asking Brown to go on a little jaunt through Harlem in an open convertible to get black votes for Humphrey.

He was pleading, but Brown had all these gigs set up and didn't want to cancel several dates and lose all that money.

I overheard Mr. Brown as he started to boil over. "Missa Humphrey, I told you three or four months ago that if you let me do it my way, I could have gotten you *all the black votes* ... but no ... you were riding high at the time, and you thought you didn't need me. I tried to tell you, but you don't realize the power I've got with the blacks—and now you're just realizing it. Do you really think that I'm gonna blow this money from the concerts and drop everything just to go get you a few black votes that's not gonna help you in the midnight hour?"

Brown was just chewing his ass out like he was just a little boy. I couldn't believe he was talking to Hubert Humphrey this way. After Brown had his say, all of a sudden, the whole tone and mood changed. "By the way Hubert," it was *Hubert* and not *Mr. Humphrey,* "how's the family?"

For Brown, this was his typical chitchat to get ready to hang up the phone. I knew what was comin'.

"I hope you have a lot of luck in your election, and tell your wife I said 'hello'." I love 'em ... I love you ... See ya later Hubert ... Bye."

He hung up the phone and shook his head and said, "Missa Humphrey is a good man, but these people don't listen. They don't know how powerful I am. And then they come up, and they're grasping at straws like a drowning man, trying to get everything he can, because he knows he's fixin' to lose this election. If he would have let me get the black votes, I told him I would—but he didn't think he needed them at the time. I ain't gonna waste my time like that ... because nobody would appreciate it. Now he comes on his knees to me."

While I worked for Brown, there was at least two occasions that I went by to see Hubert Humphrey to ask for favors ... usually about the IRS. He would say, "You go tell Missa Humphrey about it ... he's my friend and he needs to do something about this."

I was also sent to plead Mr. Brown's case in front of other senators ... like Herman Talmadge ... and when I would go to see Strom Thurmond, I'd always go to his aide, Lee Atwater, who was just a little peon who laid back and plucked on his guitar. He was a big James Brown fan, but he was just a little flunky. The next thing I know, he's the head of the Republicans and was a big part of helping George H. W. Bush get elected. Unfortunately, Lee died with brain cancer at about 40 years old. Just a typical fraternity-guy, good ol' boy.

The last time James Brown and I saw Mr. Humphrey was in late 1977. He was dying from cancer, and Mr. Brown wanted to pay his last respects. Brown hated to go to hospitals and funerals … so this was his absolute last chance.

Humphrey's hair was falling out and his skin looked milky white. He was very gaunt, but his cheeks were kinda rosy and ruddy looking. And his knuckles were very bony … he was wasting away right before our eyes.

We got together and had lunch in the Senate dining room, where one of the waiters gave me a menu as a souvenir. Humphrey sat there and didn't finish his meal. In fact, none of us ate too much. Then Humphrey was called away to go vote on something, and he gave me a pass, so I watched him vote from the upstairs gallery in the Senate.

After that, the three of us talked for about 30 minutes in his Senate office. He looked like he was about to die while we were there. But he was smiling and in good spirits. He talked about his illness and how it had sapped his strength, but he said that he "still had things to do … I need to be in the office to finish up some things."

We all knew that it was a farewell. We shook hands and hugged his neck and as Brown and I left his office, we stood in the hall and Brown remarked, "That'll be the last time we see him." It was. Hubert Humphrey died soon after that on January 13, 1978.

A few months later, I walked into Brown's office and noticed a photograph on the wall … on the opposite wall from his desk … a location that would always be in his direct line of sight. It was a framed and matted photograph of Humphrey's gravestone. I don't know where it came from, but it was an obvious conversation piece so that everyone who came in would comment about it.

When they did, Brown would always get this distant look in his eyes, and he would always say what a good man Hubert Humphrey was, and how much he loved him. I never could grasp the importance of having a picture of his grave. You could go back and shoot another picture and that tombstone will be there. If you need a picture, go shoot another one. It wasn't like it was an intimate picture of a person who had passed away. But the photograph was one of James Brown's most cherished possessions.

Only a few people were able to get James Brown's attention and respect … but even with that respect, he would still get pissed off at you, chew you out, and rub it in your face … and he'd talk down to you, kinda like, *I'll show you!* That's the kind of environment he came from … you couldn't get a lot of sympathy from James Brown.

* * *

When I tell people that I worked for James Brown the first thing they want to know is why I left such a glamorous job. It was glamorous. I don't know how many five-star hotel suites I've slept in, how many limousines and private jets I've been in and what unbelievable money I was making.

Well, the glamour wore off after about two years, and then it became just a damn job, and it was getting more demanding and frustrating every day. At the end of my time with Brown, he had divested himself of his radio stations. Before that, I had used the radio stations as my refuge. After he sold them, I was forced to spend more and more time in the Augusta office rather than having the freedom of going to the Baltimore or Knoxville radio stations. This was also during the time when he started smoking PCP. He became a changed person. He was mean, erratic and unpredictable, and I was always hanging out with him in the office. He became obsessed with the smallest details in the contracts … he found fault in everything and disagreed with all my business decisions. He was not running the business right, and there were a couple of days that we had a falling out, but it washed itself out after a few days. Finally, I came to the decision to resign. I was all stressed out and called in sick for a couple of days, but he knew what was going on. James Brown didn't believe in getting sick. He pulled out a bag of antibiotics he had lying around and told me to take some, like, "Just get yourself a good handful of pills and you'll feel better real soon."

I didn't know how to quit. If I walked out, Brown would blame all his bad business dealings on me, and I'd have no defense. I'd probably go to jail for all the millions of unpaid tax problems he had created so I had to ease out slowly and cover my tracks. I also had to make copies of all the documents to prove that I was not responsible for his arrogant disregard for the law.

My Dad got wind of my situation, and while he was in Augusta for a visit he told me to quit. "Make it simple, and just say, 'I quit', and walk out—it's that easy." So Dad came to the office and helped me gather my personal possessions, when he and Mr. Brown began discussing the matter. After a few minutes, Dad said, "Mr. Brown, I'm not going to stand here and listen to anymore of your bullshit." Then Daddy turned and walked away down the hall. Brown was hurt … he hated to be rejected but my Dad was like a father figure to him. Brown called his own father "Pop"—he called my father "Pop", too.

As my Dad walked down the hall, Brown was following him like a puppy. "Pop, Pop … hang on a minute, I'm not through talking." Nobody in the world ever talked to James Brown like that. This was serious.

Brown drifted back down the hall and into the office. I was getting some stuff out the drawers and laid my keys to the office up on the desk. "Mr. Daviss, you can't leave me."

I said, "Mr. Brown, we'll still be family, but we can't keep on going on this way. Things have changed too much—you won't let me do my job."

The exchange went back and forth—starting with mutual affection and then turning into him pleading, and then into anger.

I said, "Mr. Brown, any time you need me, just give me a call."

Then I saw a dazed look come over his face. Reality. He knew that I knew too much about his dealings—his money, his deals, his secrets. I turned and walked down the hall, but his anger kept growing with each step. He was dogging me step by step, and he was crowding up so close behind me that I could feel his chest rub up against my back. When I got to the door leading out to the courtyard, I stopped abruptly, but since he was crowding me so much, he lost his balance and his chin wound up resting on my right shoulder. We were both stuck in the doorway, and I was getting really pissed. I snapped my head around, and we were eye to eye—about three inches apart.

I gritted my teeth and said, "Mr. Brown, back off!" And I was drawing up my hand into a tight fist. He knew that I would swing on him, and I could see that he had the same stance—his fist was cocked back like he was just waiting for an easy excuse to swing. But he didn't—he stepped back a little

I said, "Mr. Brown, I'm just quitting the job—I'm not leaving you. You can always call me if you need me."

So my Dad and got in the car and headed up Interstate 20 going home. I was relieved but kind of felt out of sorts, you know. Then, no more than a day or so went by when Brown called me for a casual talk, just like I was still working for him. After that, we were talking on a daily basis, and we continued to do deals together through the years. It was true ... with James Brown, you could quit but you could never leave.

* * *

Even after I resigned from James Brown, we were still in touch on the phone every day. When I found out he was having some new dental implants in a downtown Atlanta hospital, I decided to make the two hour trip with my second wife, Cynthia, to visit him as he recovered. When I first saw him in the hospital bed, he looked awful. He was drugged up on Demerol or whatever, and his face was really swollen.

When Cynthia and Mrs. Brown left the room to go to the coffee shop, I sat down beside Mr. Brown on the bed. He held my hand and told me the helluva time he was going through with the surgery. Then he mentioned that he was also having some tax problems. He had found a stock certificate from the Chemical Bank in New York tucked behind a picture frame and had decided to cash it in and transfer the money directly to his bank account. Apparently the tax people got wind of it, and they had put a lien on the money. He asked if I could come to

Augusta for a few days and sort the problem out—he'd pay my expenses. I agreed. The next day, Sunday, he was released and drove back to Beech Island, South Carolina, and we made plans to get together on Tuesday at 11 o'clock.

When I ran into James Brown in the hall of his office complex, I was shocked. I had never seen him in this condition ... he was sweaty—he had on this silk shirt that he had obviously been wearing for several days. His wife told me that had not been to sleep since they had left the hospital on Sunday afternoon ... and this was Tuesday.

Mr. Brown was having trouble talking. He was so high—he was trying to get the words out, but what really bothered me was the fact that all the employees in the office were so shocked to see him in this condition. It was embarrassing. Many times I had seen James Brown smoke a joint late at night in his hotel suite after a concert and then he'd be all right the next day, but this time the PCP had really gotten into his system.

The girls in his office and his receptionist didn't know what to think. I sat there and heard him on the phone, trying to do business, and he was stuttering so bad. It was obvious that he was out of control—and I was unable to help him. I spoke with his wife, and she didn't know what to do about the drugs. I told her, "Just flush the stuff down the commode." But she didn't—she was using the stuff, too. Had the stuff in nasal sprays hidden in her bra.

I told her that he needed some type of intervention. I'd do it for him, but I had no authority, I was not a member of the family—I wasn't even an employee anymore.

I continued to deal with the tax issue on Tuesday and Wednesday. Brown would come into the office a few times, but I didn't know what was really going on at night at his home. I wrapped everything up and had made plans to drop by his house on Thursday evening and pick up a check for my expenses before I headed back home. When I got there, I discovered that Mr. Brown hadn't slept or eaten since he left the hospital on Sunday. Now it was Thursday night. When I walked in the front door, I found Mr. Brown wearing red silk pajamas and his bedroom slippers. He was smiling and grinning, high as a kite, and he was standing in a real formal stance … like a military parade rest except that he had his hands on his hips. He raised his finger to gesture but as he tried to talk, he was just sputtering his words.

I said, "Mr. Brown, you're gonna be alright." He smiled and gestured for us to sit down in two wing chairs separated by a huge globe. I started the conversation. "Let me get you some help."

Then I noticed that he was not really there mentally. It was like talking to someone when they're drunk, and they start to focus on something small—like talking to the wall or something. Brown was focusing on the globe between us, and he started showing me some things in Africa. He had enough sense that he knew the country names but it was just meaningless babbling. Finally I said, "Mr. Brown, we can talk about this later, but now we need to talk about getting you some help. Please let me help you."

He was smiling but he kept on talking and changing the subject. Then I got hold of his shoulders and got my face up close to his face and made close eye contact. I said, "Mr. Brown, you need some help, brother. I'm your friend—let me get some help."

All of a sudden there was silence. I stared at him and I said, "Please let me get you some help, Mr. Brown. I know about drugs, and you're way out on a tangent and can't get back to where you can handle yourself."

All of a sudden he looked at me and nodded his head and just broke out crying. I held him and he leaned over and laid his head on my shoulder and cried like a baby. I could hear the words softly coming into my ear, "Yes, Mr. Daviss … please get me some help." I leaned back and I smiled at him.

"I'm glad you realize that … I'll call the doctor … " I reached in my pocket to get a small telephone address book.

Then all of a sudden, he freaked out and hunched up like a child, hugging himself with his hands crossed up on his shoulders, very child-like. He yelled out, "No doctors! … no doctors!"

"Mr. Brown, you don't have to be afraid. I will sit there as long as it takes—I will hold your hand, and I'm not gonna let anybody hurt you or take advantage of you in any way."

His wife came in and dished up some cream corn, which was one of his favorite foods, and maybe some mashed potatoes. She slammed the plate down the kitchen bar and tore off back to the bedroom in disgust. I didn't know what to do. I knew I had lost an opportunity when I said the word "doctor." I mentioned that it was getting late so I went back to the master bedroom with Mr. Brown. He just sat there in a daze as his wife paid me for my expenses.

I left his home on Thursday night—I got home about 1 o'clock Friday morning. On Sunday morning, the news broke about Mr. Brown—he'd been arrested. The first thing I did was call his home. His wife explained that he had been arrested twice—once on Friday night and then when she got him out of jail, he got the car keys and was arrested again on Saturday night.

So this was the start of it all—the car chase and his stay in prison, which happened about a week later. I had come close to making a breakthrough with Mr. Brown, but as usual, he wanted to do things his way—and he did.

* * *

Besides me, the other person James Brown really cared about was Mr. Charles Bobbit. He is a black guy from New York who became Brown's personal manager. While I managed all of Brown's financial business, Bobbit took care of all the details of Brown's day-to-day needs.

Their relationship began in the mid-1960s and continued for several years until we went to play a private concert for President Omar Bongo in Gabon. Brown's entire entourage went to Africa, and Bongo was quite generous. While Mr. Bobbit was trying to tell Bongo that he couldn't speak French, Bongo picked up four $10,000 packs of $100 bills lying on a table and gave them to Bobbit. $40,000! Of course, James Brown didn't like that at all!

After the concert, we were flying back over the Atlantic when Leon Austin, Mr. Brown's hairdresser, presented him with Bobbit's letter of resignation. Bobbit had stayed back in Gabon to work for Bongo! Well,

Mr. Brown blew a fuze! It just ate him up that Mr. Bobbit had resigned, and he couldn't stand it because Mr. Bobbit was making all this money, in fact, Mr. Bobbit later bought his own private jet. Brown was so jealous of Bobbit, and when Brown would mention him in a conversation, he would always add *what a rat* Mr. Bobbit was.

Mr. Bobbit ended up working for Mr. Bongo for probably 15 or 16 years, and when he returned, it surprised me when he went back to work with Mr. Brown, more or less on a consultant basis. For several years, Mr. Bobbit also worked for Michael Jackson.

Mr. Bobbit was, and is, a good man. He's done a lot of good things for a lot of people, helping them out financially. He's always remembered where he came from, and he always remained loyal to Mr. Brown.

He was with him in the hospital on the night he died. Mr. Bobbit told me about it … told me that James Brown raised up in bed and said, "Missa Bobbit, I'm fixin' to leave you."

Bobbit replied, "Mr. Brown, if you're talking about what I think you're talking about … that's one trip I'm not goin' to make with you."

As James Brown was sitting on the side of the bed, he couldn't breathe good, and he said, "No, Missa Bobbit, I'm serious. I'm fixin' to leave you." Then he laid back on the bed. Bobbit bent over to cover him up where his gown had come open, and then he just quit breathing. And that was the end.

In the early morning hours after Mr. Brown had died, Mr. Bobbit and I talked on the telephone, and we both cried. It's funny how things come back full circle. After all those years when Mr. Bobbit left him, Brown really had his mouth stuck out about Mr. Bobbit. He was a rat … and I'm sure after I left Brown, I was a rat, too. Brown never wanted people to leave … he couldn't understand that we had our own lives … but we were always loyal.

Of all the people that Brown knew over the years, the two closest people to him would have been me and Mr. Bobbit. He loved both of us … he trusted both of us … but Brown used to tell me, "If I really want to let my hair down, it's gotta be with Missa Bobbit, 'cause culturally, Missa Daviss … we're different. But just 'cause I love Missa Bobbit, doesn't mean I don't love you. I do." And he did, so I'm glad Mr. Bobbit was with James Brown on the night he died … I can't think of a better person … I'm just thankful that Mr. Brown wasn't by himself.

That's because James Brown was really a vulnerable person … a little uptight, a little private, but he had to be because he was a celebrity. His fans need to know that he had a human side—that James Brown put on his pants just like us … however … he was an awesome man … extremely talented … and brilliant … I mean, this man could turn lawyers inside out and spit 'em out!

I've told a lot of stories about James Brown … I've laughed about him, but I'm not making fun of him or anybody else. If somebody told the same stories about me, I'd laugh, too … we're all human whether we're black or white … we can all identify with these stories. Life is short, and we've got to learn to laugh at ourselves and see the humor in our journey through life.

* * *

It's good we can laugh, because telling this last story always make me tear up a little. Not sad tears … glad tears.

The thing that used to impress me about Brown was that he would help the little white kids as much as he would help the little black kids. Brown was a sucker for kids … I guess it was because of his upbringing-never having any store-bought pairs of underwear until he was seven years old.

One time, we were in a stretch limo on the way to a concert at the Apollo Theater, and we were going through a seedy, dilapidated part of town as we were heading to Harlem. All of a sudden, Brown hollered for the driver to stop … and I was wondering why the hell we were stopping—it was a tough neighborhood. Brown let his window down, and there's this little grubby-looking white kid … a street urchin about 9 or 10 years old … and he's got his corner staked out with his little shoeshine box. I don't know why anybody in that neighborhood could possibly want a shoeshine—but the kid was out there trying to make some money, plus it was early evening, but still daylight.

Brown said, "Come here, son," but the little boy was real street wise, and leery-like, *Who is the hell is in that big ol' limo?* Very suspiciously, the little boy kinda sidled up to the limo window, and Brown looked at him and said, "Yep, it's me."

The little boy's eyes got so big, and you could tell he recognized James Brown, but the little boy stuttered and pointed, "You, you, you're … oh, man! … you're James Brown!" He was in awe. He said that he had some of Brown's records and really liked his music … even hummed a few bars.

James Brown was flattered and laughed as he sized up the boy. He was nasty, and had shoe polish all over him … his blond hair was hanging in his eyes, and the knees were torn outta his jeans. He had ol' beat up tennis shoes on, and he looked like he hadn't had a bath in days, but he was standing there, protecting his shoeshine box.

After a moment, Brown asked, "Have you ever seen a James Brown concert?" The boy said he hadn't—he never had the money to buy a ticket. Then Mr. Brown asked him if he wanted to go see his concert that night.

"I told you … I don't have any money for a ticket."

"You don't need any money … you can work for it, then you can be my guest and I'll get you in."

And the little boy looked at him like, *What's the hook here? What's the hustle?*—getting a little paranoid. The boy said that he couldn't go to a concert … he could still make some more money before the end of the day.

Then Brown provided a counter offer. "I really need you to shine some shoes for me. I got a bunch of shoes, and I'll pay you good money if you go to the concert with me."

The boy was still a little apprehensive … he would have to let his mama know. The family didn't have a phone—the neighbors did. The boy and Brown worked out a deal where his parents would be called once we got to the theater.

Once he got in the limo and started riding down the street and looking out the window, he got a little more comfortable with us, but when we got to the Apollo it really got fun for the boy … we met the entourage at the stage door, and Brown goes strutting in and everybody gets to hopping around and all the ass kissers were running around saying, "Good afternoon, Mr. Brown!"

Miss Sanders, who was his wardrobe mistress, was always grumpy and griping about everything … and she was one of the few people who got away with calling him "James" … and was always limping around on her bad leg and always had an iron in her hand. She ran the dressing room like a drill sergeant.

And we walked in, she said, "Lawd kno', Missa Brown, where did you get that raggedy-looking little thing?"

And Brown shot back, "Miss Sanders, he's working for us tonight. You take care of *your business* and me and Missa Daviss will take care of *our business*." And Miss Sanders went off grumbling like she had a mouth full of marbles or something.

Then Brown told me that I needed to put the boy on the payroll for that night. I said, "Yessir, Mr. Brown," and that made the kid feel so important.

Once we got in the dressing room, the boy saw all of Brown's uniforms and outfits—at least 100 of 'em hanging on the rack … and 100 pairs of perfectly shined shoes and boots, all neatly lined up. I'm sure the little boy had never seen any $300 or $400 boots—his eyes were big as saucers. Then he got down on his knees and started rubbing and buffing the six pairs of boots that Brown had picked out … the boy was going to town, and it didn't take long to get the job done.

In the dressing room, James Brown called his family and said, "I want y'all to come over as my guest of the show tonight, and I'll send a limo to pick you up, and you can bring the boy some shoes. We've got plenty of dressing facilities here—he can take him a shower, so bring him a change of clothes … as a matter of fact, if you tell me his size, I'll get a guy to go out and buy him some new clothes."

When the daddy, the mama, and little sister arrived, Mr. Brown met them backstage, introduced himself, and made sure they knew their child was alright. And as we were talking, I couldn't help but notice that these were just some pitiful-looking people. But they were grateful, and we offered them some fried chicken off the buffet table. Then, as the boy took a shower, his family was escorted to a box seat … the best seats in the house, right off the end of the stage.

Once the boy got cleaned up we could finally see the freckles on his nose that had been hiding underneath all the dirt. He got dressed in his new clothes and was sitting next to James Brown, *The Superstar,* at the same dressing table with the mirror surrounded by lights. They were both combing their hair in the mirror … the boy was looking like he was ready to go on stage himself! And it made the boy even prouder when James Brown put on the shoes he had just shined and wore them for his performance.

During the concert, the boy sat with his family for a while and then wandered around backstage with his All Access pass. We all treated him good, and he had a nice buffet dinner and musta drunk about 15 damn Pepsi Colas … just like Forrest Gump drinking all those Dr. Peppers at the White House.

When the show was over, his parents came back to the dressing room, and we stood around and had a little chit chat with Mr. Brown until he mentioned, "Oh by the way, Missa Daviss … we owe him some money—have you paid him yet?" I said that I hadn't and didn't know how much to pay.

Brown stood there and said to the boy, "I'm fixin' to pay you for shining these shoes," and he reached into his coat and pulled out a wad of $100s … and he pulled a $100 bill off, and he spread that bill out right in front of the boy's eyes and said, "This hundred is for shining my shoes. Is that enough money?"

The little boy was about to shit. "Oh man, you don't owe me any money!"

"No, you did a good job," he said as he put his arm around him and gave him a hug. Then Brown asked him what grade he was in and so forth, and asked him, "Do you plan on going to college?" … but the boy said his family couldn't afford it … and they really were such pitiful looking folks.

Brown said, "I tell you what, I want to see you go to college. I want you to get all the education you can and then you can end up making more money than me. You need to get that education … and you stay in school … don't be a dropout."

"Oh naw, I make good grades now!"

Then Mr. Brown peeled off five more $100s. He said, "I'm gonna give you five more hundreds. I'm gonna give this five hundred to your mama. I want y'all to put this in the bank to start him a college fund. Every week when you're shining these shoes, I want you to add a little bit to it. Now if y'all get in an emergency or anything and you need some money, take it out and use it because you'll be able to put it back later. But what I want you to know … this is the start of his college money. You can build it up by the time you're ready to go to college. I tell you what, by that time we'll probably talk some more, and when you're ready to go to college, we'll still be in touch … and I will help you. But I want to see how much money you're gonna add to this. Missa Daviss, I want you to give him your business card where they can get in touch with you. (Brown would never give anybody his personal number!) If you have any emergency come up, you can call Missa Daviss. Now, I'm gonna have the limo carry you out for a late supper … let you celebrate a little bit … celebrate going to college."

The lady broke down and started crying, and she hugged his neck. You could tell that that was probably the first time she ever thought about hugging a black man. It was like they hit the lottery, and the little boy started crying, and I started to get a lump in my throat.

And Brown concluded by saying, "Son, I really want you to stay in school … because I know, you can become anything you want."

At that point, even Miss Sanders got tears in her eyes … and she was a hard nut. I know Brown didn't want Miss Sanders, or me, or nobody else to see his soft side. He didn't want to, or need to impress anybody, but that night he let some of his real feelings out. For weeks after that, we'd all whisper to each other about it… *Did you see the tears in Mr. Brown's eyes?* And if you said anything to him about it, he would have denied the whole thing.

James Brown did a lot of things that were never publicized. I can't count the times that James Brown would meet people in the elevator or in a hotel lobby and give them a motorized wheelchair, and when I first met James Brown, they were giving them bicycles during the intermission of the shows. In all, it added up to at least 20,000 bicycles. Most people don't know that. At Thanksgiving, he gave away thousands of turkeys to deserving families. And he paid for many funerals for needy families ... and nobody knew about it but us.

I told him that he needed a foundation to write this stuff off, but he said, "Naw, then they'll think I'm trying to show off."

Brown had a good heart, but on other days he'd kill you over $10. He had a soft spot for kids because of what he went through as a kid. He loved little kids, and I saw him many times getting down on his knees so that he could talk to them at eye level. I saw him do that with Kelley and Pepper ... he'd squat down on their level and set them down on his knee. The public has never seen that side of James Brown, and they've never heard about the shoeshine boy.

We never heard from him or his family unless they wrote to Brown, and he didn't mention it. But because of this one little evening, I became really impressed with James Brown, The Man ... not James Brown, The Legend.

And I've wondered many times if the little kid went to school ... and I hope that kid reads this book and gets in touch with me because I want to know what eventually happened in his life, and what kind of impact James Brown's generosity had on him ... because it had a helluva impact on me! I get tears in my eyes just thinking about the story.

And despite all the stuff that went on ... the violence, the women, the drugs, the cruelty, pettiness and jealousy ... mostly, there was a lotta love.

The End

THANK YOU!

FAMILY FIRST

It's impossible to thank all the people who have supported and encouraged me through the years. Without them, I would not be the person I am today and would not have been able to have had such a rich and unbelievable life.

To begin, I'd like to acknowledge the coolest wife in the world—**Cynthia**. She is so good to me, and so forgiving when I frequently step out of line. Best of all, she's such a friendly and happy person who can put up with almost anything. As an example—on one of our first dates we went along with James Brown to wash his car. That's what we did! He drove his Lincoln Town Car into one of those self-service places, and he's out there in his outfit spraying down the car and such. Not the glamorous life most people would envision. Then Mr. Brown gave Cynthia the ultimate compliment, "Missa Daviss, I'm glad that you finally got a woman with some spank." He was a butt man. Cynthia and Brown got along very well—and most of that was because she was so understanding and flexible.

Her parents, **Jack** and **Claudia Fowler**, raised her well, and even though they've both left us.

My Daddy, **Bill Daviss**, has also departed. He gave me great guidance throughout my entire life. Not only did Daddy raise me with strength and integrity, he also shared those same qualities with James Brown and sorta became his surrogate father. Brown respected Daddy because Daddy had the real-life experience that his own father, Pop, never had. Daddy toured with Brown on several occasions, and I believe that they both thrived on each other's company.

I have great appreciation for my first wife, **June**. When James Brown came into my life, June and I were just kids with a new baby, and we were living out the American dream. Then I began spending more time with Brown than with June and was often absent in my daughters' lives. I was running around living like a rock star while June stayed at home raising the girls. June is a great mother, and that's evident by the fact that Kelley and Pepper are both strong, independent businesswomen. We're still a tight and loving family—**Kelley Daviss, Karen Lineberry** and **Pepper, Kolby** and **Mark Ware.**

The family also includes my former brother-in-law, **Ernest "Bubba" Whitfield**. He is an accountant, and he really saved me early in my career with Brown. Brown had all these receipts and scraps of paper stuffed in paper bags, and since I was his Money Man, I was responsible for all the money coming in and going out. I was on the verge of pulling my hair out (that's when I used to have it) but Bubba stepped in and made sense of Brown's chaotic bookkeeping. Thanks, Bubba!

A lot of my personality related to my **McKinstry cousins: Jimmy**; **Tom**; and **Gilbert**. They're all brilliant, and crazy and funny as hell, and I believe their memoirs would be far more interesting than mine. They always encouraged me and were always eager to hear my James Brown stories. I really appreciate y'all—I really do.

Jerry Ridley came into my life after Daddy had a stroke and was confined to his bed in my in-law suite. Jerry was with him 24 hours a day, and after a while Jerry became more than a caretaker, he was my right-hand-man taking care of my stuff as well. After Daddy died, Jerry continued to live in the in-law suite for several years. He was family, and even though we didn't share any DNA or even the same race, Jerry had become my main man. Jerry, I can't thank you enough.

IN THE MIDST OF PROFESSIONALS

I have worked with some of the greatest entertainers and creative people in show business. I'd like to recognize several who have shown their commitment in helping me write this book and to capture my stories on video. Several years ago, I went to Memphis to see **George Klein** (his memoir is "Elvis: My Best Man"). The last time I had seen him was the night when James Brown and I made a visitation to Graceland when Elvis died. After the interview on The George Klein Show on Elvis 24/7 Sirius XM Radio, George extended an invitation to return. What a nice man.

I've had several people really dedicated to helping me, including **Barb Paresi**. Barb is a force of nature!—full of ideas and energy—and she sure isn't a quitter!

Helen Halton is another creative force. Her specialty is marketing and promotion. She believed in this book from our very first meeting—and that's a very gratifying feeling.

Chris Savas is a professional photographer who shoots the celebrities—***the beautiful people***. I suppose he made an exception in my case. Chris is one of the nicest and most talented guys you could ever meet!

We decided to produce a one-man show of me telling my stories before a live audience. We enlisted some seasoned broadcast producers to put the show together—cameras, lights, audio. It was a pleasure working with the crew, especially **Steven Panayioto, Neal Pruitt** and his son, **Alec**. You made me look good.

R. J. Smith included me in his James Brown biography, "The One, The Life and Music of James Brown". Later, we continued a friendship and he decided to visit me at home, but his car was slammed by an 18-wheeler on a rain slick interstate, and he barely escaped death. Life is very fragile, but God has a plan for all of us.

THROUGH THE YEARS

My life has been filled with an amazing mix of characters. Some good, some bad. And some of them even helped to change my life. **Reverend Al Sharpton** is one of those characters, and I've known him since he was a teenager. I call him "Rev", short. He's a controversial guy, but when you're with him, he's really one of the funniest guys in the world! I invited him to spend the night at my home in Georgia, but he laughed, "If your neighbors found out that I was there, they'd burn your house down!"

Former University of Georgia football coach, **Vince Dooley**, is a real gentleman. When the team was #1 in the country, James Brown and I would go into the locker room, and Brown would give Herschel Walker and the team some advice on their game. Vince, you're a class act. Thanks for putting up with us.

J. Ellis Parker III was an FCC attorney who took a special interest in helping Mr. Brown and me. I am so thankful for his graciousness. In his stately antebellum home, he had a cabinet which held his child's Sterling silver baby toys on permanent exhibit. Feeling somewhat intimidated, I tried to one-up him by mentioning that when I had my appendix out as a child my mother had proudly placed it in a little specimen jar and displayed it on a living room table—it looked like a little shrimp. Thank you Mr. Parker for being kind.

I was producer of Brown's TV dance show, "Future Shock". At that time, **Ted Turner** had his TV station on West Peachtree Street in Atlanta. He drove a Toyota, but we all knew that he had great things in his future. Ted, you gave us a great exposure—those shows were so unusual, they could never be produced like that now.

Sen. Richard L. Greene is one of those guys who needs more recognition. He was the most pivotal person in the creation of the Georgia Music Hall of Fame, and yet he's never been inducted. It was a pleasure working with you to get the thing going.

In my hometown, I know of several people who always ask me about the progress I'm making in writing my memoir. Over the years, **Larry**

Walker, a local attorney, has always expressed his interest in the project. It made me feel good. Thanks, Larry.

Another group of my "followers" is the employees of Warner Robins Supply, including **Eddie Oliver** and **Howell Tabor.** I'm always in there buying building supplies, and I can't leave until they make me tell a James Brown story. Now there's no need for them to buy the book, I've already told y'all the stories!

Dr. Mausa Alwawi is another local citizen of my hometown. His job is to keep me healthy and alive—I'm glad somebody is responsible for doing that. Every time I go to see him, he is always so interested in my James Brown stories, and I know he'll actually enjoy the book—but after reading the book, he may think that I'm sicker than he thought!

Mike Chitty was one of my Daddy's caretakers, and he was a pall-bearer at his funeral. He's also one of the best house framers in Middle Georgia. While I was writing the memoir he'd always ask if he was gonna be in the book. I said, "I don't think so." But he kept asking me, and I'd say that I'd promise he'd be in the book. In the end, I didn't mention him. But a promise is a promise—so Mike Chitty, ya finally made it in buddy!

FRIENDS ALWAYS

Some people go beyond being mere friends. They become a part of you, and that makes it even worse when they leave. **Bob Patton** was the coolest guy I ever met. He dressed like a rock star, and people would assume he was. Bob was Brown's promotional director and later he worked for Jerry Lee Lewis. His little black address book held all the names and numbers of everyone in show business. He was a people person, and even though he was always short on money, he'd give you the shirt off his back. He came to my rescue many times. He died suddenly at age 70 soon after completing his own memoir.

Diamond Jim Sears was a close friend of mine. He was a DJ at Brown's Baltimore radio station, WEBB. Jim was a real operator, and we'd pull some crazy stunts in order to keep Mr. Brown happy. Coincidentally, Jim's mother-in-law retired in my little hometown, and I built her a custom house just down the road from me.

I'm so proud of **Joel Katz**. I met him when he was starting out as a lawyer. After I got to know him, I recommended him to become James Brown's lawyer. Brown was his first entertainer client, and now Joel is one of the top entertainment lawyers in America.

Al Garner was the "other white boy" who worked with me. He had that deep radio voice that helped him to talk his way out of many tight situations. Together, the two of us had to justify the chaotic financial situation that Brown had created. I'm glad we were both young at that time—that kind of wheeling-dealing would kill us now.

Some of my friends I rarely see, like **Chris Neilsen**, a stockbroker in New York. He's always been a James Brown fan—and he's always been a trusted friend.

Many times, friends come in married pairs. Cynthia and I often have parties and dinners together with these couples—we even go on trips together. These friends have all heard my stories—they never get tired of them either, so I have to mention them and how much they mean to Cynthia and me—**Pete and Lavern Lauritsen, Wendell and Marylena Cockrell, Jim and Becky Speer and Steve and Joyce Barker**.

PEOPLE & ORGANIZATIONS

There are several organization I must publically thank for their support. I previously mentioned George Klein ... he helped me to be interviewed on the **Graceland Legacy Program** which is available on the Internet. I want to recognize **Mike and Julie Stewart** at the **Hawkinsville Opera House** and the local **Hawkinsville Arts Council** for their support of my stage show—also **Sheila Jones** at the **Perry Arts Council** who graciously supported my presentation there along with the **Perry Area Convention and Visitors Bureau.**

SPECIAL RECOGNITION

There are a few other people who deserve some special recognition for their lasting support. **Charles Bobbit** was Brown's personal manager and later became Michael Jackson's personal manager. He also managed the personal business of Premier Omar Bongo of Gabon. He was a busy man. So was I, and while we were working we had little time to develop a deep, personal relationship, but I always had a strong respect for him. He didn't smoke or drink, and he was always honest and reliable. He still is. I've known him since the mid 1960s, and he's an unusually close friend.

James Brown's family and his second wife **Deidre (Deedee)** will always be a part of my family. Brown's two daughters, **Yamma and Deanna**, were about the same age as my daughters, Kelley and Pepper. I carried school photographs of his daughters in my wallet and Mr. Brown carried photos of my girls in his wallet. We were some kind of family! My wife, June, was jealous of me spending time with James Brown, and I'm sure Brown's wife was jealous of me for spending so much time with her husband. Show business is not easy, but some relationships endure through almost anything.

There are over seven billion people in this world, and the best person in that crowd to write my memoir is **Jones DeVere**. That's his pen name (I think he may be in the witness protection program). He understands the complex Southern culture—in words, he has captured my speech, my expressions, my dialect and speech cadence—and he has had the patience to sit at my kitchen table and listen to me retell my stories, year after year. While he was writing Bob Patton's memoir, Bob introduced him to me so, in reality, he was writing two memoirs at the same time. At this point, he's probably the literary authority on the personal life of James Brown.

My greatest thanks go to **James Brown**. It took 125,000 words to explain this relationship, but the bottom line is that he changed the direction of my life one day at the Atlanta airport when I said, "I know who you are—you're James Brown." After that, everything changed. It's been an unbelievable adventure, and I hope you enjoy reading "James Brown and his Money Man".

Index

A

B

C

D

E

F

G

H

I

J

K

L

M

N

O

P

R

S

T

V

W